Using Your Portable Studio

A complete course to the art of using a portable studio.
Over 30 recording "recipes" throughout the book and in the special
Portable Studio Cookbook section can show you how to produce
professional results on a home-studio budget.

by Peter McIan

Cover photograph courtesy of TEAC/Tascam
Project editors: Roland Ottewell and Peter Pickow
Interior design and layout: Len Vogler

Order No. AM 92232
US International Standard Book Number: 0.8256.1437.6
UK International Standard Book Number: 0.7119.4357.5

Exclusive Distributors:
Music Sales Corporation
257 Park Avenue South, New York, NY 10010 USA
Music Sales Limited
8/9 Frith Street, London W1V 5TZ England
Music Sales Pty. Limited
120 Rothschild Street, Rosebery, Sydney, NSW 2018, Australia

Printed in the United States of America by
Vicks Lithograph and Printing Corporation

Amsco Publications
New York/London/Sydney

Acknowledgements

My thanks go first to Dave McCumiskey, who has had the faith and the patience of Job throughout this whole project; Peter Pickow and Roland Ottewell, whose editing talent and support brought this all together; and Garson and Stefanie Leder, who kept asking me when the book was going to be finished.

Contents

Preface

Warning! Before you read any further you should be advised that the use of any recording equipment can rapidly become an addictive habit.

Me and my best friend John Douglas showed up at the small studio in downtown Baltimore, Maryland. Our avowed purpose was simple enough; to immortalize ourselves through our music. We'd saved up for quite a while to be able to invest in our future as rock and roll stars. We knew that the sacrifices—the dates we didn't go on and the movies we didn't see—were all going to be worth it. We had it all worked out: We were going to record our song and send demos to the record companies and get a record deal and go on tour with like the Rolling Stones and never ever be turned down for a date again. We were sixteen. We had high hopes.

It was the first time I'd ever set foot in a recording studio, and while I pretended to be cool, I can easily recall my real reaction as I walked into the control room; I was intimidated, awed, confused, and downright bowled over by the Star Trekiness of it all. A zillion pulsing lights, anodized knobs, dials, and meters were patiently waiting for the engineer's command. All that thrumming power at his beck and call; like a James T. Kirk he was the captain of this sonic USS Enterprise. I saw all this stuff and thought the recording engineer must have the knowledge of mysteries as deep as a bishop of some secret religion. Mind you, I'd never met a real recording engineer before, so I didn't know quite what to expect. I was a little taken aback when he walked into the control room. He looked like a perfectly normal mad scientist, with hair style by hand grenade and piercing pale eyes with which I was sure he had no trouble seeing the actual electrons that coursed through the console wires. His name was Lennie. He greeted us with a disparaging "hmph" reserved for rank amateurs and pointed vaguely to where we were to set up our instruments. Lennie was, to put it politely, a jerk. During the setup and after a brief and loud summary from Lennie of how much I didn't know, my cool was pretty much in tatters by the time John and I set sail on our musical adventure together. The rest as they say is history. The demo didn't turn out so good. John went on to become an English teacher, and I went back to the musical drawing board realizing that I had a whole lot to learn. I did resolve one thing however, I was determined one day to "show Lennie."

And learn I did. Anyway I could. I hung around music instrument stores and checked out what gear my older, wiser brethren were using. I listened to records incessantly and began to dissect them; not, mind you, with any analytical plan in mind, just trying to isolate what it was that I liked or didn't like about a particular record. I began to **discover** that even as much as I was in love with writing and playing music, I was also falling in love with SOUND.

It was two years before I got the chance to go back into the studio. This time I was like a sponge, soaking up every molecule of experience, asking annoying questions, pretending I understood the answers and nodding wisely. That began the second (and in fact ongoing) phase of my recording education. The total immersion in the "studio experience" . . . the constant learning and experience of the good . . . the creation of a breakthrough sound and the bad . . . the 312th cup of dark, chewy coffee. So, this is a warning: take it from one who's been there—working in a studio is addictive. I'm still hooked all these years later.

When I started, it was of course back in the dark ages before the invention of the portable studio (or pre-PS). In those days the process of recording a demo nearly always involved a professional studio (or a very expensive home setup), a professional (or talented amateur) recording engineer, and a fair amount of money. Now of course, with equipment improving by leaps and bounds and prices falling yearly, you can make excellent demos in your bedroom for a fraction of the cost of renting a studio to do your recording.

The fact that the equipment is reasonably available should ease the impediments to getting your musical vision on tape. Well, sort of. When you went to the studio and shelled out that dough, not only were you paying for the use of the space and equipment but also for the expertise of the engineer. So now, even though the gear is available to take home, the engineering and producing skill unfortunately doesn't come in the box when you buy your portable studio.

And so the genesis of this book. Its purpose is to give you a ready resource to help you through every stage of the recording process (including the dreaded 3:00 A.M. "Oops, what do I do now" and "Why doesn't that work?" and "What's that gurgling sound on the vocal track?"). But also, and perhaps more importantly, this book is designed to give you a working knowledge of why and how these techniques work. Only by understanding the raw material of recording can you hope to be inventive in its use. That raw material is of course sound.

The goal of this book is to equip you the recordist with sound knowledge you can apply to any recording situation. The idea is to give you tools that you will never outgrow; the basic concepts and techniques explained here remain the same whether you're working in the world of portable studios or the most sophisticated multitrack facility. You can readily adapt the information in this book to each circumstance.

The book is organized in four sections. I highly recommend you first read it through in sequence before you begin to use it as a reference. The book could be called a "cookbook" for a number of reasons. Partly of course, because it contains recipes, but also because it will teach you the techniques required to "cook"; it is a text on the nature of the ingredients and how to prepare them to add to the mix. So the material in the chapters are the "pathway" to the recipes in back. Once you have a clear understanding of the chapter material you will see how the recipes make sense. Furthermore, you will be able to find ways to creatively adapt the recipes to suit your own taste.

The book's four sections each address a different stage of the recording process. The book is sequential, building a foundation for each subject upon which the next can be built.

Section 1: Why You're Doing What You're Doing

In this section I discuss the basic material of recording: sound. This is where it all begins, and I hope to give you a new perspective on how to be aware of the richness in the sonic world around you; what you're hearing. Just as a painter looks at light in a way different from the rest of us, so too the professional recordist listens to sound in a very specific way. This section is designed to introduce you to how to listen and what to listen for before you begin the process of capturing it on tape.

Section 2: What You're Going to Do It With

This section is concerned with the mechanics of getting sound on tape. In order to manipulate the recording gear creatively the recordist must have a firm grasp of what the gear does and how it works. This section is a mostly nontechnical guide to the inner workings of the equipment you paid so much money for. It also includes one of the most tortured analogies I've ever written involving wildebeests and oxen.

Section 3: How You're Going to Do It

This part of the book is the getting down to it section. It is filled with hands-on information on everything from "good sound every time" basic recording technique, to top advanced techniques that "push the envelope" of the portable studio's capabilities. In this section I deal with techniques specific to recording drums, vocals, guitars, bass, and keyboards.

Section 4: Doing It

This section is dedicated to a step-by-step guide to recording and mixing a track. It includes the practical and aesthetic considerations that go into a successful recording. Also included is the concept of "bouncing," or combining, tracks to make your four-track portable studio do the work of many more tracks.

This is also the home of "The Recipe Section." These pages contain instant reference on specific techniques to accomplish particular tasks. I wanted an information source that functioned easily for those wee hours after recording for twelve days and operating on seven dim brain cells; occasions when you needed to find an answer to a problem or discover a way to enhance your sound.

Just a few final notes and I'll let you get to it.

I've been incredibly lucky in my life to be exposed to and learn firsthand from some of the true greats in audio recording. People like Mick Gausauski (Earth Wind and Fire among many others), Andy Johns (Led Zeppelin, Rolling Stones), Roger Nichols (Steely Dan and a million others), and Roy Thomas Baker (the genius behind Foreigner, the Cars, Journey, and half the records you've ever heard). These people were a gifted resource to me and influenced me greatly in my own career. I hope that this book will serve to pass on some of what I learned from them as well as the knowledge that resulted from a thousand experiments and mistakes I made quite on my own. So this book is designed to get you started, and keep you going. To allow you to benefit from my mistakes so that *you* won't have to make them. Enjoy.

Oh, and just one more thing: *HEY, LENNIE!HA!*

INTRODUCTION

Applying Pro Techniques to Recording with the Portable Studio

Unless you're an auto mechanic, looking under the hood of your car can be an intimidating experience. There seems to be so much stuff — hoses, wires, and other unidentifiable things. I've seen people with a non-starting car actually talk pleadingly to the ton or so of inanimate steel they're sitting in. It makes perfect sense to me, because that's the way we deal with what we know, namely people. We try to talk the car into doing something (in this case firing up and moving down the road). If we don't know how the car works we can only hope that the magical automobile gods are listening to how nice we're talking. Or that somehow our car has the intelligence to know that we really care about its well-being. So we reason with it and promise it an oil change or a wash or something. (What's worse is if the car *happens* to start, then the next time we have trouble we'll talk to it even longer and then get mad when it doesn't listen to us.)

But to an auto mechanic that stuff under the hood is no mystery at all. He or she knows that the components of an engine were put together by humans in an orderly fashion that allows it to perform its function. Well, the use of recording gear is just like that. When it doesn't do what you want it to, it's not because the recording gods are angry at you or the machine is having a hissy fit. No amount of talking to it, yelling at it, or promising it recorder treats is going to make a difference. The only thing you can do is to learn how it works and then how to make it work the way you want it to. You've taken a pretty good first step — you bought this book.

To go back to our car analogy, the modern internal combustion engine didn't spring full-blown from some fertile mind in Detroit or Stuttgart. It evolved over the course of many years under the influence of many talented people and in response to changing needs. In its earliest incarnation you didn't need to be a rocket scientist to understand the basic principle of a gasoline motor. An explosion forces a piston to move, which moves something else. One form of energy is **transduced** into another; heat and concussion energy (explosion) is converted into mechanical energy (work). Remember the term **transduction;** it will come up later and is central to understanding recording.

As time went on the creative minds interested in such things began to improve the combustion engine. They added automatic spark distributors and starters so you didn't have to crank the motor by hand anymore, automatic transmissions, and, for my money, one of the most important developments of all — the air conditioner.

Now after all these years of development when we look under the hood it feels like a daunting task to try and understand an engine. But if you take each element and examine its purpose individually, the bits and pieces become comprehensible, and once you understand each one, then putting the whole car together makes sense. All of these devices were relatively simple in their original form. The concept behind them led to the engineering required to develop them. If you understand *why* they work then you are most of the way to understanding *how* they work. What's more, and perhaps most important, is that if you understand the components you will also be able to customize their application to suit your creative vision. That's how we get hot rods.

The recording process is no different. Knowing the bits and pieces is how you take advantage of the system as a whole. Each and every piece of gear was developed to meet a sensible need. And you don't have to be a rocket scientist to understand how this stuff works. Once you do, you'll see how you can adapt your recording to get the most out of your circumstances. That's the way you apply pro techniques to the home studio environment: by knowing how to take full advantage of everything you have available to you.

Me

The very first time I walked into a professional studio I was completely overwhelmed by what looked like an incomprehensible array of buttons and knobs and blinking lights. All I knew was that I wanted to make music, and all the stuff in that room was somehow going to help me do it. After that first experience I was hooked. Once I saw how sound could be created and shaped and colored and then permanently captured, that was it. I knew that this was what I wanted to spend as much time as possible doing. So I began to learn whenever I could, and I experimented whenever I could with whatever gear I had. I made some really horrible noises and got to meet a lot of my neighbors under less than ideal circumstances. The main thing I did was make lots and lots of mistakes and learn from them.

Along the way I wrote about a million bad songs and a few good ones, enough to get me a record deal and the opportunity to work with some great engineers from whom I learned what it was to really know what you're doing. They were patient and I was all ears, so to speak, and I got the best grounding in the real world of recording that I can imagine.

Shortly thereafter, through a series of fortunate circumstances, I found myself in Australia producing and engineering a new band called Men at Work. It was the first record I had ever engineered completely and was an amazing, exciting, and nerve-racking experience. But through it all I had been given the confidence to do it because I had been taught by the best how to break a complex job into understandable pieces. I was comfortable with the basic concept of what each piece of gear did, and from that I could see how each piece of gear fit into the scheme of the recording. Finally, I had learned from some of the greatest how to make the equipment work transparently in the service of the artistic vision. As a friend of mine once said, "Any time you hear the gear workin', you ain't workin' it right."

This Book

While I was making all those mistakes I was in a way doing research for this book. Hopefully my having made the mistakes means that you won't have to. But there's more to my idea of a helpful book then simply guiding you around a few potholes on the highway to learning. The idea here is to give you not only techniques but also an understanding of concepts — both the how and the why of recording. With this understanding you can then go on to modify and invent techniques of your own. My purpose with this book then is to give you the tools and understanding to hot-rod your own recordings.

If you follow the blueprints that I lay out you will always have good recording results, I guarantee it. But my techniques are certainly not the only way to do things. So this book is just a starting point. If you do as I hope you will, you'll use the book as a road map, a solid reference point from which you can travel your own route and experiment along the way.

I've organized the book into four sections:

Why You're Doing What You're Doing, which is a brief user-friendly explanation of how sound ends up on tape;

What You're Going to Do It With, which discusses the equipment itself;

How You're Going to Do It, which is a section full of techniques, tips, and tricks for recording; and finally,

Doing It, which contains a blow-by-blow recording scheme and a special "recipe" section to help you apply pro techniques to your portable studio experience.

You

The most important tool for good recording is the one on your shoulders that wears all the hats. Ingenuity and creativity combined with learning, experience, and experimentation are the keys to any successful recording. This is especially true when you are dealing with limited recording circumstances and equipment budgets. In the real world you have to substitute smarts for bucks, and knowing how the basics work will allow you to improvise successfully.

Why You're Doing
What You're Doing:
The Foundation of Recording

What Is Sound?

The rest of this book is dedicated to an understanding of the tools of the studio and how to use them. But for the next few pages I want to spend a little ink reacquainting you with the most important recording tool of all...your ears.

When we experience the booming roll of thunder, the buzz of an annoying mosquito, a whisper, a scream, or Jerry Garcia's guitar solos, our perception of these sonic events is due to a marvelous interaction between the physics of sound and the ability of our brain to interpret the world. In order to understand the recording process and how to use the tools of the trade effectively, it is necessary to know something about the raw materials you're trying to record. No, this chapter isn't going to be a visit to Mr. Wizard's science lab; it's simply a user's manual on the mechanics of sound and their effect on your recording.

A Definition of Sound: In Space, No One Can Hear You Scream

Sound is the transformation of one kind of energy into another, as expressed by the movement of molecules in a medium (like air or water or bourbon). Or, as the American Heritage *Dictionary* says, sound is "a vibratory disturbance." Sound is of course only one type of energy transference. The action of a piano hitting the sidewalk after falling from a six-story window causes a great deal of energy transference of various types. The energy of the fall is converted into kinetic energy when the piano hits the pavement. This conversion at impact finds expression in the immediate manufacture of a whole lot of expensive Steinway matchsticks. Another product of the transfer of energy is the CRASH! KABOOM! SPROING! you would hear — in short, sound. The kinetic energy at contact displaces not only molecules of Steinway but also molecules of air. These molecules displace other molecules until the sound reaches your ear. Think of the process as a ripple in a carpet. You give one end a little flip and the ripple carries through the rug all the way to the other end. What's happening is that energy is being transferred, is traveling through the medium of the carpet. It travels in an **analog**, or picture, of the physics of the original event — that is, the wave of the original action of the carpet flip (more about analog in the next chapter). Sonic energy moves like the ripple in the carpet, only the medium is air instead of 100% genuine nylon shag.

BANG!!!! Your kid sister just dropped a barbell on the hood of your car. And you heard it all the way through the fog of a deep and righteous sleep. Let's calmly analyze, shall we, how it is you heard the dent being made in your car. It works like this: the kinetic event (action) takes place (barbell contacts metal) and generates a sound pressure (sort of like wind) that creates a sonic picture of the noise event. This analog radiates out from the site of the energy transfer (your car's hood) and vibrates air molecules, which then enter that incredible mechanism called the human ear. The ear has a complex system for turning that sound into electrical energy. This now transformed electrical information is then sent along a specialized set of nerves to the brain, which interprets the electrical impulses into meaningful information like BANG!!!! Your brain interprets as "Hey, $#*#! Somebody just dropped a #$%&@ barbell on my car!" All of this energy transfer business is called **transduction** and is the heart of the recording process — but we'll get into that in the next section.

(Note: As you have undoubtedly figured out by now, the reason that "in space no one can hear you scream" is that space is a vacuum: there are no air molecules to excite.)

Surfing the Sound Wave

Okay, we know the general mechanics of sound, that sound moves air around. But what does sound look like while it's doing this? If you look at an *oscilloscope* (an electronic device that can create a visual display of sound) you will see that sound travels in *waves,* and different sounds draw different wave lines on the screen. For instance, a barbell dropping on the hood of your car has a different sonic signature than the sound your cat makes when you accidentally step on its tail. But both events are made up of the same stuff — sound waves — and each has its own characteristics. That's how we distinguish one sound from another.

Cycle, Frequency, and Amplitude

A sound wave is made up of three elements: frequency; period, or cycle; and amplitude. Simply put, a **cycle** is one complete back and forth vibration (oscillation), **frequency** is the number of cycles occurring over time (usually expressed in cycles per second), and **amplitude** is good old-fashioned loudness. Any alteration in a sound is the result of a change in one of these three components. Below is a diagram of a wave at two cycles per second (which by the way is too low for a human to hear but works well for diagrams).

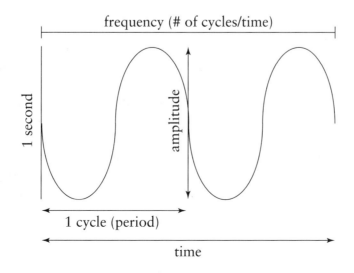

It's probably easiest to visualize a cycle if you think of the movement of a piano string. When the hammer comes down the string moves out of its resting position in response to being struck. If you think of its resting point as "zero," the string moves away from zero in one direction, comes back and passes through zero, and goes the opposite direction. This is an oscillating pendulum movement with the string moving an equal distance from rest in each direction, slowing until the string is at rest again.

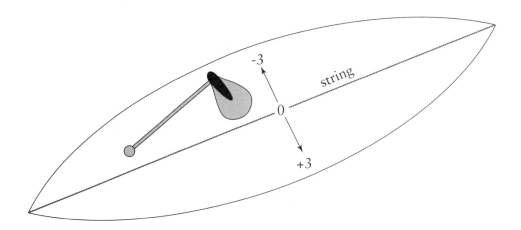

Everything that happens in sound can be described with this little model of vibration — just substitute bell, reed, column of air, or yowling cat larynx. The oscillating medium displaces the air molecules and a sound is born.

Where Does It Hertz?

There is a term that you should know before we go any further. Maybe you already do know it but bear with me — it's only a paragraph. The word is **hertz**, named after Heinrich Hertz, a German physicist (not the rental car people). A hertz is a unit of frequency with a value of one cycle per second. The symbol for hertz is **Hz** (pronounced "hurts," not "aitchzie"). All frequencies are made up of some quantity of hertz. For instance, 1 cycle per second is 1 Hz, 100 cycles is 100 Hz, etc. However, when we get to 1000 Hertz we refer to **Kilo**hertz (*kilo* is Greek for "1,000"). This is symbolized by using the letter K (pronounced "kay"). Three thousand cycles is 3 K, 1,000 cycles is 1 K, and 2,500 cycles is 2.5 K, but 999 cycles is 999 Hz. Okay, now we can move on.

The Components of a Sound

Frequency

Let's deal with frequency first. Frequency is really the determinant of pitch. The higher the pitch of the sound the greater the number of cycles occurring each second. Whenever you're talking about how many times something happens you're talking about its frequency ("I go to the refrigerator with alarming frequency"). The note A440 has 440 complete back-and-forth vibrations (oscillations) happening each second, meaning that the string will go to its outermost extremes 440 times each second. If the event occurs twice as often (two times the frequency equals 880 times), the note will be an octave higher; halve the number of events (half the frequency equals 220 times) and the note will be an octave lower, and so on. So frequency is determined by the rate of oscillation.

Cycle

The second component of a sound wave is the cycle itself. This is described as a **period**, meaning a discrete something that has a beginning and an end. The cycle begins when the string gets as far as it's going to go from zero in one direction, and the cycle ends after the string has come back through zero and gone as far as it's going to go in the other direction. One complete cycle is the unit of frequency.

Amplitude

The third component of a sound wave is amplitude, which is a measure of how far from zero the string travels. The greater the energy used to strike the string the farther the string will travel, and therefore the greater the loudness of the sound. As the string moves more vigorously it compresses more air molecules, which results in greater volume. The volume of a sound (loudness) is expressed in **decibels (dB)**. To give you an idea of relative loudness, the sound of a gentle breeze through the magnolias is about 20 dB, the sound of normal street noise is about 70 dB, the sound of nearby thunder is around 120 dB, and the sound of your heart as you get pulled over by the cops is about 170 dB.

So to summarize our model sound wave: the piano hammer transfers energy to the string, causing it to move back and forth (a cycle); the number of times the cycle is repeated in a second determines the pitch (frequency); and the distance the string travels from where it was before you hit it determines how loud it is (amplitude).

The Sound of Music

Timbre: Instrumental Signature

That's cool as far as it goes. But there is a minor problem here. If sound is determined by pitch alone how come I can tell the difference between a bass fiddle and a bassoon even when they're playing the same pitch? After all, frequencies are frequencies, right? How come the instruments sound different?

The explanation for the differences in instrumental tonality has to do with the complex interaction of sounds that make up what is called **timbre**. Timbre is musical sound composed of interrelated frequencies produced simultaneously. The timbre of an instrument is what identifies it sonically.

There are three components that make up the sound of an instrument: tone, non-tone, and overtone. **Tone** is the pure pitch of an instrument. This is frequency information devoid of coloration. Pure pitch rarely exists outside of a synthesizer. **Non-tone** is that sound that is produced as a by-product of the instrument. For instance, the stick as it hits the drum, the bow as it attacks the string, the fingers as they move on the fretboard. These sounds are accompaniment to the act of playing an instrument and are more or less noticeable depending on the instrument. **Overtone** is the complement of harmonics that are produced in sympathy to the fundamental tone. Overtones are the signature characteristics of the instrument. They are determined by the type of instrument, the shape and form of the instrument, the materials the instrument is made of, and the person playing it. It is in the overtones that the identity of an instrument lives.

All instruments are a combination of these three elements. The way an instrument sounds is largely determined by the emphasis you the recordist place on each element. For instance, a snare drum has an important non-tone component, the bang when the stick hits the skin. This is called the **transient**. A transient is a momentary explosion of sound that in loudness is well above the level of the tone of the instrument. Another transient non-tone is the attack of the pick on a guitar string, or a "thumb hammer" on a bass guitar. Generally speaking, the transient comes first, causing the tone of the instrument to follow, like the stick striking the drum and producing the tone and overtone. But there are other types of non-tone that are also important. The snare drum has snares, which are also non-tonal elements but are very much a part of the sound of the drum.

Outside of synthesizers I suppose the instrument that produces the closest thing to a pure tone is the flute. But even the flute has an overtone series that, while less complex than some, is nonetheless unique and identifiable as its timbre.

A flute creates sound by vibrating a column of air. When a note is played the flute will produce relatively few overtones — an octave and a sixth above are the two predominant harmonics. These pitches are softer than the original note, and because they are related to the fundamental they reinforce it. That's why the flute has such a pure tone; the overtones are **consonant** with (in the scale of) the fundamental. In the case of a sax, the sound is created by a vibrating reed that is amplified by a column of air through the horn. The reed produces a rich variety of overtones, many of which are **dissonant** to the fundamental and each other. Consequently, the sound you hear has a sort of buzzing quality produced by the clash of harmonics. These overtones have frequencies of their own that are carried on the sound wave of the original note. It is in the overtones that distinctive sound lives. I will say lots more about this when we get to the discussion of equalization of specific instruments. Now we have a working idea of what constitutes musical sound. But what, from the recordist's point of view, is music?

A Definition of Music

A reasonably accurate definition of music would be that music is the ordered production of sound: a deliberate sequence of noises sent out into the world by the design of a musician.

The Art of Listening

Learning how to order that sound in the most musically effective manner is the goal of the recordist. This is a process of learning from our environment and each other. We are living in a stupendous classroom and concert hall, and all we have to do to learn is listen. While we humans are programmed to pay more attention to our own noises we sometimes forget that we are surrounded by the music of the world.

There are sounds to learn from all around us, everywhere we listen there are lessons to be learned. When a developing visual artist is still a student he or she is sent out to draw the world from observation. By paying attention to the environment the artist can then recreate what is seen and incorporate it into an artistic vision. The process of learning to create with sound is the same except that instead of a pencil and paper we use our ears to observe and record. I recommend that you start out your listening practice in the natural world rather than the musical one. I suggest this because it's very easy to get seduced into listening to the music instead of analyzing the sound. So in my seminars we spend time listening to the environment and to the forms of sounds that precede the content of music. Most of the sounds you will ever record are found in nature, in the simple experience of living. You just have to be aware. Reverb? Listen as you pass through a tunnel or speak in a warehouse. Echo? Find a canyon, either man-made or natural, and shout. Listen to how your voice returns to you. Listen to the sound of traffic for other tricks of the ear like phase-shifting. Listen to the pitch change as a train goes past. Close your eyes and let your ears guide your impressions of the environment you're in. I can't emphasize enough the importance of learning to really hear. Remember that the impression you get of a space or sound will probably be the same impression most other people will get. Without getting too philosophical here, I think it's fair to say that communication is common understanding of the same language, and the language that you speak in when you're recording is sound. If you want to communicate a sonic mood to articulate your music you need to understand the components of the sound you're trying to create.

Listening Tips

- Whenever possible notice the sound of the room you're in. Close your eyes and listen to the way the sound bounces off the walls and ceiling. Start to notice the difference between the sound of a room with hard surfaces and those with carpet and drapes. Notice how long a sound bounces around the walls and relate it to the size of the room.

- Keep a "sound journal." Try to memorize interesting sounds and describe them in a few words. The entries don't need to be precise, just reminders to jog the sound file in your head. "Use the sound of the Klingon space ship for the treatment of the power guitar;" "The reverb in the empty gym for the background vocals." Creating sound is largely a matter of having a clear idea in your head of what characteristic you want to capture.

- Try the "clap test." One way to learn the sound of different environments is to clap your hands once sharply and listen to the sound off the walls. You will begin to notice the components of the sound. Try asking yourself these questions; How long did the sound bounce around? Was the sound "bright" or "deep"? What was the difference when I stood close to the wall and when I stood farther away? The clap test is invaluable aid for microphone placement. As you learn to differentiate between different sound environments you will be able to position the microphone to take advantage of the sound characteristics of the space you're in.

Practice Listening

After you've spent some time learning to pay attention to your environment then you're ready for the other great source of listening and learning: other people's recordings.

When I'm listening to a CD I usually listen for several different things. First off, like anyone else I listen just to decide if I like how it sounds or not. Next I listen for how well the recording enhances the music. Then I begin to look for what I can learn from other folks who record for a living. I listen for the types of reverbs and echos used. From experience I can analyze the size of the "imaginary room" the artist has created and what effect it has on the mood of the song. I listen for the frequencies that dominate the recording. Does it sound edgy? Warm? All of these things are components of the success or failure of a particular recording to enhance the music.

That's the beginning of real recording, learning to listen to the sound all around you and compare it to what you're trying to communicate. Once you are able to do that you have a palette of colors that you can use to bring your recording to life.

Now that you have some idea of what to listen for, the next bit of information offers a perspective on exactly what you're listening to.

Frequency and Pitch and the Size of the Wave

As I discussed above, pitch is the result of the number of cycles occurring per second in a vibrating medium (string, kazoo, etc.). And the pitch of a *sound* is the rate at which *air molecules* vibrate in response to the pitch of that medium. Yeah, so? This is a pompous way of saying that sound waves have physical dimensions every bit as real as ocean waves; we just can't see them. As you will see later, in the discussion on creating your studio ("The Recording Studio Kit Chapter"), the size of a sound wave is a very important attribute and can make a big difference in how you perceive your recording.

By size I mean physical size, the amount of distance it takes for a complete cycle to develop. This dimension in terms of space is called **wavelength**. It is the amount of real estate that one cycle of a pitch takes to develop. To go back to our rug-flipping analogy, each ripple in the carpet takes up a definite amount of space. So does a cycle of sound. There is a fairly easy formula for figuring out how much distance comprises the wavelength of a particular frequency. For example, take an A440 Hz on the piano. Sound travels at 1,100 feet per second (thank you, Mr. Wizard). At a frequency of 440 cycles per second the distance it takes to complete one cycle is about two and a half feet.

$$\frac{1{,}100 \text{ feet per second}}{440 \text{ cycles per second}} = 2\tfrac{1}{2} \text{ feet}$$

You already know that the lower the note the fewer the number of oscillations (cycles) per second. Therefore it would take more room to complete one wavelength the lower you go. For example if you play a bass note of 110 Hz the number of feet to complete a cycle would be:

$$\frac{1{,}100 \text{ feet per second}}{110 \text{ cycles per second (Hz)}} = 10 \text{ feet}$$

Now 110 Hz isn't really all that low. Generally, the bottom end of a recording averages somewhere below 100 Hz. What does this mean to your listening? It means that if you're too close to the source of the sound you are not hearing a realistic representation of the bottom end. You need to be ten feet away to hear one complete cycle! Try sticking your head in a bass cabinet and you won't hear anywhere near the amount of bass you'd hear across the room. The waveform hasn't had room to develop.

Conversely, the higher the frequency the less distance needed to create a complete wave form. Let's take a guitar overtone at 3 K. Using our formula:

$$\frac{1{,}100 \text{ feet per second}}{3{,}000 \text{ cycles per second (3 K)}} = .36 \text{ feet} = 4 \text{ inches}$$

This means that it only takes about four inches to hear this very prominent frequency. If you're too close the upper midrange will seem too loud and you will have a tendency to lower this frequency. The result of this will be an imbalance in the frequency spectrum in your recording; you will have manipulated the sound based on a false picture of what is there.

This matter of distance from the sound source is much more than abstract semi-interesting theory. It is a very real-world issue. As a good recordist you are always striving to record sounds that meet your musical vision. In order to do that you need to understand how far to place a microphone from a sound source, how the size and shape of a room will affect the frequency characteristics of the sound you want to record, and how accurate a representation you're hearing of what's on tape. Remember this fact as you record: The ability to be aware of and adjust the physical elements of recording are even more important when you are limited in the electronics you have available to you for manipulating sound. In other words, what you don't have in good gear you need to make up for with good ears.

In later chapters on constructing your studio as well as in "The Mixdown Chapter," I'll give you some techniques for creating an accurate listening environment, as well as how to compensate for unavoidable limitations of room size, electronics, and budget you may encounter.

What Sound Tells Us

We've just looked at how the physics of sound interact with the room, but how do they interact with your head? As you no doubt know, there is a continuum of frequencies in the range of human hearing. This range is from about 20 Hz to somewhere around 20 K. (Pretty impressive, but when it comes with hearing we humans are fairly limited compared to other animals. A dog can hear about five times more information than we can. Of course on the plus side we don't have to drink out of the toilet.) Though we have a fairly broad range, we don't hear particularly well at either extreme of the spectrum. When we get up to 20 K we are barely aware that something is tickling our ear hairs. However, our full range of hearing is used at all times to sample our environment. Even frequencies at the top and bottom of our range provide us with important spatial information.

We humans for the most part have stereo hearing. That is, we hear the world through two receptors (ears) on either side of our heads. In our ancestors, this stereo hearing was, as are most of our attributes, very useful to basic survival. By comparing when the sound reaches one ear to when it reaches the other it's possible, with some help from our brain cells, to determine where a sound is coming from. This stereo experience wasn't just for Cro-Magnon listening pleasure; it was first and foremost a way to find food while at the same time avoiding becoming food.

How does this impact on effective recording? Well, our brain interprets re-corded sound as it does any other sound. It takes in the information and com-pares it to a file of audio snapshots that we've gathered from the experience of a lifetime. From these comparisons the old gray matter creates a picture of the world it is listening to, a representation with space and size and nearness and distance, measured by the familiar. And the art of recording? By knowing the brain's expectations and manipulating sound accordingly we can create effects that fool us into thinking that we are somewhere we are not — in a concert hall, driving through a tunnel, or floating in the air. Stereo hearing creates an audio world of three dimensions, which, you will see as we go along, is the canvas that the recordist paints. The process of modern recording is one of capturing and then manipulating and recreating the stereo audio environment. As you will see, a good deal of what we will be talking about in this book will be techniques for shaping sound in what is called the "stereo spectrum." This is the miniature world we create in the final mix. The key component in the musical world the recordist creates is the perception of nearness and position. Here's how our human perceptions of sound in the real world are used to create perceptions in our recorded musical world.

Bottom end, low end (low frequencies) = distance

Top end, high end (high frequencies) = direction

The statement above pretty much sums up the situation as far as our hearing is concerned. We tell how far away something is from us by information con-tained in the lower frequencies. We tell the position of something by the informa-tion contained in the upper frequencies. This little bit of information will come in very handy when you decide how to mix a song.

What exactly is low end? For the purposes of this discussion *only*, I'm going to define it as anything below 200 Hz (for recording I would call it below 100 Hz). Conversely, anything above 200 Hz is high end.

The equipment we have on either side of our skulls is pretty sophisticated. When it comes to differentiation of direction, our hearing is so acute that we can close our eyes and still follow the rapid changes in the location of a mosquito as it dive-bombs our skin. We can also judge when a herd of stampeding buffalo is about to arrive by listening to the rumble, even from relatively great distance.

The difference between the way our brain interprets low- and high-frequency information is very important to creating our stereo world. To use our above examples, we can tell from the low-end rumble that there is a buffalo herd com-ing closer, but guess what? We can't tell where it's coming from. The sound seems to be all around us. When the herd gets closer we can tell where it is be-cause we can hear more high-frequency information.

In the case of the mosquito, we have an excellent idea of whether it's in front or behind, left or right, but it's much more difficult to guess how far away it is. Think of a fly buzzing around in your bedroom at night. It seems just as loud and annoying wherever it is. In fact, if you pay attention some time you may find that the soundtrack to a fly is pretty much either you hear it or you don't.

From a recording standpoint this translates into two important facts: 1. *Bottom end is mono* and is not specifically positionable in the stereo spectrum — it seems to come from everywhere; 2. *Top end is the stereo positioner* — the more top end the easier it is to pick out placement.

This leads to some very important points to keep in mind. First, the more low end of an instrument you hear, the less definite is its position in the stereo spectrum. In other words, muddy recordings mask spatial definition. The more high end you hear, the more the sound will be "up front," because we can't detect distance without low-end reference. Too much high end on each sound and they all end up lacking depth and fighting for the same space and psychological attention. As you will see ad nauseam, balance of sound is the whole deal to successful recording.

The Squeaky-Wheel Frequencies: The Upper Midrange

There is a category of frequencies that is the equivalent of the class hell-raiser. These frequencies call our attention out of all proportion to how loud they are. They are what is termed "psycho-acoustically active" and are hard to miss. As with all of this stuff, we have to go back to our ancestors to understand why some frequencies are more dominant than others. There were certain noises that were very important to survival, one of which was the sound of the human voice, the cry of a baby. Our brains are hardwired to be acutely sensitive to this range of frequencies, which live in the **upper midrange** of audition (from 1 K to 5 K). We will hear them louder than other frequencies that are in fact registering much louder on the meter. What this means is that these dominant sounds are more likely to grab our attention, but it also means that they are also more likely to sound irritating if our threshold is exceeded. Now guess which instruments are apt to leap to center stage? How about guitar leads? trumpet solos? sax solos? That's why they call it a lead instrument — it takes center stage with little effort. As a contrast, think of trombone, bassoon, or bass solos. They have to be much louder than the other instruments in order to be heard clearly. Yes, the instruments that play in the psycho-acoustically active range have an unfair advantage. We humans are hardwired to pay more attention to them, so consequently they "cut" through the track. These magical frequencies from about 1 K to 5 K are a source of great recording joy and migraine headaches.

A Final Word on the Listening Animal

As you progress through the book you will see how you can use the basic facts of how humans perceive sound to your benefit. Especially when you're confronted with limited resources, a good ear and a knowledge of the way we hear are great equalizers, in every sense of the word.

Getting the Sound to Tape: A Brief but Necessary History of Recording

In the last chapter I discussed the physical characteristics of sound. In this section you're going to get a brief overview of how the sound gets onto the tape.

Recording

If I were to ask a hundred musicians, "What is the purpose of recording?" I'd probably get a hundred different answers. Some would involve artistic passion, some would have to do with fame and fortune, and some answers would be all about improving a dim social life or hot-rodding dating prospects. (Hey kids! Be the coolest on your block! Learn to record, make big money!) All of these reasons are, well... reasons, but not answers to the question I asked. The question they answer is, "Why do you want to record?" So, with an eye to reexamining the commonplace let me rephrase the question slightly to: "Why was recording invented?"

I don't think ol' Thomas Edison had a music career or dating in mind when he gave birth to the recording process; so, to state the obvious, the recording machine was invented to make a "record" of an occurrence. Record equals recording. Sort of like a seismograph makes a record of an earthquake, or a court reporter takes down testimony as a record of a trial. The difference was that Edison's machine not only gave us an accurate record of a sonic event, but for the first time in history allowed us also to experience it. Edison literally created a time machine that allowed us to capture a piece of the past and save it for future listening. Prior to this time, in the late nineteenth century, if you wanted to hear the Rolling Stones you would have had to go to the town where they were playing and sit near the bandstand in the park. The best you could do to recreate the event when you got back to the folks back home was to hum them a few bars of "Satisfaction" and hope their imaginations could fill in the blanks. But Edison changed all that. Now you and your friends could sit around in the living room and listen to a tinfoil- or wax-covered cylinder with the actual sounds of the Rolling Stones scribed into it. You could listen over and over and reexperience the event. So why am I waxing so rhapsodic about ancient history? The reason is that the principles that Edison used back then to create early cylinder recordings are, notwithstanding some evolution, the same principles that are used today to create recordings on your portable studio.

Let's continue and reexamine some definitions you may take for granted. Here's one: no matter how you employ it, audio recording is simply a method of storing sound information onto a medium so that it can later be replayed. The better the storage, the truer the reproduction. The better the recordist, the better the storage. Knowing how the process works is essential to good recording.

Sticking Sound onto the Tape Soundscape

In the last chapter there was a discussion about the makeup of sound and how it was transmitted to our ears. To recap, sound consists of a vibration (cycle), multiplied many times to form a frequency (number of cycles per second, expressed in hertz), which causes vibrations in the air of some amplitude (loudness). Sound is of course the raw material from which recordings are made. But how does sound get from the air onto the tape?

Mary Had a Little Lamb: Analogs

Here we need to take another brief excursion down the path of history to get a true perspective on how fundamentally brilliant and simple recording is. Trust me, once you understand the basic principles invented a hundred or so years ago then all the other stuff in this book will make logical sense.

It took someone of Edison's genius to figure out a method of capturing and storing the invisible — sound waves. The sound itself was not stored (if you hold a Springsteen cassette up to your ear all you'll hear is the ocean) so how'd he do that? Pay attention here because your recording career will be one big pop quiz on this stuff. What Edison did was find a medium in which he could literally carve a sonic picture, or **analog**, of a sound. Edison figured out a way to store an exact representation of the energy pattern that was the signature of the sound.

(Note: here's another definition to add to your storehouse: an analog is a constant stream of information related to an event. A seismograph pen scratches an analog of an earthquake on a piece of paper. Analog recording is the continuous recording of sonic event. Digital comes later.)

So where did the picture come from? Easy: from sound waves vibrating a material. Initially the analog was created by talking into a tube, and the sound vibrated a piece of metal (think of how a kazoo vibrates when you hum into it). This piece of metal had a cutting stylus attached to it. It was passed over a rotating cylinder covered in tinfoil. As Edison spoke the immortal words "Mary had a little lamb" into the tube, the stylus vibrated on the surface of the foil, scratching a pattern. This pattern was an exact duplicate of the vibrations made by the cutting stylus. In order to hear back what was recorded he replaced the cutting stylus with a needle. The needle vibrated as it tracked across the scratches previously made by the stylus, and the vibrations created sound. Thus from "Mary had a little lamb" spoken into a tube the recording industry was born.

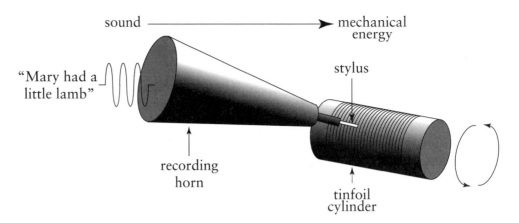

Tinfoil on the surface of the rotating cylinder is scratched as the cutting stylus moves across. The placement and depth of the scratches are due to the stylus responding to the frequency and amplitude of the electrical signal.

Now let's jump ahead to 1925 or so. Recording was still done by variations on the Edison method. Music was recorded onto acetate-coated discs (instead of cylinders) by acoustic means. A big tube or funnel-looking thing called a recording horn was set up in front of the band. When the band played, the sound went down the tube, so to speak, and vibrated a much better cutting stylus on a much fancier machine to make nicer scratches on the disc material. Better than before, but still a little primitive even by 1925 standards of technology. Then, in the never-ending march of progress, someone came up with the idea of using electricity to do the recording. The microphone had been invented some time before and was used by radio to send sound through the air; why not use it to transmit to the recorder? Good idea — have the cutting stylus respond to an electrical analog of the sound instead of a direct sound wave. No more big funnel-looking thing.

Electricity Is Our Friend

Converting sound into electricity was by this time pretty commonplace. It was accomplished by a process called **transduction**. As you know by now, transduction is the process of converting one form of energy into another. A **transducer** is any device that does the converting. So what the commercial studios of 1925 did was to start using a microphone (transducer) to convert sound energy into electrical energy. (More about how a mic does this in "The Microphone Chapter.") Without getting too technical, the recording process went like this: sound was converted to electrical energy, which was transferred over a wire to the recording machine where the electrical energy was converted (transduced) into mechanical energy to move the cutting stylus up and down, digging grooves into the master disc (sound energy to electrical energy to mechanical energy). The pattern that was scratched into the walls of the grooves was an analog, or picture, of the frequency of the sound vibrations, and the amplitude (loudness) of the sound was created by how deep the needle dug into the surface of the disc.

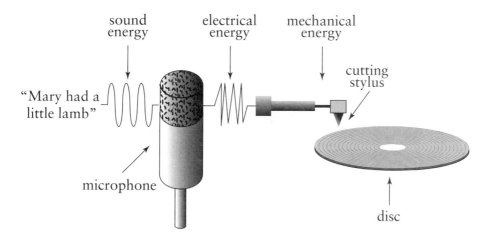

The microphone transduces sound energy into electrical energy which is sent to the cutting stylus. The stylus vibrates cutting a continuous analog of the sound into the disc for storage.

Okay, so far so good, the stylus has made marks in the acetate disc, but how do we reconvert the marks back into sound? By reversing the process. On play-back, a needle is allowed to move as it traces the marks in the grooves. This vibration of the needle is detected by changes in a magnetic field and is converted back into electrical energy. This is then amplified and the energy is sent to alter a magnetic field that in turn moves a membrane diaphragm (the speaker), which vibrates the air in an analog of the marks made on the acetate. Voilà! Sound (mechanical energy to electrical energy to sound energy).

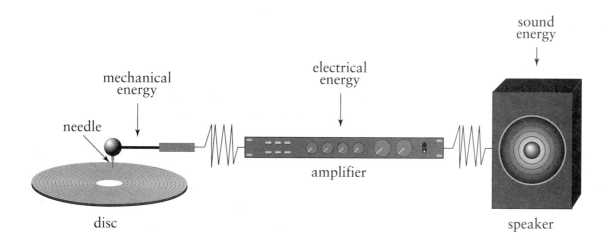

The needle tracks along the groove in the surface of the disc and vibrates as a result of the cuts made by the stylus. As the needle vibrates it causes shifts in a magnetic field and mechanical energy is converted to electrical. This is sent to an amplifier which sends the energy to a speaker where it is converted back in to sound. A reversal of transduction from the recording process.

This ingenious method stood more or less intact for generations, through all kinds of renovation and improvement. But in the middle of our disc story there was a revolutionary development.

Tape Recording

In the 1940s there were some technological advances that brought about major changes in the way recorded information was stored. For a long time there had been a desire to get away from the cumbersome method of cutting into a plastic plate to store sonic information. Various alternatives were tried. Eventually the one with the most to recommend it was the **magnetic tape recorder**. Its invention was the result of a number of earlier discoveries in the film and scientific communities. This was a tremendous innovation, a storage medium with huge advantages over the disc. It represented a breakthrough equal to the invention of the CD in the 1980s.

The way tape recording works is relatively simple in concept. A narrow strip of plastic tape is coated with a magnetically sensitive powdered oxide. The tape is pulled by the machine motors across the recording head of the machine. When you record, the head emits a stream of electronic impulses, which charge particles of the tape in the exact pattern of the energy transduced from sound. These charged particles line up on the tape to form an analog of the sound experience. The particles remain in that pattern like ants frozen in an ice cube. As long as nothing is done to disturb the pattern it will always stay the same.

When you want to play back the stored information the playback head simply reverses the process. As the tape passes over the head the pattern of charged particles on the tape is read by the playback head and converted back into electrical energy, which is sent be retransduced into sound.

Without getting over-technical (there are a bunch of good books specifically on the science behind recording if you want more information), the entire process involves manipulating minute changes in a magnetic field. This issue of manipulating magnetism has some practical ramifications for the recordist, as you'll see later.

So far I think you can see the logical similarities between storing information on a phonograph disc and storing it on tape (at least I hope so; that's why I did the song and dance with Edison). Both obtain their information by converting sound into electrical energy. Both create a pattern that is readable by reversing the recording process. And both methods convert an analog of energy back into sound.

Right from its inception, however, tape recording was a vastly superior method to "cutting vinyl." Indeed, there are several ways in which magnetic tape beats the cutting disc hands down. The idea of a stylus bumping along cutting dents and furrows on the surface of a vinyl disc, and the idea of a needle scraping across that surface to reproduce the sound seems pretty primitive. Major music stars were committing their performances to a medium that was, to say the least, fairly fragile and prone to scratching and melting. But with magnetic tape the recordist could store and retrieve the information completely electronically, with less concern for material handling and deterioriation.

Another factor was the desire to keep unwanted noise to a minimum. One of the inherent problems with disc recording was that noise was introduced onto the recording by the movement of the cutting head, the rumble of the lathe-turning machine, and flaws in the vinyl itself. And when you combined the noise of the recording process with the noise made by the playback method of scratching a needle across the vinyl you got a lot of noise that made a recording sound like music played in a monsoon. (Listen sometime to early vinyl recordings and you'll see what I mean.) Tape was a vastly quieter medium. The improvement was dramatic; for the first time the storage medium was relatively transparent and didn't interfere with the music.

Tape was also much more flexible to work with. For most of the history of recording, a lathe cut the music onto discs while the musicians were actually playing. A recording lathe was, to put it mildly, a cumbersome piece of equipment. Imagine plugging a microphone into something that was a cross between the world's biggest record player and a piece of heavy industrial equipment. Weighing in somewhere around an instant hernia, it was not a piece of gear to be taken lightly. The musicians had to come to *it* (hence the development of the recording studio). Recording on location at clubs or concerts was pretty much out of the question.

Another reality that lowered the recording fun factor was the time limitation of the disc itself. As previously noted, the lathe cut live to disc, one take per disc, with a time limit of around three minutes per take. Screw up or run overtime and you'd have to chuck out the disc. In fact I'm told that in the 1930s you could usually tell a good band from a bad one by how much acetate debris was lying around the lathe at the end of a session.

When magnetic tape became practical it offered solutions to a lot of the inconveniences and restrictions of cutting to disc. But there was one factor that would have perhaps the biggest impact on the art of recording. Once you cut to a disc it was done, fini, kaput, no possibility of altering what was on it. Magnetic tape, on the other hand, offered a new kind of flexibility to the artist. The artistic process didn't have to stop when the performance was done. The recordist could enhance the performance — in a sense return to the scene of the musical crime and rewrite history. Music could be added or subtracted by editing the tape through cutting and splicing. And of course the biggie, magnetic tape could be re-recorded entirely or even in sections. Want to fix something? All you had to do was send a new pattern of electric impulses to the tape and the particles would obediently reorient themselves to the new information. To use my previous analogy, the ants would get thawed out and then refrozen into a new configuration (I'm starting to feel sorry for the ants).

So even though the bulk of the *process* of converting sound was basically the same as in the days of Edison, the change in the storage medium from disc to magnetic tape was as profound as the progress from pen and paper to computer. For the first time in recording history the medium of storage became part of the artist's tool kit. The recordist went from being only able to take a snapshot of a performance to being able to use production artistry to enhance a performance. To borrow an analogy from film, it was like going from making documentaries to making movies.

Edison with a Six-String: Les Paul and Multitracking

The buzz this newfound flexibility caused among the music community led to a further development by another genius, a rock-and-roll Thomas Edison named Les Paul. By the 1950s this guy (one of my personal heroes) had not only given us a practical electric guitar but had also developed multitrack recording in his garage. He did all this as part of his desire to experiment with his own music. Oh, did I leave out that he and his partner Mary Ford were also major hit recording artists? The first commercial use of multitrack was two-track recording, a little thing called "stereo."

What Les Paul did was to take two sets of mono tape-recorder heads and stack them one on top of another. Then, using a double-wide tape, he was able to get two tracks of recording room side by side on the same machine. By recording on only one track when he played the first time he could then use the second track to record an accompaniment without erasing the original. Voilà, two-track recording, and the first use of overdubbing. Eventually Paul would stack eight tracks onto one machine, the world's first genuine eight-track multi-recorder.

This kind of innovation was to open the floodgates of musical creativity. With the use of magnetic tape, nothing was written in stone. If you messed up you could fix it by re-recording. You could go back after the fact and change what you had stored. You could overdub and add instruments and musical ideas. You could speed up the tape and slow it down to alter pitch. Basically, you could sculpt and resculpt your music until you were happy with it.

I'm giving you this little history spiel for a reason. I want you to realize that all of recording is basically multiples of a few principles. If you understand the relationship between sound vibrations and what ends up on tape then the ways to manipulate sound and to care for it become logical. It's easy to get lost in all of the recording technobabble, all the gear, all the specs, all the stuff. But the bottom line is that if you understand how Edison did it, then you know how it's done. Everything else follows from that. A forty-track multi-machine is really forty mono machines stacked one on top of the other. If you understand how one works you understand how they all work. Magnetic tape, multitracking, and frequency manipulation are all brilliant variations on Edison's basic theme.

Edison's Recipe for Recording

To record, take a sonic vibration and convert it into a form of energy to be stored in an impressionable medium. To play back the information, reverse the process, use the information stored, and reconvert it so it vibrates something and makes sound.

So later if it starts to get a little confusing, try to reduce the amount of unnecessary noise in your head by rereading the above and chanting "Edison, Edison, Edison...."

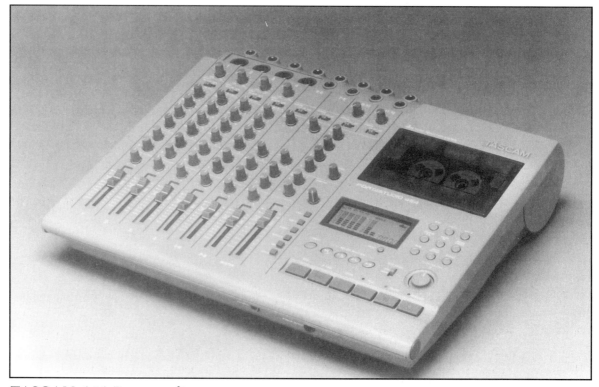

TASCAM 464 Portastudio

How a Tape Recorder Does What It Does

In the last chapter we discussed the concepts that lie at the heart of the recording process and a little history about the developments that got us to here and now, recordingly speaking. In this chapter I'm going to focus on how a tape recorder actually works and, perhaps more importantly, what this means to you when it comes to getting great sounds.

Transduction, as you no doubt are getting tired of hearing, is simply the process of converting one form of energy to another. In our particular area of interest that would be sound energy into electrical energy. This is done by the transducer (usually a microphone) before anything goes to the tape recorder. A simple analogy: the telephone mouthpiece converts a voice to electricity, and it goes over a wire and ends up in your ear. What happens then? It gets stored as information in your brain. The tape recorder's job is analogous to your memory — it stores the information that results from the conversion of sound to electricity. So the function of the tape recorder is storage. That's it. Period.

Unfortunately, unlike your brain the tape recorder doesn't discriminate between what's valuable information and what's just meaningless junk. For instance, you know that your Swiss bank account number is worth remembering and so you allocate brain cells to it, whereas Aunt Livia's detailed and grisly gall bladder story is probably not going to rate much memory space. We humans have the discretionary ability to filter out the information that we want to ignore. Now, think of the bank account number as signal and the gall bladder story as noise and you have the basic principle of good recording. You want to help the tape recorder allocate as much memory to valuable stuff and as little to noise as possible.

The Portable Studio Configuration

For this chapter I think the concepts are easier to explain if you think of the portable studio as two separate units packaged together. Kind of like a duplex apartment. Two complete living arrangements that happen to share some plumbing and wiring. One half of the portable studio is the **console** and the other half is the **tape recorder**. I'll go into this in greater depth as the book goes on, but I mention it because for now there'll be less room for confusion if you think of the tape unit as a detached piece of machinery.

The Basic Machinery

All tape recorders are operationally pretty much the same. This is true whether you're talking about your portable studio or a $125,000 24-track machine. They function by using a motor to pull a strip of magnetically sensitive tape across magnetically active heads, which transmit an amplified signal onto the tape. The machine then retrieves the signal and sends it out to be reconverted into sound.

Three Heads Are Better than One

This process requires three heads for each track of tape: an **erase** head, a **record** head, and a **playback** head.

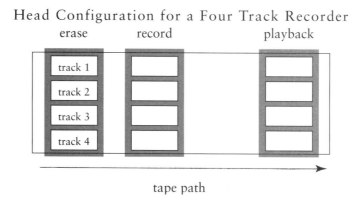

Head Configuration for a Four Track Recorder

erase   record   playback

track 1
track 2
track 3
track 4

tape path

The three heads are lined up one after the other. The erase head is first in line. When you put the machine in record the erase head cleans all previous electronic information off the tape so that a new alignment of particles can be achieved. Then the tape is sent to the record head. This head applies the signal to the tape, aligning the particles into a coherent signal. Finally, the tape gets to the playback head. Its function is to read what the record head wrote and report it to the amplifier for output.

This orderly assembly-line progression from erase head to record head to playback head is perfectly fine — that is, until you want to overdub.

Overdubs and the Sync Head

Overdubbing, as you probably know, is the process of recording a track as an accompaniment to another previously recorded track. This is accomplished by listening to the first track and playing or singing along to record to another track. This capability is certainly one of the revolutionary features of multitrack recording, allowing any recordist to be a one-man band, because recording different instruments can be done sequentially. However, when people first started overdubbing they encountered a problem. They had to guess when to start playing and singing. Why?

Because the record head and playback head were in different locations, with a time lag in between. If you look at the above diagram you'll see that you could not be recording and listening to the same part of the tape at the same time. They are separated by some distance. So in order to create a more perfect union, so to speak, Ampex Corporation came up with a new wrinkle. Someone invented the Selectable Synchronizer Head, better known as Sel-Sync, or today just the sync head.

What Ampex did was to add a less sensitive playback head in the same location as the record head. In this very clever way they put the reference tracks you are listening to in the same physical place as what you are putting on tape, making them in sync with one another when you overdub.

Guided Tour of the Tape Machine

I think the easiest way to lay all this out is to take you on a Cook's tour of the tape machine to show you what happens where.

The Input to Tape

I'm deliberately going to deal with this information in a way that is as simple as I can make it because I want to show the interrelated processes as building blocks. Even if you're familiar with all of this, bear with me because I'm going to approach it from a functional standpoint, which is a little different from a technical one.

When you press the record button, the first thing that happens is that the sound (I know, it's not sound, it's electrical impulses transduced from sound, but sound has fewer letters than electrical impulses so I'm going to call it sound) is admitted to the machine. This is accomplished at the input point (plug) on the machine. The amount of sound admitted by the input is controlled by an amplifier with a volume or gain control. You can see how much sound is going into the machine by watching the meters on the front of the unit. These indicate in decibels how much gain is going to go to tape when it's recorded.

The next step in the process is that the erase head sends a blast of magnetic energy to the tape to delete whatever's there and get the tape ready to record. After that, the input electrical impulses are sent through wires to the record heads. These heads consist of coils that transmit signal to pieces of magnetically active metal through which an ordered signal is transmitted to the tape.

Note: The angle of the heads relative to the tape is called the **azimuth**. This physical relationship is very important because if the heads are not making good contact with the tape, the signal is only being partially recorded.

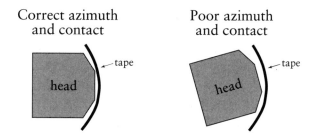

The Tape

The tape is a strip of thin polymer coated with magnetically sensitive particles called oxide. The tape is stored on reels which the recorder motors spool to allow the tape to pass across the heads at a predetermined speed. As the signal is transmitted through the head to the tape the oxide particles line up in response to the electrical pattern. The combinations of patterns make a continuous trail of particles oriented by the magnetic field of the head. This continuous trail is an analog, an uninterrupted record of the event, hence the name "analog recording." Just to firmly fix the picture in your mind in a particularly disgusting fashion, picture the trail of slime a garden slug leaves on the sidewalk as it moves. From the trail you can recreate the journey the slug took. The slime trail is an analog of a slug out for a stroll.

Those are the basic mechanics of how the tape recorder works and how sound gets onto tape. Seems simple enough.

Simple? So How Come My Recording Sounds Borderline Lousy?

Oh yeah. That's because there's a lot of opportunity for error in the process. The key term that I will pound away on is **signal-to-noise ratio**; that is, the relationship between what you want to hear and what you don't. Noise is what you don't want to hear. At all. Ever. Unfortunately, some noise is an inherent part of the recording process. And so the battle begins. Remember: noise is the enemy — it is Darth Vader to your Obi-Wan Kenobi, it is the dark side, the yin to your yang, the Riddler to your Batman, and so on ad nauseam. In short, noise is a bad thing. But it can be defeated if, as the old saying goes, you "know thine enemy" and are ever vigilant. A big part of the rest of this book is devoted to getting rid of noise in one way or another.

Noise

Music is organized sonic energy. Noise, quite simply, is random, unorganized energy. If you want to see what noise looks like, check out your TV picture when you're flipping between stations. All those white dots called "snow" are noise. They show the presence of energy transmitted to the tube that doesn't add up to anything recognizable (unless you are, shall we say, a very unusual person).

When we're talking about audio recording, noise is *the random excitation of oxide particles on the tape*. When the energy going to tape is organized you have an analog of whatever you're recording. When the energy going to tape is disorganized you have the auditory equivalent of snow.

So Noise Sucks! Well, Mostly.

Here's a general rule. Whenever signal is being transmitted there is the possibility of noise, and an effort has to be made to avoid it. But not all noise is unintentional. A very specific kind of noise is actually necessary to the recording process. This is called **bias signal**.

Bias

The subject of bias can be one of the great black holes of recording education. The physics of bias and magnetic fluxivity have been the topic of whole incredibly technical dissertations. Real high-octane stuff read and used by genuine brainiacs. I don't think we need that just now. So let me describe it in a little more functional way. All you really need to know is that tape recorder bias is a high-frequency low-level signal sent to the tape by an oscillator in the machine whose function is to get the molecules of oxide moving around so they are ready to accept signal. You see, molecules of oxide won't move unless they have to (which is often the case with me, too). The biasing signal is sort of a little electronic goosing used to overcome inertia so the molecules are ready to line up and go to work when called upon.

Magnetic tape before charging by recording

thin plastic backing—oxide particles are randomly distributed

Put into record mode

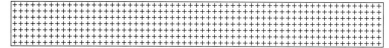

bias signal is sent to initialize tape

Signal is recorded

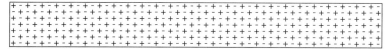

record head organizes particles in response to input from source

Why this becomes important to you, the recordist, is that the bias signal, while necessary, is for all its noble purpose, noise. It is a random excitation of molecules. Your recorded signal on the other hand is hopefully not noise, but the *organized* excitation of molecules.

So what we have is the bias signal being sent with the record signal. But what happens to the biased (excited) molecules that your signal doesn't line up? They remain as background noise. Just like if you have poor reception on your TV — you get electronic snow interfering with your enjoyment of *Gilligan's Island*.

A Small Side-Trip

Some time when you can't sleep and it's too dark to stack BBs, try this. If you want to hear the difference between biased and unbiased tape, put a brand new cassette into your machine and play a little of it. Listen carefully. You should be hearing the sound of pretty much nothing. Now put the machine into record and let the tape roll but don't plug anything in. That is, record a little nothing (no, this isn't a Zen thing). When you play back the portion of the tape that you put into record you will hear a different kind of nothing. What you're hearing is the bias signal, a hissing sound that we're all too familiar with.

(Note: If you are putting a master tape of several songs together make sure that the tape between the songs is biased. By this I mean tape that has been put into record without input signal. Pure blank tape will make the recorded program sound noisy by comparison when the song starts.)

Now you know that the instant you go into record, even before you have recorded note one, there is already noise going onto your nice clean tape. Fortunately this bias noise is at very low level per track. Unfortunately, as you will see, you are going to multiply the noise by the number of tracks you record and multiply that by the number of times you premix. That's why it's crucial that you try to minimize the noise and optimize the signal at each step along the way.

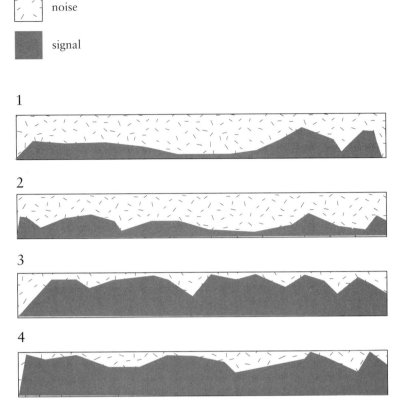

noise

signal

1

2

3

4

Track 1 and 2 have a relatively poor signal-to-noise ratio, while 3 and 4 are more desirable. If you add tracks 1, 2, 3, and 4 in the mix you can see that the combined noise will be almost equal to the combined signal.

Recording with a Good Signal-to-Noise Ratio

The first thing to notice about the diagram above is that the desired signal (sound) takes up some physical portion of the tape. More accurately, it occupies some percentage of the total number of oxide particles on the tape. These particles act sort of like brain cells, with each contributing to the storage of a given memory.

Now to take this brain cell thing one step further, if I were searching for my long-lost love in the forest I would listen for her voice amid all the other noises in the forest. I would try to remove any noises from my consciousness except the sound of her voice. My brain would be sorting as best it could for the sound I want to hear. But if she were very far away and calling my name, the amount of her voice that I hear would be relatively less than the accumulated sounds in the forest. Valuable ear and brain space would be taken up by information that was only background. As I got closer to her, I would hear relatively more of her voice than the sounds in the forest, until ideally as I got near her I would hear almost no background sounds, only her sweet voice saying, "For crying out loud, get this $&%#@Y log off me, willya!"

Well, bias noise is the constant background. And in order for it to disappear, the sound you want to hear has to take up relatively more storage space. The easiest way to describe good recording technique is to say that you want the signal to reach the tape with as much level as possible and still remain below the threshold of distortion.

Tape Distortion and Saturation

What that means in real-world terms is most easily explained by looking at the storage medium (magnetic tape) and reiterating a principal characteristic. Magnetic tape is not magnetic. It's the gazillion or so little particles that coat the tape that are magnetic. This molecular worm's-eye perspective makes it easier to understand how signal level can cause tape distortion.

A Definition of Distortion

Distortion is the deforming of something from its natural state. The American Heritage Dictionary defines to distort as, "To twist out of a proper or natural relation of parts; misshape." If you accidentally stomp on your grandmother's locket, chances are that the pictures inside are going to be distorted. On the other hand, if you heat up and bend a steel bar into a horseshoe you are also distorting the form of the steel bar. But you are doing it deliberately; it is a controlled form of distortion. I mention this because there is a matter of intent to distort. Not all distortion is bad (as any guitar player will tell you). But for the purposes of this book, unless otherwise noted I'm talking about unintentional distortion.

Back to Tape Distortion and Saturation

Earlier we talked about amplitude and frequency as components of recorded signal. When it comes to the tape the amplitude of the signal is expressed as the number of oxide particles that are charged by it. The frequency of the signal is expressed by the arrangement of the pattern of particles.

When a signal is properly recorded a high percentage of the oxide particles is excited by the organized signal from the input. This balance is maintained throughout the entire analog of the signal. We know what happens when the signal is too soft — we get noise. But what happens if the signal is too loud? Then we get what amounts to an overload. This is exactly equivalent to overexposing a photograph. The particles of oxide are used up, every particle stuffed, the volume is on "11," the cup runneth over. What you get instead of a nice orderly amplitude pattern is saturation. Tape saturation is the point at which there are no more oxide particles left to charge. This means there is no contrast between levels of loudness, because all the particles are as excited as they can get. Like in the case of overexposed film, where there is so much light that the picture is distorted.

Transient Response

Tape saturation is usually an undesirable situation, because it limits transient response, the ability of a tape recorder to express the attack of a sound and accurately reflect the tonality that follows the attack. As you know, when you hit a drum there is a sharp "bang" followed by the tone of the drum. The bang is relatively louder than the tone. The bang is of course the transient. However, if you set the input signal to tape so that the tone is at saturation level, then all the particles will be equally excited, and the bang and the tone will be of equal volume. To put it intuitively, the tape quite simply couldn't get any louder.

By saturating the tape you are removing dynamics. For reasons that will become obvious later in the book, this is also called tape compression. This means that when you're recording you have to be careful about saturation on tracks where the transient is very important to preserve — things like drums and cymbals, clean guitar parts, and so on. This is also especially true of vocals, where you want to retain as much of the character of the voice as possible. If the dynamic contrasts are missing because the overall level is too loud to tape, you will limit your possibilities of nuance or shading.

How Much Is Too Much?

So now you can see why proper recording technique is a balancing act between signal and noise. Too little level and you get unwanted bias noise. Too much level and you get tape saturation and distortion. How much is too much? A reasonable rule of thumb is that you should try to keep your recording level such that the peaks only momentarily touch the top of the meter and the lows don't dip much below -3 dB unless the sound is fading out (decaying).

Using Tape Compression for Dynamic Control

For those of you who are more advanced, tape compression can be used deliberately to provide dynamic control over certain sounds where unpleasant peaks are a problem. This, however, requires practice with your specific machine. You need to know how much level your machine can take to make sure that the results are musical.

TIPS ON TAPE

Magnetic tape is a volatile medium. There are a number of environmental factors that can affect it. I can't stress enough the importance of taking care of the tape itself. It is important not only from the standpoint of caring for your work but for your equipment as well.

- Use new tape for important recordings. Much-recorded-over tape will have some oxide rubbed off, and high-end response will suffer as a result.

- If you must record on a cassette that is more than 6 months out of the package, be sure to check the heads on your tape machine frequently for shedding problems.

- Store your masters in a dark space with a stable median temperature. Avoid extremes of temperature. *Never* leave a master recording in your car.

- *Never, never, never put your cassettes on a speaker.* There is a big magnet in the voice-coil of a speaker. The material on your cassette is magnetized particles. Put them near a big magnet and POOF! They'll be partially erased.

- The more times you pass the tape over the heads the more oxide will be rubbed off and the poorer the high-frequency response will be. So when you premix (see "The Step-by-Step Recording and Mixdown chapter") record the mix back onto a fresh cassette, particularly if the original is much used.

Another Source of Noise: Generation Loss

When you record a recording of a recording you are liable to get what's referred to as **generation loss**. A "generation" in this case refers to a copy once removed from the source. For instance, a mixdown is a first-generation copy. A copy of the mix is a second-generation copy, and so on.

Generation loss is characterized by an increase in noise and a decrease in clarity. The reason this happens is that each time you make a copy of a copy the noise from the first copy is transmitted along with the signal to be recorded on the second-generation copy. The second generation makes its own noise, which is combined with the noise from the previous generation. This noise takes up oxide molecules, leaving less room for the signal. Think of a Xerox of a Xerox of a Xerox. By the time you get done there are dots all over the paper and you can just barely make out the dirty joke. Enough generations of copying and there is likely to be more noise than signal.

Defeating Noise: A Shorthand List of What to Do

Here are some guidelines for controlling noise in your recordings.

- **Consider the tape itself:** The first area of noise concern is the type of tape you use and the way it's been handled. To begin with, a very good thing to do is to use the type of tape (not necessarily the brand) recommended by the manufacturer of your machine. The amount of bias signal generated by the machine is determined by the designers. This bias signal is usually optimized for a high bias (CrO_2) cassette, which allows for a better high frequency imprint on the tape. Using a tape that matches those specs will help in the noise war.

- **Record nothing when you're not recording something:** When recording try to keep the input off in between actual present signal. For instance, if a guitar part only occurs intermittently, try to pull the fader down between parts. This will help remove some extra noise. (This is also a good idea when mixing: "Dip" the volume of a track when it isn't playing to help with noise.)

- **Clean the heads frequently:** Not keeping the heads clean of dirt and "tape shedding" (particles of oxide rubbed off on the metal of the heads from friction) can result in a radical loss of top-end sensitivity and increased noise. Heads should be cleaned before you start to record and every thirty or so minutes of use.

- **Use the highest possible tape speed:** Now that you know that the more particles that are exposed to the input signal the better, you can guess that the faster the tape passes over the heads the more particles are going to be available for creating a picture of the sound. This is most noticeable in the top end, where the complexities of high-frequency information require a lot of charged particles to be accurate. So except when you are using your porta as a musical sketch pad use the top speed available.

- **Use noise reduction (Dolby, DBX, etc.):** The way a noise-reduction unit works is to create an exaggerated dynamic relationship between the noise you don't want and the sound you do. These units are very specific forms of compressor-type devices. They combine noise and signal in such a way that when the signal is decoded the noise level is relatively lower than the signal. (Important note: If you "encode" [record with] a noise-reduction signal, you must decode it in order to get the expected result. Undecoded noise-reduced tracks sound overly bright and hissy.)

- **Check the azimuth:** This problem is usually manifest as an absence of high-frequency response and a peculiar rise in the noise floor of the top end. If your cymbals sound dull (and the heads are clean) take the unit to a shop to see if the azimuth needs to be aligned.

- **Check the bias adjustment:** If after doing all of the above you still get what you feel is an extraordinary amount of noise, you need to have the bias checked. This will require a trip to the shop, where they can check to be sure that the bias is properly optimized.

A Final Reminder on Signal-to-Noise Ratio

Make sure the signal-to-noise ratio is optimized at every step of the way, including during the mixes and premixes.

What You're Going to Do It With: The Tools of Recording and How They Work

The Portable Studio

When the portable studio was first invented by the whiz guys at TEAC Corporation in the late 1970s it was immediately recognized as one of those brilliantly simple ideas whose time had clearly come. The idea was to take the two key components of the recording process and combine them into one unit. And so a **console** was joined to a **tape machine**. Then, before the thing got out of the prototype stage, some wise boffin said, "Hey, let's use a cassette deck as our recording device instead of a reel-to-reel recorder and we can make this thing truly portable. Make it relatively inexpensive, make it so it can fit in a one-room apartment." Zowie! Build it and they will come! This was it, a recording revolution, a recorder for the unheard masses, a machine for Everyman, a rabble recorder for proletariat pop. There must have been a zillion people in the tape recorder business who smacked themselves in the head and said, "Why didn't I think of that?"

Two, Two, Two Machines in One

As I said, the portable studio is basically composed of two parts: a console, or mixer, section that acts as a switchboard for directing and routing signals, and a tape machine, which is used to imprint the signals you want to remember and retrieve later.

I think the easiest way to deal with the relationship between the main components of the portable studio is to break them up and discuss them separately. I adopt this approach probably because my personal orientation is to think of the console and tape machine separately, as two distinct parts of a recording system. So I'm going to take an ax and divide the portable studio between two chapters. In the next chapter I'll discuss the console, and then I'll give you an overview of the tape machine. Finally I'll give you some recommendations with regard to features to look for in purchasing or upgrading your portable studio.

The Console

When you walk into a professional studio the first thing you usually notice is the **console** (sometimes called a **desk** or **board,** depending where you're from). This impressive *Star Trek*–ian collection of knobs and glowing lights is command central for most of the activities that will take place in the studio. It is the brain of the recording process, the place where the ears connect and the sound is interpreted and routed to the appropriate location.

The first time I saw a pro console I thought of it as some kind of alien intelligence, winking and blinking at the engineer but indecipherable and mute to the uninitiated (like me), and intimidating as all get out to mere mortals (like me). It was only later in my career when I began to use the equipment myself that I had a revelation — of those million or so knobs, not all, but most, just make the damn thing louder. No, really, it's true. And the flashing lights? Those, for the most part, tell you how much louder you've made it. And when you've made it too loud they turn red.

Another Trip Down Magnetic Memory Lane

Okay, I'm oversimplifying a little. Which I will proudly do again. What a console does is to receive an electronic signal that has been converted from a sound (transduced by a microphone for example) and send it to the tape machine to be recorded. In its simplest form the console is just a thing that plugs into the tape machine and acts like a big extension cord. In fact, you don't even have to have it. You could plug the mic directly into the tape recorder and save all the trouble and expense (not to mention all the packing material the console came in). However, like all stuff in the recording world, the console was created to meet a need.

Way back in the dark ages of recording there was a need to be able to plug more than one mic at a time into the recording device. In order to do this, some kind of a mixer was required to collect all the mic signals and gather them up and send them to one place (that is, the recording machine). So somebody put together a bunch of inputs and had all the signals wired so they would go to the same output (many in/one out). This single output could then be plugged into the input of the recording device. There you have a simple mono console. A bunch of signals come in, but only one combined signal goes out.

In addition to combining all the signals, a mixer had to able to balance levels of microphones so that the instruments blended. Kind of like fixing the temperature of your shower. You want just the right amount of cold and hot to come out of the shower head. You alter the volume of each separate source of water in order to blend the two so you don't scald yourself or permafreeze your skin into tundra goosebumps. The mixer works the same way. It allows the volume of each sound to be increased or decreased in the blend.

Well, after they got the volume-mixing thing happening someone thought that it might be a good idea to be able to alter the sound as it was on its way to the recording machine. So they added equalization to the list of functions. In this way not only could the volume be changed but the tone could be modified and noise removed as well.

Then a little while later someone needed to send the signal to more than one recording machine at the same time. So a circuit was designed that would split the signal and send it to two places. This became what's known as the auxiliary (or effect) send and could be used to route the signal.

Now you had a piece of gear that could: 1. collect several signals together; 2. alter the sound of the signals; 3. blend the relative volumes of the signals; and 4. send the output signal to one or more machines. So what started out as an extension cord had become a sophisticated piece of artistic-enhancement equipment. And that is basically the modern console.

Before We Go Further

Throughout the following chapters I'll introduce you to some terms that are commonly used in recording. Most of the meanings of these lingoisms succumb to common sense, but please bear with me even if you know them because hidden in these words are the clues to how all the pieces fit together. For this reason I'll emphasize certain terms and define them as they are used in recording. At the end of the chapter there is a glossary of the most common ones.

The Chain of Events

Here's the whole deal from beginning to end: Something goes into the console section of the portable studio and then comes out on its way to the tape machine. Along the way it has picked up some different characteristics. I'm going to use a "think of the signal as water" analogy to paint the picture. It's not entirely accurate, but I think it's better than using the "think of the signal as peanut butter" analogy favored in certain circles.

A Virtual-Reality Experience

Imagine a stream coming down out of the mountains. It is pure and crystal-clear. You are a livestock owner who wants to channel the water to feed your oxen and wildebeests. So you dig a canal. When the water gets to your canal you need a valve that controls how much water flows in. As the water passes through the canal it picks up dirt. It's no longer pure and crystal clear — it's brown. Now, since you're a conscientious sort of wildebeest owner you don't want your animals drinking dirt, so you want to purify the water to get it back to its crystal clarity. With another valve you divert the flow from the canal to your own little purifying plant where, through the magic of processing, the water is returned to its pristine state. Now you have repurified the water coming out of the purifying plant and it's heading to the animals' troughs.

Your past experience as an animal owner tells you that the oxen and wildebeests don't like to drink from the same trough (something about ox slobber offends the wildebeests). So you have to make an adjustment and route the water to two different places. You turn a valve that splits the water flow and sends it to two different pipes and so to two different locations. So there's water that goes to the oxen and water that goes to the wildebeests. Now as it turns out, you have not one but four wildebeest troughs, and you want to get the water to the one you designate. So you use a diverter valve that routes the water to the trough you want (and only the trough you want). Finally, you know that the troughs can only hold so much water at a time; you have to adjust the flow so that each trough is filled up but not overflowing. You do so by means of a big valve between the pipes and the troughs.

To recap: the water enters through a valve where its volume is controlled and then it is purified. Then it is sent to a valve that splits its flow and sends it to separate places, one path to the oxen and the other to the wildebeests. A choice is made as to which wildebeest trough the water is going to. Finally, another valve is used to control the amount of water that goes to the wildebeests. Okay, so now you know how to set up a livestock irrigation scheme. But let's get back to consoles.

Trading Water for Electrons

Here's how the analogy plays out. When the signal enters a channel of the console via the input (the valve to the canal) it may be degraded by noise from components or unwanted frequencies (dirt). The sound is therefore sent to the equalizer (purifying plant), which allows you to purify, modify, and enhance the sound by adding (or subtracting) frequencies to it. Then from there the signal returns to the main "stream" and you are presented with the choice of whether or not to split it in order to send it to two places. For instance, one signal might go to a reverb unit for processing (the oxen). This is done with the auxiliary (effects) send. The other signal goes to a tape track of the multitrack (the wildebeests). But how does it know which tape track to go to? Another kind of valve called a **buss assign**, or **track assign**, is the diverter valve that sluices the signal to the correct trough.

Some Definitions

Assigning a signal is the act of routing it to a particular destination.

A **buss** is a circuit that is capable of carrying *several* signals at once to a *single* destination.

A **circuit** is a hardwired signal pathway.

The business of assigning and bussing lies at the heart of the functioning of a console. It is from this activity that the path of a signal is chosen. Most commonly in the world of the portable studio, the **pan pot** functions as the selector for bussing the signal. By manipulating the pan you can change the destination of the signal as it goes out of the channel.

This is where some confusion about the function of the pan pot can result. The portable studio manufacturer uses the pan pot in two different ways, depending on the stage of recording. For recording to a specific track on the portable studio tape machine the pan is used as a buss assign. For stereo mixing the pan pot functions as a device for placement of a signal in the stereo spectrum.

Being Assigned to the Right Buss to Get Safely to School

Think of a buss as a vehicle for transporting a group of signals to the same place. Like a school bus, it stops along the way to let different little signals get on and then delivers them all to the same school. The buss assign (also called the track assign) is the button (or pan pot) you use that sends the little signal on that particular vehicle.

For instance, if you have a four-track recorder there are obviously four choices of where to send the signal to be recorded. Let's say you want to send a guitar to track 4. You would assign the signal to track 4 by using the control designated for track 4. The signal would then travel down the circuit that addressed track 4 of the tape machine. So far in this chapter we have dealt with only one channel on the console. But let's say that there are *several* channels that you want to combine to go to a single place. Now here's where it can get a little tricky.

Let's say you want to add a keyboard and yodel-harp along with the guitar to track 4 at the same time. No problem. If you want to combine more than one signal to track 4 you would assign all of their respective channels to buss 4. Then they're *all* going to be combined and transported to the same destination. You have to balance the level of each in order to be able to hear it individually in the blend, and that brings us to the next stage. (By the way, I think it only fair to point out that in this little section alone you've had schoolbuses, little signal kids, wildebeests, canals, streams, guitars, keyboards, and a yodel-harp. If that isn't value for money then I don't know what is.)

The Last Stage in the "Console as Irrigation" Scheme

Finally, the volume of the signal that is going to the buss — and ultimately to the track of the tape machine — is controlled by another sort of a big valve, the **fader.**

Diagram: The Signal Path

At each stage of the process you have the option to perform or not perform some operation. Just like the valves and canals, the console will route the signal through the passages you assign it.

Basic Console Routing
(to record to track 4)

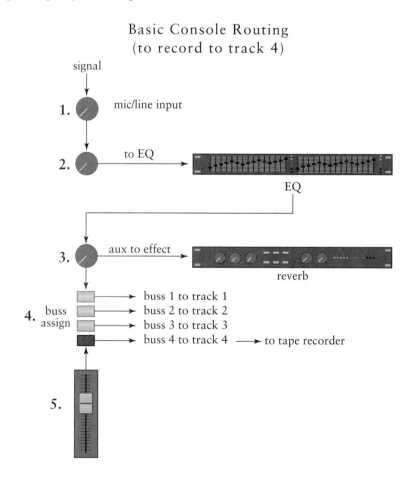

The signal comes into the channel module and is then subject to a series of decisions as to where it will go and how it will be treated.

1. The decision is whether the signal is from a microphone or a line source and how much of it should come into the channel
2. This decision is whether or not to send the signal to the equalizer and, if so, how much equalization should take place.
3. The decision here is whether to send some part of the signal to an additional tape machine or effect.
4. This decision is which buss and therefore which track to send the signal to.
5. The final decision is how much of the signal to send.

First, Some More Terms...

The **recording chain** is the combination of all elements that go into the recording and playback process. These might include the microphone to the console to the reverb to the tape recorder and so on.("Everything was all set up in the recording chain but I started to smell a burning odor. Is that what they mean by chain smoking?")

The signal route that you define using the console is called the **signal path**. Makes pretty good intuitive sense. The term simply describes where the signal is going. ("The EQ was faulty and interrupted the signal path.")

A **channel** is the location of the signal path. To go back to our analogy of the wildebeest ranch, a channel is like a canal to divert the water down a specific path. It is the combination of valves and canal that controls the signal path. ("I input the signal into the channel but somehow it got routed to my television.") The channel is often referred to as a **console module** because channels are modular; independent of one another but using the same resources (power, for instance).

The **console** is the collection of all the channels, the group of canals through which all the signals are flowing down their respective signal paths. ("I've got all these channels on the console. Which one is ESPN?")

A **clean signal** is one that is unencumbered by a bunch of unwanted extraneous electronic information, such as noise. ("I couldn't get a clean signal out of the console, so I took it outside and hosed it down. Now all I get is BZZZT!#*!")

A **send** is a circuit that sends the signal outside the console to another location in the recording chain. A send is an output of the console. Each send has its own control circuitry. ("I sent the guitar signal out to the reverb but it still hasn't come back.")

A **return** is a circuit that accepts the signal back into the console. A return is an input to the console. ("I sent the signal out to the reverb and returned it to channel 4 through the line input in the back of the console.")

Decisions, Decisions

In your role of recordist you have decisions to make at each stage of the console, such as which valves to turn and where to send the signal. The first decision is *what kind* and *how much* of a signal to input to the console. The second is how you wish to *alter* the signal. The third decision is whether or not you want to send some portion of the signal to *another processor*. Finally, you use the console to implement your decision as to *how much* of the signal you want to go to tape and to which track. And so we march forward to the console controls.

Anatomy of a Portable Studio: The Channel Modules

Channeling the Signal without Going Into a Trance

Behold, a diagram of a channel, which when combined with other channels and some other stuff makes up the console. In this diagram you see a bunch of numbered locations. These are approximate in position but conventional in console construction.

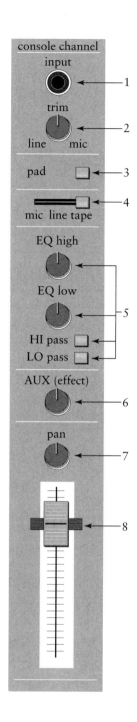

But First, an Introduction to the "Goes-Inta" and the "Goes-Outta"

A substantial number of the components of a console could be described as goes-intas and goes-outtas. As in: something goes into here and goes out of there. In fact a whole lot of the recording process could be described as a chain of goes-intas and goes-outtas. The vocal mic goes inta the input of the channel, where something happens to it, and then it goes outta the input and goes inta the equalizer of the channel and goes outta there and inta the effect send and then goes outta the effect send and goes inta the effect return and then goes... and so on. So, on our tour be on the lookout for the various goes-intas and goes-outtas and what they go into and out of.

Tour of a Channel Module

1. Input stage

The **input stage** is the place where a signal is introduced into the console for routing. This is the first stop on our channel road map. This is the place where it all begins, the input to the channel, the place where the cable carrying the signal gets plugged in.

How it works:

Sex!!! The input is a female connector that will accommodate a specific type of male plug that is mated to the circuitry inside. For the most part the entry-level or less expensive portable studios have as an input a 1/4" phono jack like that on a guitar, and the input stage circuitry is rigged to operate with high-impedance devices. The more sophisticated portable studios may have an additional type of plug called an *XLR,* or *multi-pin,* plug which is usually associated with low-impedance devices, particularly microphones.

Balanced and Unbalanced Inputs

The distinction between plug types is more than just a matter of aesthetics. The type of plug used usually indicates whether or not a console's input is balanced or unbalanced. This is an indication of the signal's level of protection from broadcast radio frequency (RF) and electromagnetic interference (EMF). A **balanced** low-impedance line uses the XLR connector described above. This is the more effective shield against having Oldies radio or electronic noise from Aunt Hildy's hair dryer getting onto your tape. Without getting overly technical, the XLR plug uses separate connector poles that are out of phase with each other to eliminate noise. That's why there are three plugs and holes. An **unbalanced** high-impedance device relies on a passive shield such as a metal foil to keep RF and EMF from the wires and therefore from transmission to the console. (Note: The subject of **impedance** itself is beyond the scope of this book, but there are many good electronic references out there if you want to investigate the subject further.)

How to use it:

Plug the appropriate plug into the appropriate hole.

2. Trim pot

The **trim pot** is the volume control for the channel input. The word "pot" is an abbreviation of **potentiometer**, a fancy way of saying gain control, or volume knob.

How it works:

It operates by controlling a preamplifier that can boost the signal as it enters the input stage of the module.

How to use it:

For instance, if the microphone level is too low for a good signal-to-noise ratio, the trim is used to raise the level before it interacts with any potential noise-producing circuitry farther on in the channel. The trim pot on some units also controls the level of the line inputs (for "direct in" instruments) as well. Check your manual.

3. Pad

Some consoles are equipped with an **attenuation pad**. The pad is usually a simple on/off switch that reduces the level by a fixed amount. **Attenuation** refers to the loss of a signal's strength either through natural resistance or by electronic means.

How it works:

This little goodie is used to "pad down," or lower the gain of, the incoming signal. It is a sort of one-position volume control that is inserted into the signal chain, reducing the input gain *before* it gets to the input circuitry. As I noted above, the gain reduction is by a predetermined amount. Check your portable studio manual for the amount of reduction accomplished by engaging the switch.

How to use it:

You would engage the pad in a situation where the signal coming into the console is overloading the input circuitry, making nasty distortion buzzes.

4. Mic/line/tape switch

The **mic/line/tape** is usually a click-stop three-position switch that tells the console where to get its signal from and what circuit to address with the signal.

How it works:

Mic level is the gain of the signal generated by a microphone, which is very low (as low as -60 dB), and it is therefore boosted by a preamplifier circuit.

Line level is the gain level of a signal generated by a guitar or signal-processing device. With high-impedance devices this level is usually -10 dB.

Tape level is the level of the output from the tape recorder section of the portable studio.

How to use it:

When you plug something into the channel you need to know what level the device is in order to set the selector properly. Check your device and console manuals to see what's appropriate. An improper matchup can cause a lot of unwanted noise.

5. Equalizer section

Throughout this book you will see the terms **equalization** or **equalizer** abbreviated to **EQ**. A functional definition of a console equalizer is that it is a circuit built into the console that is used to make certain selected *component* frequencies in the makeup of a sound louder or softer. This action is controlled by one or more pots, depending on the complexity and type of equalizer circuit.

Equalizers

The controls and discrimination allowed the recordist vary with the type of equalizer (see EQ types below), but whatever the type they all have controls labeled "boost" or "cut." **Boost,** as you will no doubt guess, makes the selected frequency louder. **Cut** makes the frequency softer.

In effect the EQ circuit is a volume control for *parts* of a signal (see, I told you most of the knobs just made stuff louder). In this manner the equalizer can be used to bring out the best qualities of a sound or to hide some of its warts and zits. For instance, if the signal coming from the vocal microphone is indistinct-sounding, you would use the EQ to boost the "presence" frequencies of the upper midrange to clarify the vocal. If you wanted to get rid of an unseemly flatulence from the bassoon you might cut the low frequencies.

Some General EQ Characteristics

An equalizer works by affecting a band of frequencies. This is accomplished through a sophisticated phase-relationship altering process, all you need to know of which is that it is tunable to affect the appropriate frequencies.

Basically there are two approaches to EQ design. Either the EQ is tuned permanently by the manufacturer, or it is constructed so that the recordist is able to vary the tuning at his or her discretion. The tuning of the equalizer determines which frequency band will be affected (just like a radio when you tune in a station).

An **EQ band** is an area of frequencies affected by an equalizer.

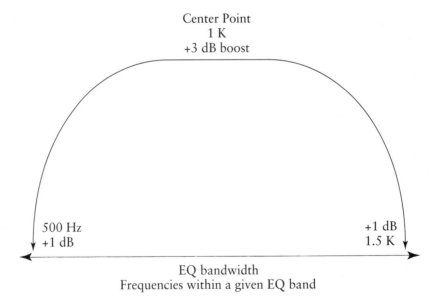

Center Point
1 K
+3 dB boost

500 Hz
+1 dB

+1 dB
1.5 K

EQ bandwidth
Frequencies within a given EQ band

In the above example of a **tone control equalizer,** the frequency of the band was set by the manufacturer. As you boost or cut the equalizer you are affecting not only the center frequency but also other frequencies within that band. How many of these frequencies are affected is determined by the manufacturer's design. It should be made clear that as the frequencies get farther away from the center point there is a diminishing effect on their level. In other words, if 1 K is boosted by 3 dB, 500 Hz and 1.5 K may only be boosted by 1 dB or less, depending on the designer's specifications. Most portable studios that have EQ have at least two bands, a high and a low.

Types of Equalizers

Later in the book I deal extensively with the types of equalizers reasonably available to the home recordist and the distinctions between them. In this section I'm going to give you an overview of the types and configurations of EQ found specifically on portable studios. Most of the portable studio machines out there use one or more of three basic types in combination. What you have on your particular machine is largely a function of price. The more expensive the unit, the more flexible the EQ.

The first type, the one most commonly seen, is the **tone control** equalizer. This is a control similar in type to what you'd find on a stereo. Usually the controls are labeled "treble" and "bass," or some variation like "high" and "low," and so on. This circuit was designed by the manufacturer to affect what it determined was the most useful frequencies in each range. The center frequency is fixed and the recordist has control over boost and cut functions only. So a tone control is a fixed-frequency equalizer. You need to refer to your manual to find out what frequencies are affected by each control.

tone-control-type equalizer

The second type of equalizer often found on portable studios is the **sweepable equalizer.** This circuitry adds another element to the tone-control type. The sweepable equalizer allows the recordist to select which frequency he or she wants to boost or cut.

This frequency selection is available within certain frequency boundaries set by the manufacturer. For instance, the most common application of this circuit is to the midrange EQ. The selectable frequencies may run from 1 K to 3 K and all points in between. This sweepable EQ is usually combined with two bands of tone control EQ for the high and low frequency ranges.

The third variety of equalizer frequently found on portable studio is the **click stop,** or **position switch,** type, usually reserved for the top and bottom frequencies. This type of EQ when engaged affects not only a *fixed frequency range,* but also gives a *fixed amount of boost or cut,* as determined by the manufacturer. The recordist controls only whether or not the EQ is on. This type of EQ is often used for *shelving,* which means boosting all the frequencies above or below a certain point. For instance, if the shelf is set by the designer at 10 K then engaging it will boost all the frequencies above 10 K.

How to use it:
One of the key skills of any recordist is the use of the equalizer. It is a skill that I have never stopped learning about. The EQ section of the console is really the first place in the recording chain where you can directly manipulate the frequency of the incoming signal. An equalizer can be used to enhance the signal itself by adding (or subtracting) particular frequencies; it is also frequently used as a problem-solver to remove elements that don't belong with the signal but

came along for the ride. These might include noise or rumble. In short, the EQ section is where you manipulate the sound of the sound that is coming into the channel.

The very first thing you need to know about how to use an equalizer is that you don't always have to. A rule of thumb and forefinger, before you twist that knob: *Any circuit that is engaged* will *contribute some noise to the signal path.* So if you don't have to use the EQ because you've done such a great job inputting the signal then so much the better.

Most recordists when we first got our hands on an equalizer assumed that boosting frequencies is what an EQ is for. It's natural to feel that improving a problem sound is a matter of adding something. So I, for one, was merrily cranking away, piling on the "freaks." Actually, with time and experience the "cut" function becomes just as important. Shaping a sound is always a matter of there being "more than one way to skin a nanoweber."

Here's what I mean. Let's say that the problem you have is an overall muddiness on the vocal track. You can either boost the presence range (upper midrange) to clear up the vocal, or cut some of the low-end interference that's causing the lack of clarity, or do both. The way I go about making a decision like that is to first work from the perspective of naturalness. Which approach is going to afford me the least "EQed"-sounding result? If I boost the presence range I'm boosting a whole bunch of frequencies that may not be entirely beneficial in order to get the one I want (remember that the manufacturer has preset the bandwidth of the frequencies I'm manipulating). On the other hand, if I remove some of the low end it may clear up the vocal without affecting the critical presence range and therefore may be a more subtle way to go. If I find that isn't getting the job done I might then also boost some of the high band. Get it? The process of EQing is one of balancing EQ ranges to get the most natural result. It's a yin and yang thing, a matter of finding the best balance.

(Just so you know — later on in the book I deal with a type of equalizer that is variable not only with regard to frequency selection and boost and cut but also bandwidth as well, called a parametric equalizer. Check out "The Effects Chapter" for more info on it and graphic equalizers.)

EQ and Signal Strength

The idea of an equalizer as a volume control carries with it an important implication that you need to be aware of: *When you boost a frequency you are making the total signal louder; when you cut a frequency you are making the total signal softer.* This means that even though you are affecting only a portion of the signal directly, you are still affecting the output of the whole signal. This becomes very important with regard to level to tape (or compressors — see "The Effects Chapter"). Adding EQ will add level to the signal, and therefore you need to adjust your level to tape *after* you equalize to avoid potential distortion problems. Every time you add EQ you add loudness, and so you need to check tape level after each EQ change.

High Pass and Low Pass Filters

These are highly specialized types of frequency manipulators that are found on higher-end equipment. They are on/off position switches, but their function is the opposite of the shelving equalizer. The job of these EQs is to remove (filter out) a range of frequencies above or below a fixed point.

The terminology can be a little confusing here. A **high pass filter** is a circuit that will let all sounds *above,* or higher than, the filter point pass through. Think of it as one of those signs you see before you get on a roller coaster: "If you're above this tall you can ride. If you're not then go get some lemonade kid cause you ain't gettin' through." Therefore a high pass filter cuts *lows*. It is very useful for getting rid of rumble and extreme lows.

A **low pass filter**, as the name would suggest, is a filter that will only allow frequencies *below* the filter point pass through. Like a tunnel where only the short can pass. Any frequency too tall gets its head knocked off. So, a low pass filter cuts *highs*. This filter is useful if you have some high-frequency noise that isn't a component of the instrument that you want to get rid of.

EQ in Mixing

An equalizer is not just used when the signal is first sent to tape. It can also be used during the mixdown stage. This is because the tape tracks are routed back through the circuitry of the console in order to be mixed to the stereo tape machine (more about that in "The Mixdown Chapter"). What this means is that you can do "compound equalization." You can apply EQ to the same signal at two different stages of the recording process.

Let's say that I am recording a guitar and I know that it will take a boost at both 500 Hz and 3 K to make me happy with the sound. The problem is that I only have one band of sweepable EQ, so I can't EQ both ranges at the same time when I lay the track to tape. What I would do is EQ the 3 K frequency as the guitar is first recorded, knowing that I will EQ the 500 Hz range when it comes time to mix the track. In effect I'm using one equalizer to function as two. The trick here is to have a mental picture of how you'd like the part to sound and then plan out your EQ accordingly. One way to do this is to test-record the guitar with the first EQ and play it back and apply the second-stage EQ and see how the two work together.

6. Auxiliary (effect) send

The **auxiliary (aux) send** (also called the **effect send**) is a routing device that splits (parallels) a signal and directs one signal arm to a specific auxiliary output.

How it works:

The knob on the auxiliary send will tell the circuit how much of the signal to send to its output. In this sense the auxiliary send is really both a volume knob and a directional device. If it's engaged it will send the amount of the signal that you determine to the auxiliary output of the console. You can then plug anything you want to be fed from the auxiliary output. An aux send is really a splitter box or Y-splitter with a volume control. So if your plug goes-outta (auxiliary send or output) with a cable to the goes-inta of a reverb, whatever level of volume you determine by the effect knob will be sent from the channel to the reverb via the auxiliary output.

Confusion, Maybe?

In this particular case an example will help. Let's say that you have only one reverb device but you'd like to hear it on both the guitar and the vocal. Not only that, but you want to hear different levels of the effect on each. The auxiliary send acts as a separate mixer for the reverb — just like a small console specifically for the reverb. You can send one volume of signal from the guitar track to the reverb and a different level from the vocal track, thereby mixing them in proportion as they are inputted to the reverb. Not only that, but you of course can plug anything you want into the auxiliary output. It doesn't have to be a reverb — it could be a compressor, a phaser, whatever a burst of creativity requires.

Actually, you got a bit of the story about effects sends in the discussion about busses. Remember, the circuit that goes between the knob and the output is called a buss. Anything you send to that circuit will end up at the same destination, in this case the effects output. In fact, you can dazzle your friends by referring to this function as the "auxiliary buss," harrumphing at anyone who calls it a reverb knob.

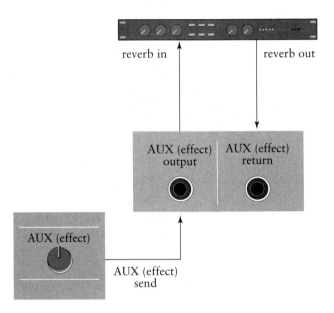

reverb in   reverb out

AUX (effect) output   AUX (effect) return

AUX (effect)

AUX (effect) send

Getting the Signal Back

Now here's where it gets a little tricky. Okay, you've got the signal going out the auxiliary send to the reverb. Now, how do you hear the reverb, and where does it go? The answer is: that depends. Here you have basically two choices to make. You can *record* the reverb onto the same track as the instrument, or you can *monitor* it and not record it at all.

Here's where you need to put on a set of functional perspective glasses. You need to think about what you want the device the auxiliary send is plugged into to *do*, not what it *is*.

If you want to record it, you treat it like an instrument (whether it's a reverb or whatever) and send it to a channel or a buss to tape. If you want to just listen to it, you send it to the monitor section, which does not record it.

Here's an important distinction: *When you are recording to a specific track of the portable studio anything that you want to record must be inputted to a channel, but when you are mixing down to an external machine everything that is going through the console will be recorded.* I will get into this in more detail in a bit. For the moment, however, just know that I am using the console to record to tracks of the portable studio, not to a mixdown machine.

Think of it this way. Let's say you have a song on a CD that you want to record to cassette (not that I'm endorsing this potentially illegal activity, you understand). If you plugged your CD player directly into the cassette deck you would get the CD signal only. (This is referred to as a "dry" signal, meaning unreverbed.) But if you were listening to the speakers as you made the copy, the room would be providing some natural reverb that you would hear along with the music. You would not be recording the reverb from the room to your cassette copy. The reverb would simply be a temporary listening condition. This, of course, would be *monitoring* the reverb. But if you sent some of the signal out into the room via the speakers and recorded the sound of the music bouncing off the walls by adding a room mic to the CD signal, you would be treating the reverb in the room as an instrument to be *recorded* with the CD track to the cassette deck. It would become part of the recording you are making.

What this means is that unless the reverb is plugged into a channel and then routed via a buss to a tape track then the reverb will not be recorded onto a track. You will be monitoring it without recording it.

Now there is a difference between the reverb in the analogy I just gave you and the reverb box you'll most often use in the recording world. In the above, the reverb was created by the natural sound of the speakers sending the music out to the room to bounce around the walls. A reverb device, however, is an electronic ambience simulator. There are no real walls in that little box; its algorithms must be translated from a completely electronic signal into sound. In order to do this it is "returned" to the console, where its signal is processed like any other instrument inputted to the console. Here's something to remember: *the console treats the signal from a reverb or a guitar exactly the same. The console is an equal opportunity signal employer.* If it can be plugged in the same way it can be treated the same way. The implications of this will become evident as you get into the recipes at the back of the book.

The Auxiliary Return

Different portable studio configurations use different solutions to return the effects to the console. In some cases there is a separate **effects (auxiliary) return** located in the **master module** (a discussion of which follows), or sometimes the effect needs to be returned to a channel specifically set up to function for this purpose (frequently with a stereo input). Check out your manual for further info. In any case, an effect can always be returned to any channel input. Think of the device as an instrument and follow the instructions for a line input.

How to use it:
At the end of this book there is a whole section of "recipes," the majority of which use an auxiliary send as a means to accomplish some tricks. Check out this section for more information.

An Analogy to Help You Understand Sends and Returns

It is easy to think of the effects sends and returns as a whole separate category of beast in the recording process, and this can lead to some confusion. Here's a way of thinking about it that might help to clear things up. Think of a guitar and a sound processor (reverb, delay, etc.) in your guitar rack. You connect them by a cable with one end plugged into the output of the guitar and the other end plugged into the input of the processor. Then you use the volume knobs on each to balance a sound between the instrument and processor.

Using the effect send is exactly the same principle. Think of the channel as the guitar, the effect output as the guitar jack, and the effect itself as a sound processor you're plugging in to. You plug a cable into the auxiliary (effect) send jack in the back of the console and the other end of the cable into the effect input. You use the "send" control on the channel as the volume knob to control the amount of signal leaving the channel and going to the device. You use the "input level" control on the device to control the amount of signal that is allowed to enter the device. You can balance the two volume knobs to come up with the optimum signal-to-noise ratio. The important thing to recognize here is that, no matter what it's called, a send is an *output* from the portable studio that functions just like the output jack on your guitar or keyboard.

The Return

That's the effect send story. Now let's look at the other side of the equation, the effects return. To clarify this little idea it is useful to still think of the effect device as the midpoint in a chain. When you plug your guitar into the sound processor you won't hear anything unless the processor output is in turn plugged into an amplifier, which translates the signal into useful information for the speaker, which expresses the signal as sound.

In our little analogy the effect return functions in the same fashion as the input of the amplifier. It is the place we plug the signal into in order to hear it. Here's where it can get a little tricky. We could plug the processor into any of the inputs on the amplifier; any input will address the amplifier, and the sound will be heard. One channel may have effects, like reverb or EQ, while another may have only a volume control, but they all get the signal to the amp. The portable studio inputs function in roughly the same manner. The word "return" is used to describe any place where the signal can be inputted to the console. It is a functional *category*, not a not a location. You can return a signal to the console by plugging the cable into any input, whether it's labeled "channel" or "effect return." In other words, channels can be used to return effects and effect returns can be used to input instruments. they are all just inputs to get the sound into the console section of the portable studio. Why am I going on about this? An example is in order here. If you were recording a bassoon you might want to equalize it or send it to an effect before you sent it to tape. This process gives you control over the ultimate sound of the instrument. That's why you have a console in the first place, so you can modify sound to suit your musical vision. Well guess what? A reverb or effect can be treated in exactly the same way as any instrument. It too has all the the qualities of a musical instrument and can be manipulated to bring out the most desired elements, or modified with other effects to change the quality completely. So that being said, it now makes sense to realize that you have more than one place to return a musical element. The effect return, which usually has little or no sound-processing capability (e.g. no EQ, etc.) is the place to input sounds that are self-contained or that can be manipulated before they reach the console. A channel input is much more flexible. It is where you would input sounds that need to be altered by the console. So the point is that just because you used an effect send to route a signal doesn't mean you have to use an effect return to bring it back to the console. Signal is signal and can be inputted wherever there is a hole to do it. There are a bunch of recipes in the back of this book that take advantage of this fact.

7. Pan pot

(On most portable studio consoles the pan pot serves more than one function. I'm going to describe both.)

The first use of the pan pot is as a **variable sweep control** for assigning the position of a musical element within the stereo spectrum.

How it works:
The pan pot is actually one control for two signals. As you know, in order for a pan pot to serve as a placement control for stereo it has to address two tracks. Stereo position is created by splitting a signal, raising or lowering the relative level of the one sound as it is sent to each of two tracks. Identical levels sent to two tracks will result in the sound being placed in the middle. Eighty percent of the signal sent to the left track will make that signal appear eighty percent to the left, and so on.

How to use it:
The pan pot is used in a mixing situation where elements are going to be combined to two stereo (Left and Right) tracks. For instance, if there are four instruments, each can be panned to a different location in the stereo spectrum, thereby allowing for separation. The panning process involves turning the pan control indicator to the location where you desire the sound to appear in the stereo spectrum. In this manner the pan can be used for instrument placement wherever a stereo pair of tracks is created (see "The Mixdown Chapter").

The second use of the pan pot is as a three-position knob that acts as a **multiple buss assign.**

How it works:
The manufacturer has designated one side of the pan pot as a buss assign for the even-numbered tape tracks and the other side as buss assigns for the odd-numbered tracks. The middle position on the pan pot addresses both odd and even tracks. In some cases the design of the console lets you designate tracks 1 *or* 3 and tracks 2 *or* 4. In other configurations you are only able to designate all odd or all even tracks at the same time. This means that you can only record *two* different tracks at a time.

How to use it:
Position the pan pot to address the desired buss (track assign).

8. Fader

The **fader** is a sliding potentiometer used in portable studio consoles for the purpose of gain (volume) control.

How it works:
The fader is a logarithmic level control that works by raising or lowering the gain in 256 discrete steps.

How to use it:
Push it up and down, duh.

Just kidding. There actually is a lot more to the fader than just shoving the thing around. The logarithmic nature of a fader is such that as you change level you are not manipulating the sound simply arithmetically. In other words, pushing the fader up 50% doesn't increase the sound by half but by a lot more than half. Each increase of 10 dB makes the sound twice as loud, so doubling the distance of the fader throw can have a dramatic effect. This feature becomes really important when you are fading a sound. If you were to simply bring the fader down in a constant speed the fade would sound abrupt. Why? Because each 10 dB decrease is cutting the sound level *in half*. Bring it down another 10 dB and it cuts the sound in half again, and so on (see "The Mixdown Chapter" for fading technique).

Another important function of the fader is the establishing of a good signal-to-noise ratio. Actually this is done in conjunction with the trim pot at the input stage of the console. The idea is to balance the two. The trim pot is the inlet valve to the channel and the fader is the outlet valve to the tape.

To begin with, set the fader at the center point designated by the manufacturer (some use a "0" or a dot or band on the fader to show the spot). Then use the trim pot to control the level into the channel and the fader to control the level to tape. Remember, you want the input level to the channel to be as high as you can get it without distortion. If the level is too low use the fader to adjust it. However, if the level to the input is too high, back the fader down. The fader should not have to be more than slightly below the center point; if it is, back down the trim pot.

So ends our tour of the console section of the portable studio. Please step this way for a tour of the heart of the unit, the tape machine.

Anatomy of a Portable Studio: The Master Module

In the last chapter we covered what happens when the signal comes into an individual channel input, goes through the channel, and gets sent on its way to an individual track of the tape machine. That was the first stage of the recording cycle. In this section we're going to investigate the second stage: how the total of all the channels' signals get distributed via the **master module**, particularly to the headphones and the mixdown recorder.

Master Module

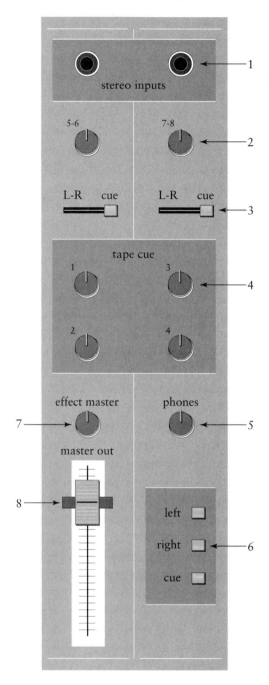

This stuff is a little like "follow the chain" or "connect the dots" or "where's Waldo" after a few rum toddies — it's easy to get lost. But once you get the idea this section will give you yet another tool for flexibility.

I need to put a small disclaimer here about the master module even before I define it. Different manufacturers include different features on this part of the console. Some models will have the effects returns and the headphone mixer section located here. Others will handle these functions in another fashion. The diagram model I'm using is for a middle-level four-track machine. Other machines will have more or fewer features depending on sophistication.

Some Definitions

The **master module** is the last stage of the console. This is where *all* the signals within the console are "summed" together and distributed to various external destinations, principally the mixdown machine and the monitors.

The effect return is a pair of inputs or a stereo input that is designated as the receptacle for signal-processing outboard gear. This circuit is the termination part of the loop begun with the effect send on the channel. This return differs from a channel input in that it typically has few of the features (such as EQ and auxiliary send) of a channel input.

Summed is recordingese for "added together" and has real technoid purpose when discussing special summing amplifiers in the portable studio that perform this function.

Tour of the Master Module

(Please keep your extremities inside the vehicle).

The master module is usually located adjacent to the last of the channel modules and looks a little different from the rest of the console.

1. Stereo inputs

In this particular model of portable studio the function of the effect return is handled by two multipurpose stereo inputs. These require a special Y-splitter that has two mono jacks on one end joined into a single cable with one stereo plug on the other end.

How they work:
Even though the stereo plug looks a lot like a mono ($^1/_4{''}$) phone plug, it differs in that its tip is divided into two contact zones, each transmitting its own signal. Inside the special jack there are two connection points instead of one as there would be for a mono $^1/_4{''}$ plug. Each connector has its own circuit that hooks up to the portable studio as if it were a single connection. The way it works is that you could take the two stereo outputs of a reverb device and the cable would combine them into the stereo plug on the other end.

How to use them:
To bring effects and premixes into the portable studio, plug each side of the mono cable into the respective sides of the outputs of the effects device (Left and Right). Then plug the stereo end into the portable studio stereo input.

2. Input trim

The channel on the master module is really two channels with one hole. This means that while you can raise or lower the level of the channel you cannot independently raise or lower the level of each side. In other words, even though the channels are labeled "5-6" you only have *one* control for both 5 and 6 and so will always affect both signals at the same time.

How it works:
This potentiometer works just like the trim controls on any other channel in that it raises or lowers the level of the signal at the input stage. It is different however in that it performs a summing (Left and Right) function.

How to use it:
Typically there is no output fader on this type of channel. Therefore the level control is entirely reliant on the input trim. Use the trim for gain control and to get a good signal-to-noise ratio.

3. Buss assign
This is a switch that can assign whatever is coming into the stereo inputs to either the monitor mix, a track of the tape machine, or the output of the whole console.

How it works:
This switch is similar to the mic/line/tape switch on the other channels. The difference is that this selector is simply selecting *where* the output of the channel is going, not *what kind* of signal is coming in. The assumption of the manufacturer is that you will not be using a microphone in this channel (because the input is stereo and most mics are mono) and you cannot use an input from the tape, because the tape will return only to the channel where it is *normalled*, or hardwired, and there are no tape channels 5 through 8. That means that the input will be used for stereo **line in** devices only. Since there is only one choice of type of signal the only thing you can select is where the signal's going.

How to use it:
This buss assign can be used in the following ways. When you are recording to a **tape track**, the assign is set to "L-R." This will route the signal coming into the stereo channel to whatever track you have in record (*e.g.*, if you are recording on track 1 the signal from the stereo input will only go down the *left* side of the buss — track 1 = pan left).

Remember that if you are recording to a single track then the signal will be mono and you will get only one side of the stereo channel. So if you want to include a reverb with a single channel you need to be aware that the result will be in mono.

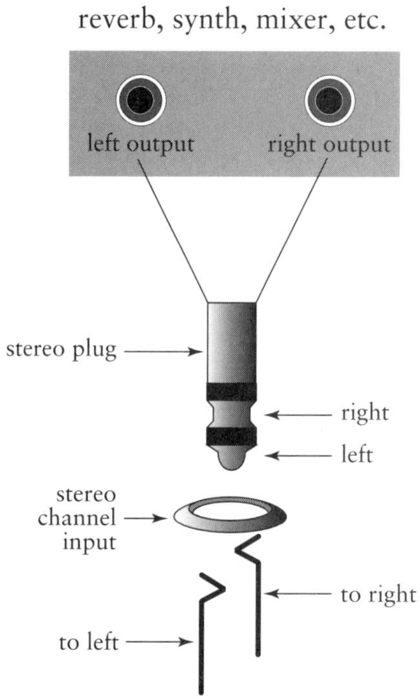

reverb, synth, mixer, etc.

left output   right output

stereo plug

right

left

stereo channel input

to right

to left

Aside from functioning to send a signal to tape, these channels also address the **master outputs** of the portable studio and therefore can be used to combine the reverb with the other signals for mixdown. This is also accomplished by pressing the "L-R" button.

When you depress the "cue" button you are sending the signal that comes through the stereo channel to the **monitor** (headphones), not to the tape. So you can listen to what's coming through the channel without affecting what you're recording.

Bringing the Outside In

In addition to being useful for adding reverb, the stereo inputs are very handy for bringing a group of premixed instruments into the portable studio to add to the mix. For example, if you have a stack of MIDI instruments that you want to input to the portable studio, you can bring a left/right premix in through the stereo inputs. This is very effective, particularly if you have control of the blend of instruments before you plug them into the portable studio (see the discussion of virtual mixing in "The Keyboard Chapter").

4. Tape cue (also called **monitor sends** or **cue sends**)

These are the volume pots that control the signal to the headphones when the buss assign is in the cue mode.

How they work:
Each of the knobs controls the volume of the track of the tape machine that it addresses. These controls are independent of the fader controls on the individual channels.

How to use them:
Balance the levels of the various controls to create a pleasing mix in the headphones. The cue section diagrammed is in mono. You can tell that at a glance because there is no pan pot or other method to asssign stereo positioning. Where this cue is concerned, the signal from all sources is summed to a mono output. Therefore all sounds will image in the center of the stereo spectrum.

5. Headphone level control

This is the overall gain control for the headphone output.

How it works:
There is a mono amplifier in the portable studio that boosts the signal to the headphones.

How to use it:
Turn it up and the whole level of the phones goes up. This means that you have overall level control with this knob and individual level control with the cue pots.

6. Headphone assign

This is a routing switch that tells the headphones what to listen to.

How it works:
It allows the headphone amp to tap into either the busses or the cue circuits.

How to use it:
If you wish to hear the monitor mix independent of what's going to tape press "cue." If you want to hear the stereo buss press "Left" and "Right." If you want to hear a combination of one buss and the cue press "cue" and the appropriate "Left or "Right" (more on that below under "Listening to Speakers or Head-phones").

7. Effect master
This is the volume control for the *all* the signals that are going out of the effects sends.

How it works:
This section controls an amplifier that sums all the signals sent to it from the effects sends of the channels and sends it to the output at the back of the portable studio labeled "effects out" (or "auxiliary out"). Typically this output would be cabled to a signal processor or reverb.

How to use it:
You use this knob to control all the level that is going to your outboard device. For example, if the input to the reverb was being overloaded by too much signal you would use the effect master to turn the level down. Conversely, if you weren't getting enough signal to the reverb for a good signal-to-noise ratio you would turn the effect master up. (See "The Recipe Section" for other uses of this output).

8. Master output fader (also called stereo buss, stereo master, L-R master)
This is the volume control over the final sum of all the signals going through the console.

How it works:
All of the signals — tape returns, reverbs and effects, premixed MIDI instruments, etc. — that are routed through the portable studio are sent internally to a stereo output amplifier. One side of this output is designated Left and the other is designated Right. Each of these sides is outputted at the back of the console at the **line out (L-R)** (also called the **master out** or **stereo out**) and can then be plugged into the corresponding inputs of the mixdown machine.

How to use it:
As you move the fader it controls both the left and right outputs of the line out in equal parts. So even though it is a stereo output it is controlled by one gain fader. The master out is where you would set the level to the mixdown machine for the best signal-to-noise ratio.

Balancing the Output

Now here's where it can get a little tricky. Remember that each of the other channels has its own level control. The combination of all of these is going to the master control for outputting. You need to balance the levels of each of these individual channels before you send the final sum out of the master. This process is called **mixing**, or **mixdown**. (I will go into the artistic nuts and bolts of mixing in its own section.) For now you only need to know two things: 1. If the sum of the channels is too loud you will distort the master; and 2. The ideal mix level of the master is at whatever your manual designates as "center" (sometimes "0," sometimes a number on the fader).

The object is to send a balance of individual channel elements to the master output, which is then used to output the sum of the signals to the mixdown machine. The signal level sent should be suitable for a good signal-to-noise ratio at the mixdown machine. If the master is set properly but the level is too low to the mixdown machine then the individual channels each need to be raised in a proportion balanced for the mix.

Mastering the Master Module

Earlier I introduced the concept of a buss as a vehicle that carries individual signals all to the same destination. In that case I was talking about the individual tape tracks, or an effect in the case of the auxiliary buss. Now I want to carry this transportation analogy a little further to give you an overview of the master module.

We've already recorded our signals from their channels to their respective tracks, and now we want to bring the signals back to the console to do something with them. The four tracks of the tape machine get returned to their respective channels of the console (when you depress the "tape" switch on each channel). The console will now act as a mixer, to blend the channels together and send the result to a pair of outputs called the **stereo buss**.

In other words, up until now the console has functioned as a way of routing signals to individual tape tracks. Now it will transform itself to perform a different function. It will become a mixer. The station where all the signals from their individual channels and inputs (including effects) mix together to be shipped out is the master module. This is where the four tracks of the tape machine get put together with effects and are then routed to the final two outputs of the portable studio before being sent to your mixdown machine.

More Definitions

The **stereo buss** (also called the **main mix**, **two-buss**, or the **master output**) is the circuit that sums all the signals in the console and distributes them to a left output of the console and a right output of the console.

The stereo buss is internally connected to two output plugs in the back of the console labeled "Left" and "Right" output. These you cable into the left and right inputs of your two-track mastering machine (more on this in "The Recording Studio Kit Chapter").

The difference between a multitrack buss and the stereo buss is that the multitrack buss is normalled to one particular track of the portable studio (1, 2, 3, or 4) while the stereo buss is the total of everything in the console and is outputted to whatever machine you want to cable it up to (usually the mixdown machine).

Normalled is a recordingism meaning that a device or a buss is hardwired up to a particular destination. Channel 1 is the *normal* place where tape track 1 returns to the console, and so on.

Hearing the Music

So follow the bouncing ball and repeat after me: the channel sends the signal to the track (when you record), the track returns the signal to a channel (for you to mix), and then the signal is sent out to the stereo buss, which is the vehicle that carries a mixture of *all* the signals in the console out to the mixdown machine.

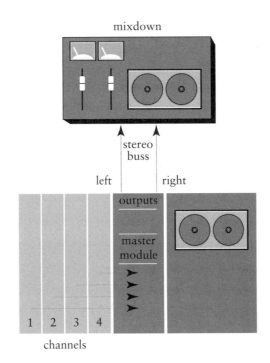

Now you know the first half of the master module story. The master module acts as a gathering depot for all the sounds you are working with. Ultimately, anything that is going through the console ends up at the master module.

Listening to Speakers or Headphones

The second half of the story is that the master module is also the "distribution center" for everything that goes through the console. There is more than one place to hear what's going through your console, depending on where you're listening from. The master module controls this function.

As a general rule, here's what happens when you are listening to your speakers. The portable studio sends the signal from the stereo buss (master out) down the cables to the mixdown machine. This machine is in record (or record/pause), which allows it to let in the signal. This machine then sends the signal out a pair of wires to the input of the stereo amplifier, which in turn drives the speakers.

A second way to hear what's on the stereo buss is to use the headphone jack built into the portable studio. If you want to use the phones to hear the output of the stereo buss (*i.e.*, what would be going to the mixdown machine) you have to depress a button (or switch) or two buttons or switches (depending on your machine) labeled something like "Left" and "Right" (see number 6 in the master module tour above). This means that you are listening to the left and right outputs of the portable studio at the stereo buss — your final mix before it leaves the portable studio to make its way to the mixdown machine. In fact, you can use the headphones in this fashion to mix down. (As you will discover, however, I strongly recommend that you use speakers as your mixdown reference and not headphones unless you don't have access to a stereo and speakers — like if you are on a tour bus or a desert island.) So by depressing the "L-R" function switch you are listening to the same thing that your mixdown machine is getting. There is, however, another way to hear what's going on inside the portable studio. It is called the **cue**, or **monitor**, function.

Now to Muddy the Waters

When you plug your headphones directly into the jack on the portable studio and depress the "cue" (or "monitor") button you are no longer listening to the output of the stereo buss but rather to a small amplifier built into the portable studio that distributes a different mix of signals that have their own controls separate from the stereo buss. You can set the mix of instruments to your headphones by using the cue sends as volume controls for each track. Another way to put it is that coming from the cue, or monitor, section you are going to hear a set of signals different from what you get when you engage the Left-Right function that addresses the stereo buss.

Here's the way it looks.

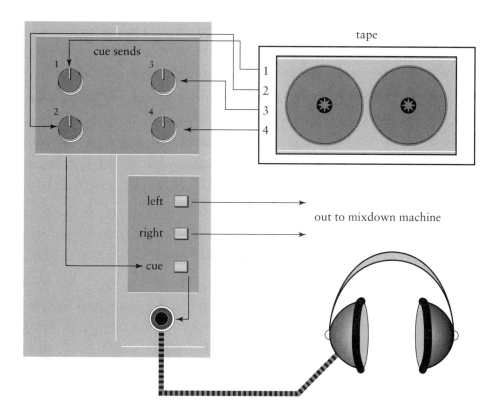

This system was devised so that the musicians could have a different mix from that of the engineer.

Here's a frequent real-world example. (Note: In order for the following example to make any sense you have to imagine that the musician is a separate person from the engineer, or at least has multiple personalities.) Let's say a guitar player, in order to monitor his performance closely, wants to hear more of himself than he hears of the MIDI sequencer instruments coming into the portable studio. The recordist, however, may be more concerned with how well the guitarist is playing in time with the other instruments, and so must hear them clearly. This is accomplished by the recordist creating two mixes: a cue mix that serves the guitar player through the headphones, and a master out (stereo buss) mix that the recordist listens to through the speakers. What this means is that the cue (headphone) mix is independent of the signal going to tape or to the stereo buss. The recordist can alter the level to the guitar player's phones without changing the level to the tape recorder. The bottom line is that no matter what you do to the cue mix, it has no effect on what is going to tape. It only affects what is going to the headphones. *So* turn up that guitar to the player's delight. You can listen to your own mix and still get the right level to tape.

CAUTION! If you are mixing using the headphones (and you know how I feel about that), be sure that you are not in cue mode. The cue mix is not the same as the master mix. You can easily make mixing errors.

Monitoring a Signal When You Overdub

Now we come to the third way to hear a mix of signals: by using a combination of the left or right busses *and* the cue mix. What? The efficient nature of the portable studio solves space and cost problems by multiplexing connections. What this means to you becomes apparent when you get ready to overdub.

If you already have instruments on tape, you need to listen to them in order to be able to overdub along with them. This part of the monitoring is done with the cue knobs. But in order to hear what is going to tape some portable studios require that you listen to the buss that is sending it. (Since there are a number of configurations from different manufacturers, you need to check your manual for the specific procedure for overdubbing.)

So now you're ready to overdub; you can listen to what you're recording by depressing a switch that connects to the buss of the channel you want to listen to. For instance, if you want to listen to what is going onto track 2 (see example below) you would follow the procedure described in your manual to do this (usually a combination of the pan pot assign plus the "Left" or "Right" switch, indicating that you are hearing the circuit that connects to a particular track of the portable studio tape machine). Now you can hear all the instruments that are being bussed to that track together *before* the buss gets to tape. In other words, you are listening to what *will be* recorded through the buss and what *has been* recorded through the cue sends.

For instance, let's say you are going to add a guitar track on track 2 to the drums you already laid down on track 1. Obviously you have to hear the drums in order to play along with with them. If the drums are recorded on track 1 you would turn up the cue for track 1 that feeds your headphones. You might even want to add reverb to the guitar for monitoring purposes. So you assign the reverb return to the cue mix also. Because the reverb is part of the cue mix it will only go to be monitored and won't go to a track of the tape machine to be recorded. This means that you can add reverb to the guitar you're recording without recording it to tape. You do this by turning up the auxiliary send on the (guitar) channel to send the signal to the reverb, and the reverb is assigned (cue is selected) to the monitor. So now you're hearing the guitar part you're laying down in combination with the other instruments and the reverb, but all that's going to track 2 is the guitar itself. (See the "Monitoring Reverb without Recording It to a Track Recipe" at the end of "The Tape Machine Chapter.")

The Cue Mix

The cue mix (also called **monitor** or **foldback**) is a circuit that is parallel to the stereo buss and allows you to distribute the signals to the headphones independently of what is going to tape or to the stereo buss.

To Recap Monitoring

There are three ways to hear the signal passing through the portable studio. First, you can listen to the stereo buss (master) output. This is the mix that would go to your mixdown machine. Its mix balance is controlled by the faders on the channels. Remember: The stereo buss is the last output stage before the mixdown machine. When you monitor this you are monitoring what is going to be recorded to your final mix.

The second way you can hear what's going on is to listen to the cue (monitor) sends. These knobs control circuits that are specifically addressed to the headphone output of the console. These circuits are parallel to the stereo buss, which means that you can hear a different mix in the headphones from what is going to tape. Anything that is assigned to the cue is only going to the headphones, not to the tape. No matter what you do to the cue it will not affect what you are recording. Turn it up, turn it down, no problem. In this case you would use the cue sends to mix the relative volumes of the signals to the headphones.

The third method is to combine listening to the buss of a particular track (what you're recording) along with a cue mix of the tracks already on tape. This is done by using two switch positions, the "Left" or "Right" plus the cue sends. This configuration is most often used for overdubbing. The volume of the instrument that is being overdubbed is controlled by a fader on the channel (level to tape) and the volumes of the prerecorded instruments to the headphones are controlled by the cue sends (level to headphones).

Anatomy of a Portable Studio: The Tape Machine

The tape machine component of the portable studio functions pretty much like any other four-track machine (as discussed in the section "How a Tape Recorder Does What It Does"). There are a few differences between a four-track cassette and a reel-to-reel that I'll get into later, but for now let's just go poke around the portable studio tape deck a little.

Some Definitions

The **basic track** (also called the **bed**) is a foundation track comprising recordings of the first reference instruments. In the process of tracking, more than one instrument may be recorded at the same time. Commonly, a basic track is referred to as *the* track, even though it may actually be more than one tape track of instruments, as opposed to *a* track, which refers to a specific track of the tape machine.

Overdubbing is the process of recording a signal along with and after a basic track reference. The overdub is a separate recording procedure that follows the recording of the basic track.

Punch-in (also called a **drop-in**): While a punch and an overdub both occur after the basic track is recorded, the overdub is generally the creation of a whole new track. The punch-in is a little different. It is the process of inserting new information into a preexisting recorded track. It is accomplished by the recordist "punching" the record function on the target track at a selected time in order to replace a section with a new performance. (See "Some Tips on Punching In" later in this chapter.)

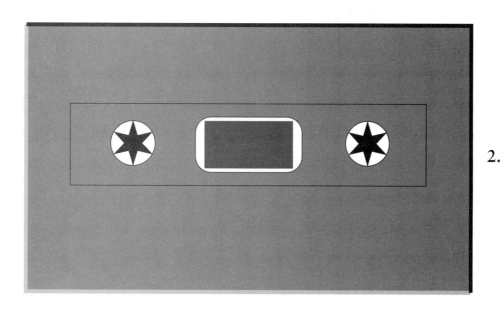

1.

2.

3.

| TRK 1 | TRK 2 | TRK 3 | TRK 4 |

DIR DIR DIR DIR

7.
enable

4. 5. 6.
DBX TAPE ZERO MEMORY

sync high stop stop

8.

PITCH CONTROL

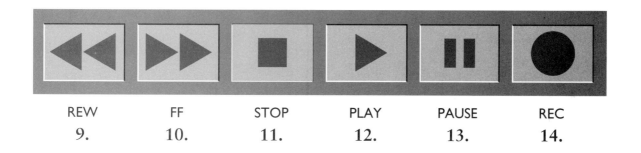

REW FF STOP PLAY PAUSE REC
9.   10. 11.   12.   13.   14.

Tour of the Tape Machine

1. Tape counter
This little gizmo is used to locate a point on the tape.

How it works:
There is a spindle inside that turns the numbers visible in the window to correspond to the amount of tape movement.

How to use it:
To store a start point for a song: At the beginning of each song you depress the button on the counter to reset it at zero. Then as tape rolls you have a beginning reference point to return to. You can of course also use the tape counter to note the position of the tape at a point where you might want to overdub or punch in.

2. Tape transport and heads
This is the place where the tape-transport motor spindles come up to drive the cassette cogs and where the electronic heads are located.

How they work:
Even though it looks like a stereo cassette deck, the four-track cassette deck works in a fundamentally different fashion. On a two-track cassette the tape has two recordable "sides." These aren't really sides, but directions. When the tape is moving one way you get side A, and when it reverses direction you get side B (hence all those auto-reverse tape decks).

The four-track cassette uses *both* sides of the tape in one direction to record its signal.

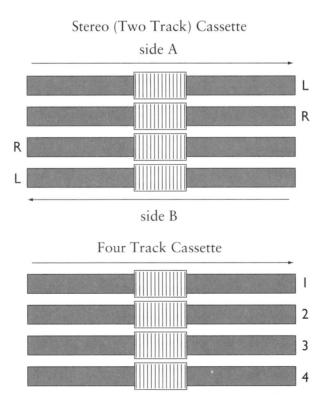

Stereo (Two Track) Cassette

side A

L

R

R

L

side B

Four Track Cassette

1

2

3

4

In other words, tracks 1, 2, 3, and 4 of the portable studio would be equivalent to Left and Right of side A *plus* Left and Right of side B on a standard cassette deck. This means that if you were to play a portable studio four-track cassette on a conventional cassette deck you would only get half the information (*e.g.*, only what's on tracks 1 and 2). You therefore need to mix the four tracks down to stereo to play them on a conventional machine. (You can, however, play a conventional cassette on a portable studio, because tracks 1 and 2 roughly line up with the left and right of the cassette. However, you would have to turn tracks 3 and 4 off or you would hear whatever's on the B side of the stereo cassette played backwards.)

Head Configuration

Earlier I described a standard tape head recording configuration as having four functions — erase, record, play, and sync. In the portable-studio world the head configuration is a little different. The erase head is still first, but a portable studio typically puts the play and record heads in the same location, allowing for the elimination of the sync head. When you are playing back the tracks you wish to overdub to, they are being read at the same location as the record head you are using to imprint the tape.

How to use them:
To record or play back, insert the cassette to be recorded in the manner your manual requires (there is a discussion of the function switches below).

3. Metering and record enable functions

This section of the tape machine is divided into two important parts. One part, the **meter bridge** (it got the name "bridge" because it often goes across the top of a console) is actually the window onto what signal level the recorder is receiving or what is already on tape, as well as having some special metering functions I'll describe.

The other function of this section of the tape machine is the **record enable** switching for routing the signal to be recorded to a designated track. This tells the tape recorder which record heads should be activated and which should not.

The Meters

The meters display a couple of different things depending on what *mode* you're in (see below), but basically they are used as a method of indicating the amplitude (volume) of a signal to the tape — in other words, how "hot" the signal is. They tell you at what level the signal is going to be stored. They also act as an indicator of optimum recording levels; when you are in danger of distorting the tape with too much level this is usually indicated with a red color. The meters are configured so that they read different stages of recording depending on the mode that you have selected (see below). (By the way, "hot" can mean loud or extremely good.)

Next to the meters there is a two-position switch that allows you to select what the meters are reading. This switch typically gives you the choice of two positions, usually labeled "tape" or "buss."

In the "tape" position the meters are set up to allow you to view a representation of the volume at different stages of the recording process: they are telling you what is going on in the tape deck. In the record, or input, mode of the track condition, the meter is reading the level *to* tape. In the play mode the meter is reading what has already been recorded to that track, the level *from* tape.

In the "buss" position the meters are reading what the manufacturer has designated for metering different stages of the console. Usually there is a specific track designation for each function (check your manual). For instance, meters 1 and 2 may read the Left-Right buss (master out) output, while meter 3 may read the effects buss output, and meter 4 may read the monitor, or cue, buss. Thus in this position the meters can be used for viewing the level that is exiting the console to the mixdown machine (L-R out), or for viewing the level going to some outboard device (effects out), or viewing how hot the signal is to the head-phones (cue).

Track Record Enable Switches

These three-position switches let you choose the source status of the signal to each individual tape track. The "direct" position sends *only* the signal from the input channel that is normalled to that track. For instance, in this position whatever is coming into channel 1 will go direct to track 1. The "Left" and "Right" positions will send signal to the target track from any source assigned to the left or right buss. This allows for the output of a combination of channels to be recorded to the target track. For instance, if input channels 1 and 3 plus reverb are combined to the left (panned left) when recording to track 1, then all of these signals will be recorded on track 1. Both the "direct" and "Left/Right" functions will typically be designated with a red light of some kind, indicating that the tracks are ready to record.

The "safe" position is a lockout that will not allow the channel to go into record even if the record button is pressed. It typically shows a green light.

Unless you are going to record something immediately, always keep the track in "safe" to avoid accidents. When you are done recording, return the track to "safe" unless you are certain you are going to do the recording again.

Track 4 (or 8) Special

On the record enable switch of track 4 of our portable studio you will see an additional position labeled "sync." This track is the one the manufacturer has selected to be used to print sync tone (to "print" something means to record it to tape). When the "sync" position is selected the tape is fed its signal from a separate MIDI input at the back of the console that is normalled to track 4. In this fashion the MIDI signal doesn't go through the channel electronics or the noise reduction circuits. This helps keep the signal free from any accidental signal processing or channel noise that might corrupt the integrity of the sync tone.

4. DBX function (some manufacturers use Dolby as an alternative system)

DBX is a noise reduction device that is built into the portable studio. It is useful for reducing hiss but also helps to a certain extent with the broadband noise associated with recording.

How it works:

Noise reduction works by using a special compression structure on an incoming signal during the encoding (recording) process. This limits the dynamic range (a topic I'll cover later) and in effect makes the noise louder. When the signal is decoded (played back) the DBX unit *expands* the signal, creating a greater dynamic range by making soft information (noise) softer and loud information (music) relatively louder. This makes the noise level lower relative to the signal. (See the discussion of compression in "The Effects Chapter.")

How to use it:
On our imaginary portable studio, the noise reduction operates off a three-position switch on the front panel. The top position is labeled "sync." This position allows the DBX to encode tracks 1–3 but disables the noise reduction to track 4 of the portable studio. This is so you can use track 4 to record MIDI sync tone without any changes in its signal integrity. MIDI tone should never be processed through any device, as corruption of the sync signal may occur. Bottom line: When recording MIDI to track 4 use the "sync" position. (Note: In eight-track models the MIDI signal is normalled to track 8.)

The "on" position will enable noise reduction on all 4 (or 8) tracks.

The "off" position will apply DBX to none of the channels.

When using the DBX you have to be aware that an overload of signal can create a tracking error in the DBX unit. This can occur even with subsonics (very low frequencies). Be sure to eliminate any suspicious extreme low end, and check the signal level on the meter to tape to make sure the signal isn't too hot.

5. Tape speed control

This is also a three-position switch that tells the cassette driver motor how fast the tape should move.

How it works:
Each position on the selector switch is related to the standard tape speed found on a conventional machine. "Normal" is $1^7/_8$ inches per second (4.8 centimeters per second). This would be the speed used on your stereo cassette deck. The "high" position is twice the speed of a conventional cassette, or $3^3/_4$ ips (9.5 cm/sec.), and the "slow" speed is half the speed of a conventional cassette, or $^{15}/_{16}$ ips (2.4 cm/sec.).

How to use it:
I would recommend always using the high tape-speed for anything you are planning to keep or play for anyone but your pet spaniel. The slower the speed, as you know, the greater the chance of introduction of noise and the less accurate the top end. Use the slow speeds only as a "notepad" to remind yourself of song ideas. (By the way, when you come up with a great idea for a song but you're not home to lay it down, call yourself and leave a melody on your answering machine. It's easier than strapping a portable studio to your back, plus it's hard to find a jacket to cover that unsightly hump.)

The downside of high speed is that you will not get the amount of time advertised on the cassette package. A C-60 cassette at high speed will give you about fifteen minutes (since the four-track uses only one side of the tape: half of sixty minutes at double the speed equals fifteen minutes). Of course, even at normal speed a C-60 will deliver approximately thirty minutes. At slow speed you get the full sixty minutes but it sounds like barrel scrapings. Slow speed is good for listening to fast musical passages to rehearse playing them, or for recording practice sessions of your Grammy acceptance speech.

6. Zero return

First of all, zero return does not refer to your rate of interest at a crummy bank. Rather it refers to a three-position switch that enables the portable to automatically locate the tape at counter mark zero.

How it works:

There is a memory circuit that will recognize when the tape has reached zero and will stop the transport.

How to use it:

This function is usually used to automatically return the tape to the beginning of the song so you won't have to do it manually. It is a real timesaver. Having this feature means that you can do something else while the tape is rewinding, like tune your guitar, practice a lick, or get back to crocheting that doily for the parlor.

The "stop" position tells the motor to automatically stop when the tape is rewound or fast-forwarded to the counter position marked zero. You should realize that the moving tape has quite a bit of energy to dissipate when the brakes are applied, so the actual stopping point will rarely be exactly "000." The faster the tape is moving when the "000" point arrives, the more error in stopping. Like a car braking on a rainy road, the tape tends to overshoot the mark. Be sure and check to make sure the location is correct before you record anything.

The "off" position is pretty easy to figure out. It means "not on."

The "play" position will tell the portable studio to automatically engage play instead of stop when it reaches the zero point. This is particularly useful when you want to hear the song repeatedly to set up your sounds during mixing.

7. Memory

The memory section consists of a three-position switch and a locate marker button. It will provide you with a locate point so that you can designate where the tape will automatically stop when in the play, rewind, or fast-forward modes.

How it works:

Pretty much like the zero return circuitry, only with a variable placement switch.

How to use it:

This little goodie is a very handy thing to have. For instance, if you wish to punch in to a particular spot the memory will locate the spot automatically and stop the tape, saving you from having to locate the spot each time you want to rehearse and perform the punch.

The first step is to establish a locate point. This is done on our imaginary portable studio by depressing the "memory enable" button at the spot where you wish to return. Usually a light will tell you that the switch is on. Once you've done that then the "stop" position on the three-position switch will (as the name implies) stop the tape at the locate spot. In this way you are ready to overdub or punch in from that location onward.

The "rewind" position will automatically rewind from the locate point. When this function is enabled the tape will go into rewind after you've done your punch-in business. This can be a good failsafe to make sure that you don't go too far while dropping into an existing track.

CAUTION: The memory function is stupid. It doesn't know what you want until you tell it. If you are recording a whole track make sure the memory is disabled to avoid accidental interruption of a take.

8. Pitch control

This is a rotary pot that allows you to continuously speed up or slow down the tape speed between the tape speed settings.

How it works:

The pot (also called a *VSO*, or variable speed oscillator) sends controlled variable levels of current to the motor that is turning the tape cogs so that the speed of the tape can be varied. More current equals faster; less current equals slower — kind of like a light dimmer.

How to use it:

This function is pretty nice to have for a bunch of problem-solving reasons. Perhaps the easiest way to explain is to give you some examples.

Problem: The singer is trying real hard, but that top note is just a little too high.

Solution: Slow the tape down slightly for the vocal overdub. By slowing the tape you are also lowering the pitch. The pitch control works on the overall tape drive and will lower the pitch on all the tracks. The singer can then sing along to the lower pitch, and then the track can be returned to normal speed. No one needs to be the wiser. However! Don't slow the pitch down too much, because when the track returns to normal speed the vocal may sound like there's a rodent singing. The trouble comes because any vibrato or tremolo the singer uses will also be sped up when the tape is returned to normal. (By the way, yes, that is basically how they did the Chipmunks recordings, by radically slowing down a track and having a regular person sing very slo-o-o-wly, then playing it back at normal speed.)

Problem: The whole track was originally recorded a little sharp. The sax player comes in to overdub and can't get in tune with the track.

Solution: "Tune" the track to the sax by slowing down the pitch control while the sax plays along. When the two sound in tune with each other that's where to set the control.

Problem: You want to record a harmony guitar lick to one that's already recorded without having to change fingering or voicing.

Solution: Play the original (melody) part on a reference instrument in unison with the recorded part you want to harmonize to. While you are doing this manipulate the pitch control to speed up or slow down the tape to create the proper harmonic relationship. Then when you've "tuned" the portable studio, record the same part onto another track at the new speed. When you play the two tracks of recorded parts back at regular speed they will harmonize. On your guitar you've played exactly the same part twice. But, because you "tuned" the portable studio, is playing the "harmony" part back a different harmonic relationship.

The pitch control can be used to create all sorts of effects. The best way to learn to add it to your sonic arsenal is to get some blank tape and play around with it.

9. Rewind button

This button when pressed will send the tape at a high rate of speed in the opposite direction from the play function.

How it works:
It controls a motor servo that reverses the motor's direction, thereby returning the tape to the supply reel of the cassette. The **supply reel**, by the way, is the reel of the cassette where the tape is coming from to be recorded upon. ("The supply reel kept going but the other reel stopped, so I got tape all over the floor.")

How to use it:
Depress the button when you wish to rewind the tape. On some machines you can slow the tape as you get close to the desired point by alternating between the rewind and play buttons.

10. Fast-forward button

This button when pressed will send the tape at a high rate of speed in the same direction as the play function.

How it works:
It controls a motor servo that accelerates the motor's direction, thereby accumulating the tape onto the takeup reel's side. The **takeup reel** is the side of the cassette where the tape is accumulated as you play or record. ("The supply reel stopped but the takeup reel kept going. Now I've got tape that's stretched as thin as spaghetti.")

How to use it:
Depress the button when you wish to fast-forward the tape to a new location.

11. Stop button

It stops the tape.

How it works:
The motor that's turning the spindle is braked to a stop. Then it stops the tape.

How to use it:
Press the button to stop the darn tape.

12. Play button

This button tells the tape transport to move the tape forward at the assigned rate. It also functions as a component of the record enable electronics.

How it works:
In one capacity this switch tells the motor to move, much like switching on a garage-door opener. In the other capacity it is a failsafe to ensure that "record" isn't accidentally pressed. In order for the record command to be activated the "play" button must first be held down.

How to use it:
Obviously, when you want the tape to play you depress the button. When you wish to record, however, you must depress "play" first, then at the appropriate location on the tape you would press "record" while still holding down the "play" button.

13. Pause button
This button is to temporarily stop the movement of the tape. But unlike the "stop" button, "pause" will not interrupt the electronic transmission of signal through the circuits.

How it works:
When the "pause" button is pressed the tape transport goes into idle, like when you put your car in neutral. You haven't shut down the motor.

How to use it:
Even though both tape conditions seem the same, the "pause" button serves a different function from the "stop" control. In the pause mode you are temporarily stopping the tape as you get ready to record or perform some other function. For example, while you are recording you can hit "pause" and the tape will stop but the signal will still be coming through, allowing you to meter what you're about to record. Then when you are ready to go you can press "play" (not "pause") and the machine will be in record from that spot.

14. Record button
The whole purpose to having a portable studio.

How it works:
The button controls an electronic circuit that sends an electronic signal which changes the magnetic field of the record head (as discussed in the chapter "How a Tape Recorder Does What It Does").

How to use it:
First, and most important of all, use it to have some fun.
When you are ready to record press the "play" button and while holding it down press "record."

SOME TIPS ON PUNCHING IN

Ever get almost to the end of the best vocal you've ever done only to choke on the final four notes? This is where the real beauty of multitracking lies, fixing screwups. There is a real art to punching in. To repair a flaw in an otherwise perfect performance you have to make the punch as consistent with the original as possible so that it remains invisible. That way when your friends ask, you can tell them how you just dashed it off in one take and no one can call you a prevaricating miscreant.

- Note the tape counter number of where you want to punch in and write it down. Sometimes one part of the song may be very similar to another, and using the tape counter to make sure you're in the right area can save you from punching in at the wrong spot (and the onset of a serious migraine headaches). *Use the memory function.*

- Never trust the counter number position to be exactly accurate. Always make sure you know where you are before you start recording. The tape counter numbers frequently drift and don't remain constant over time.

- Make sure you are aware of the VU meter level at the spot on the tape immediately before you punch in and the spot immediately after you punch out. In this fashion you can set your input levels to match your punch with what will come before and after it.

- Have the instrument or vocalist play along before the punch-in. In this manner the performance will be more natural and the levels more closely matched to the original. It also reduces the "uh-oh, here it comes, I got to do it right!" anxiety level. So sing or play along with the tape exactly as if you were recording the whole passage instead of just part of it.

- I will sometimes use the equalizer judiciously on the "fixer" punch to clean up some "mud" or unpleasant edginess inherent in that little part. (But be careful not to change the settings too radically or the punch becomes obvious.)

- For the same reason I will sometimes change comp-ressor settings for a punch.

- Finally, when you think you've got a keeper punch, take a break and leave the room for a minute or two. Come back in and listen with a fresh ear (and no reverb) to the track to make sure the levels match and the punch is "seamless."

The Recording Chain

- Signal into channel
- Channel into any or all of the following
    1. auxiliary send and return (loop)
    2. buss into cue
    3. buss to stereo buss out
- Stereo buss out to Left-Right input of cassette deck
- "Play-pause-record" pressed so you can listen to the input of the cassette deck as it goes out to stereo amplifier, which goes out to the speakers
- You can turn the gain up or down at any of these points
    1. Channel input
    2. Fader (channel output)
    3. Stereo master out fader
    4. Cassette input
    5. Cassette output
    6. Stereo amp overall gain control

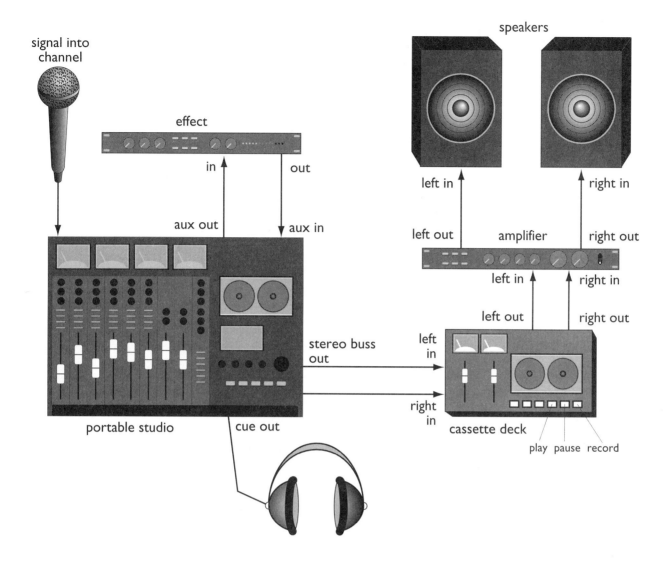

Basic Microphone Recording Recipe

Application: Fundamental recording technique
Requirements: Mic or line in* instrument, headphones

1. Plug mic into mic input at channel.
2. Switch "mic/line/tape" switch to "mic."
3. Turn pan pot to desired position (in this case left for track 1).
4. Enable track 1 using "Left" switch.
    (Note: The "direct" setting can be used when channel 1 is the only feed to track 1. This is the case here, but the pan pot is used for demonstration purposes.)
5. Set the fader level on the channel to zero or center point.
6. Make sure the mic is working and check level by looking at the meter on track 1.
7. To raise the level of signal to tape use the trim pot at the top of the channel.
8. If the signal is still not sufficient for a good signal-to-noise ratio, raise the gain of the signal to tape with the channel fader.
    (Note: Conversely, if the signal is too hot, first try to lower it at the mic trim; if it's still too hot, use the fader.)
9. Monitor the signal through the "Left-Right" buss to send it to the speakers.

* Note: To record a line in signal (direct guitar, keyboards, etc.) follow the same procedure but set the "mic/line/tape" switch to "line" and follow the instructions in your manual regarding the trim pot.

10. EQ the signal.
11. If reverb is to be monitored, set the effect send.
12. Monitor the reverb with the "cue" position of the assign selector (or "Left-Right" if you wish to send the reverb to tape).
13. Set the headphone mix by switching to "cue" and balancing with the cue mix pots.
14. Press "play," then "record" while holding "play" down to send the signal to the target track to record.

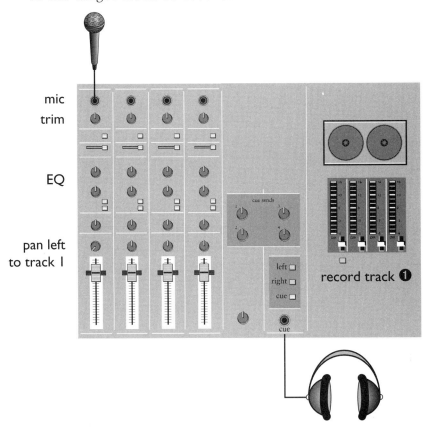

Monitoring Reverb without It Going to Tape Recipe

Application: To add reverb to the monitors to enhance the sound for performance without printing it to tape

Requirements: Mic, reverb, headphones

1. Follow the procedure above for inputting a microphone.
2. Set the pan to send to track 1 from channel 1 (L).
3. Press the "Left" button on the headphone output section of the master module (to monitor buss 1, left).
4. Press the "cue" button on the headphone output section of the master module (to monitor what's already been recorded on tracks 2–4).
5. Set cue sends 2, 3, and 4 for the headphone mix.
6. Set the effect sends channels 1 through 4 to reverb.
7. Return the reverb to a stereo channel or to the Left/Right effect return.
8. Select "cue" on the effect return.
9. Set the desired level to the headphones.

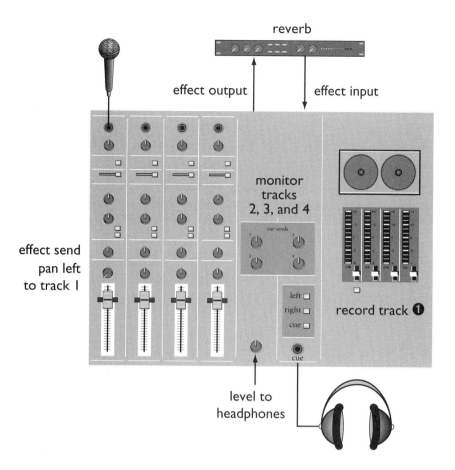

reverb

effect output   effect input

monitor
tracks
2, 3, and 4

cue sends

effect send
pan left
to track I

left ☐
right ☐
cue ☐

record track ❶

level to
headphones

cue

The Back Panel

These are the actual points of connection from your portable studio to the outside world. Different models will vary in configuration, but the functions pictured above are the most common.

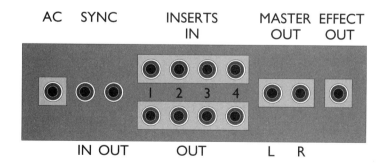

AC   SYNC   INSERTS   MASTER EFFECT
               IN   OUT   OUT

          1   2   3   4

IN OUT   OUT   L   R

I. AC in

This is where you plug the portable studio to a power source. Some machines have plug and cord arrangements, while others require a power supply (usually included with the unit).

2. Sync in and out

This is the connection point from your computer, sequencer, or other sync-tone generator. This input will frequently address track 4 or 8 directly and is set up to bypass the channel electronics and noise reduction. The **sync out** is to send what's recorded onto track 4 (or 8) back to the computer, sequencer, or other device. This allows the tape to act as the "master" machine to drive the sequencer (see "The Keyboard Chapter").

3. Inserts in and out

These are **in-line** output points on each channel that can be used to send the signal to an outboard device and then back in to the channel. Not all portable studios have insert points; in fact, it is usually only on the more sophisticated machines that you will find this feature, but it's a good one to have. For example, if you want to compress the signal coming in to channel 1 you could send the **insert out** of channel 1 to a compressor. In this fashion whatever signal is coming in to the channel would then go to the compressor. However, the insert signal path is not like the effect send. It does not send a parallel signal (mult) to the effect, but diverts the *whole* signal to the effect. Therefore, once the signal is sent out you have to have a way to return it to the channel in order for it to continue on its way for processing. This is the **insert in**, which takes the connection from the outboard device and brings it back to the channel. It is important to note that the insert point is before (pre) the equalizer and the effect (aux) send. This isn't really as confusing as it sounds. What it means is that the compressed signal when it comes back into the channel will then be subject to EQ and reverb if you so desire.

Now a Note of Caution for You Insert Owners

I'm getting a little ahead of myself here, but this seems the logical place to mention a point about using the inserts to send signal to a compressor (when you get to the section that covers compression this will make a little more sense, so come back here and take another look). Remember that an equalizer is a volume control. If you add 3 K to a signal it will make the signal louder in the 3 K range. As you will see in "The Effects Chapter," a compressor is volume (dynamic range) sensitive; therefore if you increase an EQ range you are also increasing the level of signal to the compressor. If you are using an insert, EQ the channel signal *first*, then tweak the final setting on the compressor. Also, make sure that any time you change the level to the channel you check to see if the compressor needs resetting also.

4. Master out left/right

This is where everything that is being sent through the portable studio is gonna come out. (Okay, everything except the cue mix. That comes out of the headphone jack.) These are the connector points to your mixdown tape machine and ultimately to your stereo and speakers. When I speak of monitoring on the speakers, this is the pair of outputs that I'm referring to — the output of the stereo buss.

5. Effect (aux) out

This is the output that is addressed by the effect send on each channel. Some portable studios will have more than one effect output, which means that there are two send controls on each channel, the output of each being labeled "A" and "B," or something similar. You plug the effect out from the portable studio into your reverb, for instance, and the stereo outputs of the reverb would get returned to either a stereo channel or a separate effect return.

Features, Futures, and Flexibility: Choosing the Portable Studio That's Right for You

In this chapter, what I'd like to talk about is the Holy Grail of recordists: sonic flexibility. You want as much flexibility as you can get in the equipment you purchase. This of course costs money. The more flexibility you get the more it's going to cost. So for most people choosing the right recording gear is largely a matter of a collision between absolute need, wishful desire, and cold hard cash. There is also a fair dollop of anxiety that grows with each dollar you count out into the salesman's palm. "Did I get the right machine? Did I make a terrible, life-altering mistake?"

When you go to buy a new car you have a goal in mind; namely, to drive a deal so good that the salesman is forced to leave the business and ends up mowing lawns. It's a nice thought, but it won't happen. It won't happen when you go to buy a portable studio either, but if you know exactly what you want and you can talk the talk to the salesman, that will go a long way to getting the most for your hard-earned dough.

When you go to buy a car you have a pretty good idea of what options you want to make your life easier. You make these choices based on the type of driving you do (or the kind of dates you want to attract, but that's another story). So it is when you plunk down the cash for a portable studio; you need to have a clear picture of what kind of recording you do in order to know what options you have to get to make your recording life complete.

Some features are essential to your musical vision; others are features that you want based on what you see as your musical growth and future needs; still others are purely icing on the cake, stuff you don't need right now but can brag to your friends that you have. Following are some features that appear on different kinds of portable studios and some suggestions as to how they might enhance your particular recording activities.

Multiple Tape Speeds

This feature is important for higher-quality recording. The higher the tape speed available, the better the quality of the recording, and less expensive machines usually offer fewer speed options.

Noise Reduction

Most midscale-to-upscale machines will offer either DBX or Dolby or similar noise reduction. This is an important feature to have for any serious recording. It is particularly critical for combining tracks.

Number of Channels

It seems fairly obvious that the greater the number of channels, the greater the flexiblity you have. So as a starting point let me apply a certain standard. If you are using your portable studio as anything more than a musical scratch pad you will feel frustrated with any fewer than six inputs, and generally the more the merrier. However, there does reach a point of diminishing returns in terms of dollars versus utility. For example, if you are recording synths that you are premixing to stereo you may only need two inputs to bring them all into the portable studio. That will still leave you four for other instruments or vocals. On the other hand, if you are recording live ensemble music then six inputs may be too few. You need to be aware of the possibilities for future projects. Generally speaking, the more inputs the more money the portable studio will cost. So if you're in a band, face it, it's gonna cost a little more to record effectively that if you're the lone synthesizer ranger.

Number of Tracks

The observations made about the number of channels can be made about multiple tracks as well. There are some very good eight-track cassette machines on the market, and the extra tracks will come in especially handy for live recording or extensive vocals or horn sections and the like.

If your music is predominantly synth-based and you're planning on virtual mixing, then the extra money that you'd spend for eight tracks might be better allocated for keyboards. You don't need the extra tracks for synth tracks because you record the instruments to the mixdown machine, not the multitrack.

XLR Inputs

As you know, these are for bringing low-impedence signal into the portable studio. Machines that have both phone-plug and XLR inputs are a very good idea if you plan to shoot for very high-quality recording using condenser microphones. These inputs are also useful in situations where you anticipate having to use long cables between the mic and the portable studio.

Phantom Power

To be honest, I'm not sure if any of the current crop of portable studios offer built-in 48-volt phantom power. But the way things change it wouldn't suprise me to see it on some of the more sophisticated models. This feature is for use with condenser microphones and acts as the power supply to the capsule of the mic. Most situations will call for the condenser mic to be independently powered by a battery or power supply. If, however, you anticipate using a pro quality condenser mic regularly, this feature may be desirable.

Equalizers

This is a biggie. I am going to make a bold statement. You can never have too much EQ capability. The more and better the EQ you have, the more flexible your recording can be. But the way it works in the real world is that in order to get more EQ you often have to buy a lot more machine — maybe more than you really need.

When choosing the portable studio for your particular application you need to be aware of what EQ options you already have. For instance, if you do mostly synth-type instrumentation then portable studio EQ may be less important. This is because most synths have some form of adjustable equalizer built in. The same is true for the drum sounds and bass sounds you are likely to use. So if your EQ needs are mainly one track at a time (such as overdubbed vocals or guitar) you may be able to use a single channel of outboard EQ and not spend extra on an upmarket portable studio.

On the other hand, if you are recording live band tracks, onboard EQ can be a lifesaver. There is little that is more frustrating than knowing what you want something to sound like and not being able to get at it with your limited EQ. So for complicated tracking situations I would recommend that you look for a machine with three-band equalization on each channel, with a high band some where around 10 K, a sweepable midrange from about 250 Hz to 5 K, and a low band at around 100 Hz. You may have to pay more for it, but the flexibility will be worth it.

Channel Inserts

This feature gives you an output of the channel to a device (say a compressor) and a place to send it back to the console. This output is controlled by the channel level and is therefore much easier to use than plugging the instrument directly into the device and then into the channel.

If you are tracking one instrument at a time, this feature is largely a matter of convenience. It's a nice clean way to get the signal from the input to the device (like a compressor or gate). But if you are recording several instruments simultaneously the inserts can come in very handy as ways to route the various signals to different devices and create effect loops for each channel.

Multiple Auxiliary (Effect) Sends

Having more than one effect send can be a real boon to mixing. For instance, it will allow you to apply more than one type of reverb to a mix, or more than one type of reverb even to an individual sound.

Auxiliary Effect Returns

These are special inputs for effect returns and so don't require a channel. Typically these returns don't have equalizers on the input, so any EQing of effects will have to take place outboard or on the device itself. These inputs are handy simply because they provide places to insert a signal into the portable studio without having to use a precious channel.

The Microphone Chapter

What goes on between the mic and the speaker is the entire process of recording.

There are basically two ways in which a tape recorder gets the information it records. One is from a direct line plugged into the channel, and the other is of course the microphone. For the most part I'll deal with "direct in" recording as it comes up in each of the chapters on individual instruments, but in these next few pages I want to pretend that without a microphone your portable studio just lies there like a big expensive electronic paperweight.

There is one fundamental truth about the microphone: It is very much a musical instrument itself. It has its own characteristics and colorations, and it will inevitably and unavoidably alter the sound of what you're recording. The art of miking lies in knowing how to use a mic to make those alterations positive. This little bit of observation is a not-so-subtle way of saying, "Hey you...you want good recording? Pay attention over here." This chapter is by necessity a little technical, but understanding microphones and the techniques of using them is a critical component of good, solid recording.

The microphone is the ear of the recording system. I mention this because all through this chapter I will use the ear metaphor, probably stretching it to within an inch of tolerability. Bear with me though, because it is a useful way to think of the process of **transduction**, which is the heart of recording.

Technically speaking, a transducer is any device that converts one form of energy into another. For our purposes that means that transduction is the process of turning sound waves into electrical impulses and then back into sound waves again. Both a microphone and a speaker are transducers; the microphone does and the speaker undoes, so to speak.

It is useful to think of this activity as that of translating one language into another then back again. Of course we humans do it automatically without even knowing we're doing it. For example, let's say you're in court having been arrested for wearing a pale blue polyester jumpsuit in public. You take the stand ready to defend your right to wear polyester and the bailiff asks you to raise your right hand and repeat after him, "I promise to tell the truth, the whole truth...." You take a second to absorb and store what the guy's saying, and then as soon as he stops talking you begin to repeat as requested. Simple. A no-brainer. Well...

When your ear gets spoken into, an incredible chain of events takes place. The ear translates from one language (say, bailiffese) into another. This language is the neuro-brainwave-electro-speak used to transmit to the auditory cortex in your brain. There it buzzes around for a while, gets processed and stored, and then gets retranslated so that when the time comes you can repeat it with your mouth. What I've just described is also what takes place in the recording process. The mic hears something, converts it to electrical impulses, sends it to the console for processing, the recorder for storage, the amplifier, and finally to the speakers, where it is reverse-transduced into sound waves again (ear = microphone, mouth = speaker; any opportunity for an analogy is a terrible thing to waste).

So far so good. But what if in all the excitement you forgot to take the cigarette filters out of your ears before you took the stand? What you would hear isn't exactly what the bailiff said. If the information isn't accurate in the first place no amount of processing will make it right. You will end up repeating something odd like, "I, Thomas, to sell the group, duh, fold the group...." Anyway, you get the idea. If the device used for inputting the information isn't accurate then neither is the information. To borrow from the computer world: garbage in, garbage out. Therein lies the importance of miking techniques.

Basic Transduction 101

Microphones operate in a simple but ingenious fashion. Like the human ear the mic uses a **diaphragm**, which is a thin flexible material that senses vibrations caused by sound waves crashing against its surface. How far the diaphragm travels from its resting point when struck by sound pressure translates into **amplitude** (loudness); how fast the diaphragm vibrates translates into **frequency** (pitch). An easy way to visualize this would be to use a drumhead as an example. The harder you bash it with a stick the more it stretches and rebounds. As the distance in and out traveled by the head decreases so does the volume. Simultaneously the head also vibrates, producing a pitch and overtones that are like ripples on the surface of a puddle. As the vibrations slow, the higher-frequency overtones disappear, eventually giving way to the slowest-moving frequencies as the vibration dies. As you might guess, this little factoid is important to recording. The reasons why come a little later in the discussion on mic techniques.

Microphone Types

There are several types of microphone, and each category is defined by the scheme it uses for converting sound into electrical impulses. For the purposes of this chapter, however, I want to limit the discussion to the two types that are most useful for home recording. These are the **dynamic** and **condenser** mics. Each has its advantages and disadvantages, strengths and weaknesses that should enter into the decision on which mic you choose for which application.

The Dynamic Microphone

The dynamic microphone is the one you're most likely to find in a home studio or on a nightclub stage. It operates with **passive** circuitry; that is, it transduces by using the physical mechanics of sound pressure unaided by any electronic assistance. Here's how it works.

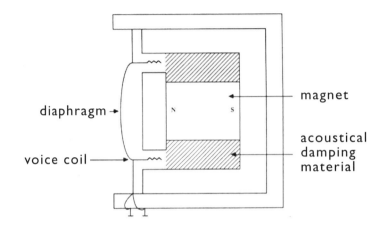

A diaphragm made of a flexible material is connected to a movable voice coil that is positioned in front of a magnet. The diaphragm acts as a sort of sail, moving the voice coil in response to the changes in **sound pressure level** (SPL). As the diaphragm moves, it changes the magnetic field (magnetic flux), and electric impulses flow in direct correlation to the diaphragm's movement. *Voilà*, the electric impulses generated in this manner are an analog, or "picture," of the sound. (See the discussion of analog recording in the chapter "Getting the Sound to Tape.")

Generally speaking, the dynamic microphone has a single response pattern that is set by the manufacturer. This means that the mic will most effectively pick up sound in a particular region around the **capsule** (the area in the head of the microphone that contains the diaphragm). Outside of the designated region the mic is very inefficient. Look to your microphone manual for specs regarding patterns.

The Condenser Microphone

This is the Rolls-Royce of the microphone world. Believe it or not, there are some condenser mics that cost upwards of $7,000 apiece. "How," you may ask, "could one condenser mic cost as much as thirty-five good dynamics? What could it possibly do that would account for the difference? Peter," say you, "why are you including a type of mic that costs as much as a pretty good used car in a book about portable studios? Are you nuts?" Read on, say I, the logic will unfold.

Here's how a condenser mic works. A razor-thin diaphragm is placed parallel to a metal perforated plate. The two elements are separated by a small gap, making a sort of an air sandwich. A small electric current is sent to each of the elements, making them act as the opposite poles of a capacitor (condenser mics are sometimes referred to as capacitor mics for this reason). This current comes from the console, from a separate power supply, or from batteries in the mic itself. When sound pressure vibrates the diaphragm, a change in electrical capacitance occurs, altering the flow of current. This electrical change then creates an analog of the sound in much the same fashion as the dynamic mic.

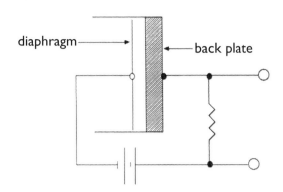

Okay, great, so what? It's just a different way to skin the same grape. Well, no. The condenser diaphragm, by virtue of its extremely low mass, can detect even minute variations in sound pressure and respond very quickly to volume changes. Also, because of the method it uses to read sound waves, the condenser mic diaphragm is more able to vibrate at high frequencies, creating a higher-resolution "picture" of the sound. What this means to the recordist is that the condenser is capable of much better frequency response than the dynamic, particularly in the top end.

There are some other major differences as well. While the dynamic mic has a preset, usually fixed, region of efficiency, a condenser mic will frequently offer the recordist a multiple choice of what are called **polar-response patterns**. These are selectable zones of directionality controlled by a switch on the mic itself. For example, setting the mic on the **cardioid** pattern will make the mic hear predominantly what's in a narrow area in front of it and reject sound outside this zone.

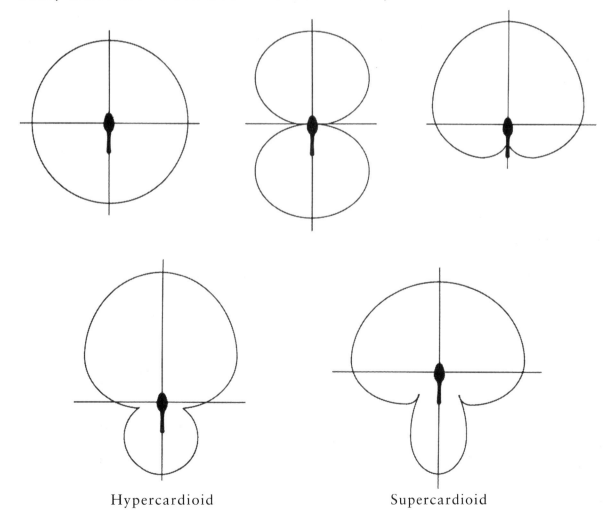

Hypercardioid   Supercardioid

Polar response pattern of omnidirectional and unidirectional microphones.

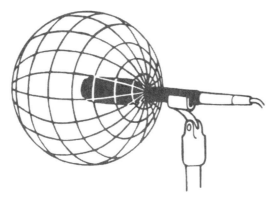
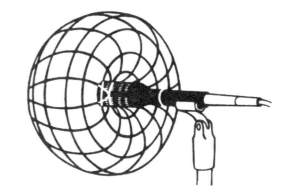

Omnidirectional Microphone   Unidirectional (Cardioid) Microphone

Three-dimensional polar response patterns.

Setting the mic on a **bidirectional** setting will allow the mic to pick up what's in front and in back of it but reject sound from the sides. Each of these patterns has its uses.

- **Cardioid:** The setting I use most often. I use it for recording single vocalists or instruments.

- **Bidirectional:** I use this setting for group vocals or duets with singers to the front and back of the microphone.

- **Hyper- and Supercardioid:** I use this for larger groups of vocals, horns, etc.

- **Omnidirectional:** I will usually use this setting in order to record a live space for ambient sound bouncing off the walls.

Another area where the condenser mic offers a choice is in the type of circuitry it uses. Some condensers use transistors (FET), while others actually use tubes. Most engineers would say that the tube mic is warmer and is preferable for fattening up or smoothing out a sound, whereas the FET mic is more precise, with truer frequency response and a more accurate top end.

There are other features added to some condensers mics that are useful for special situations. These may include a **pad** (attenuator) that acts sort of like earplugs: when selected it reduces the volume of sound before it can distort the mic. Some mics have frequency **roll-off** switches that provide a built-in equalizer of sorts to remove unwanted frequencies. It's not too suprising that the Rolls-Royce of microphones would have a lot of optional equipment available.

So which mic do you choose to add to your sonic arsenal? There are a variety of factors to consider.

Choosing a Dynamic Microphone

The Pros

1. *Dynamic mics are comparatively inexpensive.* The choice to use a dynamic mic may come down to simple economics; it's way cheaper to buy than a condenser. You can expect to spend under $200 street price for a really good dynamic, even less if you buy a used mic.

2. *Dynamic mics are durable.* They take a licking and keep on ticking. A dynamic is the "swing-it-around-your-head-by-the-cord" mic used and preferred by a lot of your rock-star lead singer types. You can almost tell whether or not a dynamic mic has been used for live shows by how many dents it has in it. Not that this is a recommended application of the mic, but if it can knock an audience member unconscious and still work in the out chorus, that tells you something.

    The reason for the durability of the dynamic mic is that it uses a relatively simple circuit that doesn't rely on delicate electronics to do the job. So dropping a dynamic doesn't mean an automatic trip to the microphone clinic.

3. *A dynamic mic can handle a lot of level before it distorts.* Microphone distortion happens when the amount of level coming into the mic exceeds the diaphragm circuitry's ability to respond. To go back to our ear analogy, if you stuck your head in a Marshall speaker cabinet while your guitar buddy was blazing away, you'd distort too. The more sensitive your ears, the quicker you'd hear nothing but white noise. One of the major factors that determines the sensitivity of a mic is how light its diaphragm is. The diaphragm of the dynamic microphone has a relatively large mass whose tolerance for movement is comparatively large. This means that it takes a fair amount of sound pressure level to push the heavy diaphragm to is limit. While any microphone can be distorted, the diaphragm characteristics of the dynamic make it slower to distort. The dynamic therefore is better equipped to deal with blasts of volume than the condenser, and is therefore more forgiving under challenging conditions.

4. *The dynamic is versatile.* If you are planning on using a mic for both live performance and recording, a dynamic mic is probably the choice for you.

5. *Power is not required to make it work.* More on this in the section on condenser mics.

The Cons

1. *Its frequency response is limited.* The very thing that makes the dynamic mic durable is also a detriment when it comes to frequency response. The mass of the diaphragm makes quick response more difficult.

2. *The response pattern of a dynamic microphone is set by the manufacturer* (see below). This can result in greater "leakage" of unwanted sounds into the mic.

Choosing a Condenser Microphone

The Pros

1., 2., 3. ... *The condenser mic sounds better.* Yeah, but seven grand's worth? Well actually the $7,000 mic category is a rare one populated with scientific calibration and "classic" (read old) mics. But it got your attention. First, there are some good condensers at substantially lower prices; secondly, as a general rule they *do* sound big dollars better for a lot of applications.

    To elaborate, the top-end improvement is more than just a nice thing to have. It results in great tonal separation and clarity. As was noted in the chapter "What Is Sound?" the thing that distinguishes an oboe from a pan flute is its timbre, the soul of which lives in the harmonic overtones accompanying a pitch. These overtones are for the most part high-frequency information. Therefore the clearer the overtones the clearer the difference between instruments. A condenser mic is more capable of reproducing top end, so in the final analysis using a condenser mic to record with makes it much easier to accomplish a pleasing mix.

The Cons

1. *A condenser mic is expensive to buy.* Ah, but there are some solutions to that (see below).
2. *Condenser mics are delicate.* The circuitry used to translate minute changes in sound into useful electrical impulses is vulnerable to damage and costly to repair. Therefore condenser mics should only be used under controlled conditions.
3. *The condenser mic requires power to work.* The power is needed to charge the diaphragm elements. And as I said earlier, there are three ways to get power to the mic. The first is called **48-volt phantom power**, which has nothing to do with the spirit world. This small current is sent directly to the mic from the console. It is activated by a switch on each channel of a console equipped with low-impedance connectors. The second source of current is a **power supply** that comes with the mic. This is for use when a console doesn't have 48-volt phantom power. It just plugs into a wall socket and steps down the current to send to the mic. The third way to power a condenser is with a **battery** in the mic itself.
4. *The condenser is much more susceptible to distortion.* It is a sensitive thing and the diaphragm is easily flattened by excessive sound pressure level. Like with the human ear, loud percussive noises can even cause permanent damage.

Miking in the Real World: Mic Placement Guidelines

I discuss some specific miking techniques in each of the instrumental chapters of this book, but here are some more general points to keep in mind. Mic placement is critical for bringing out the best in each instrument. In fact, in the old days before equalization was used, a recording engineer was prized for his skill at mic placement.

- To get the right balance between low, mid, and high frequencies there is an optimum position for the mic. Finding this position is the art of miking. It is a process of trial and error and critical listening. Placement will depend on the type of instrument, how loud it is, and what kind of tonal and ambient emphasis you wish to obtain. The process of miking is one of chipping away at a sound sculpture. Move the mic, go listen to the monitors; move it again, go listen again. This is a game of inches. Literally. You must learn to be patient. It may take many moves, but by doing so you can save yourself lots of problems come mix time.

- Avoid mud by being aware of **proximity effect**. This is a condition caused by the sound source's being too close to the mic. For example, listen to your voice twelve inches from the mic, then put your mouth right to the mic and speak. You'll notice that there is a substantial addition of low frequencies. The mic must be far enough away to avoid low-end buildup (more in "The Vocal Chapter").

- Beware of reflective surfaces that may contribute rumble. I always place a blanket or something absorbent under the mic stand to avoid reflections off the floor.

- Make sure that the mic you choose is used properly. Sounds silly, but you can improve your technique by simply reading the microphone manual or spec sheets.

- Try not to use the same mic for everything you record. As I said, each mic has its own unique characteristics, and varying mics will help to differentiate sounds. So go ye forth and borrow from friends.

- When miking try to avoid blasts of air. These can come from speakers, the soundholes of guitars, the bells of brass instruments, and, most often, from vocals. The mic hears a blast of air as what's called a "pop." This sounds like a percussive thump, and once on a track it can be very difficult to get rid of. One way to avoid this problem is to always have the mic at an angle to the potential source of air. Another is to use a pop filter (see Vocal chapter).

Money, Money, Money

If you want to add a bit of variety to your sound or want to use an expensive mic for an important part, you can find companies in most major cities that will rent pro audio equipment by the day, week, or month. If you can't locate one in the phone book under "audio," try film production houses, advertising agencies, or even some local music stores that lease PA systems.

There are some very good condenser mics in the $300–400 range. AKG makes a remarkably good one, and I'm sure that there will be new models by other manufacturers. Check out your local dealer for the latest.

Check out the classifieds for used mics. For the most part mics will either work or not work — mileage isn't really a factor. So buying used is a reasonably safe bet and you can expect to pay half or less for a mic.

Advertise for what you want. Run a classified. Who knows, there may be some guy who bought an expensive condenser, then decided to join the priesthood.

There are some less expensive **electret** condensers that have battery-powered circuitry. These are in the dynamic price range. Some of them tend to sound a bit brittle, so be sure to check out the mic for pleasing quality.

Some Favorite Mics

Every engineer has some favorite mics for certain applications. These are some of mine. By experimenting you'll find the ones that work for you.

Dynamic

Shure SM 56, 57, 58	Power guitars, drums, loud vocals
Sennheiser 421	Kick drum
Electrovoice RE 20	Bass amp

Condenser

Neumann U-89	Lead vocals, acoustic instruments
Neumann U-87	(with pad) Tom-toms, guitar amp
AKG 414	Cymbals, backing vocals, piano
Neumann U-47 (tube)	To warm up or smooth out vocals

Using Which Mics When

When I Use a Dynamic

- Loud instruments, power guitar amps, drum heads

- When I want to limit the high end due to hiss problems. The dynamic doesn't have the top-end sensitivity of a condenser, making it is easier to avoid recording an abundance of hiss along with the sound. This is particularly true of noisy effects running through an amp.

- Bass amplifiers

- Loud or "rough" vocals

When I Use a Condenser

- Most vocals

- Soft instruments

- Acoustic guitars

- Any instrument with a lot of high-frequency information (strings, saxophone, flute, etc.)

- Clean guitar amp

- Acoustic piano
  Do not use a condenser on percussion or guitar amps unless the pad is engaged.

The Effects Chapter

Smoke and Mirrors

One of my favorite things about recording is playing in space. Now, before you think I've been sniffing too much capstan cleaner, what I mean is that I enjoy the way space can be manipulated by using effects. This for me is one of the principal methods of expressing the art of recording. In "The Mixdown Chapter" I'll discuss in detail the creation of musical space, but for now I want to lay out a few ideas about what effects are and how they work.

Signal-to-Noise Ratio

In the discussion on tape recording and tape I beat the signal-to-noise thing so much that I hope you'll never forget it. Well guess what? It applies to effects units too. Oh boy. The short version is as follows: The ideal is to get as much signal as you can on the input side so you can send as little as possible out the output side. Translation: make the signal loud when you're feeding the effects unit so you don't have to keep turning the thing up to feed the portable studio.

The reason is that all electronic gear generates some of its own noise. (To confirm this just listen to a reverb unit when nothing's plugged in to it.) This is particularly true with semi-pro gear where the manufacturer has to compromise the expense of component quality to keep the unit affordable for the consumer.

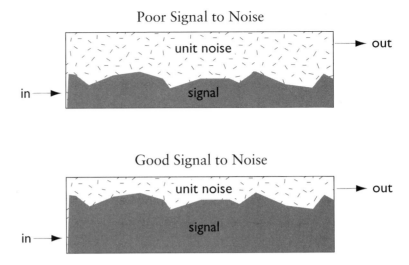

Poor Signal to Noise

Good Signal to Noise

The moral of the story is that the lower the signal to the unit the more of the unit noise you will hear at the output.

Shapers and Colorers

I consider sound-processing gear as falling into two categories: **sound shapers** and **sound colorers**. These are my own labels, but I find them useful to avoid confusion when discussing the topic.

Sound shapers are processors that bring out the inherent quality of a sound. These would include things like equalizers and compressors. Sound colorers on the other hand are those processors that alter or add to the fundamental quality of a sound in order to create a new sound. Among these I would include reverbs, echos, phasers, flangers, chorus devices, fuzzboxes, and wah-wah pedals. You get the idea. Stuff that makes stuff sound different.

Sound Shapers

Sound shapers are the sculpting tools of the recording medium. Ideally they are used to bring out the essential character of a recorded element. Michelangelo once said that when he was sculpting all he was doing by chipping and carving was removing the excess marble in order to reveal the sculpture already in the stone. The shaping tools of the recording world do the same thing with sound.

Equalizer

The equalizer is the principal tool for carving a sound. It is a sort of volume control, but with a major difference. It alters the volume of a given **frequency range** within a sound. By using an equalizer you can create an emphasis on particular characteristics of a sound. By adding or subtracting the volume of certain frequencies you can make big sounds small, small sounds bigger, and soft round sounds mean and sharp.

What an EQ does is to alter the balance of frequencies that compose a sound. As you know from earlier chapters, the sound of a musical instrument is composed of a complex of frequencies. The mixture of frequencies that make up a sound is different from instrument to instrument even within the same type. No two guitars sound exactly alike and so on. Not only that, but different micro-phones also have varying frequency characteristics. In the early days of recording there were even bigger problems to deal with, like low-end rumble and high-end noise. The electronic boffins of those days came up with the idea that if they could filter out unwanted frequencies the sound would be clearer and they wouldn't be using up precious disc space to record what sounded like subway noises. So the first equalizers were actually built to respond to the problem of noise. Once they had the idea and the technology, some unnamed person figured out that if a filter could take away certain frequencies it could also be used to add others, thereby smoothing out the sound. So — badda-bing, badda-boom — the equalizer was born. It was designed to make equal the disparities in the frequency configuration of a sound.

When the principal function of equalizers shifted from filtering to sound shaping there were some necessary modifications. The early filters were dedi-cated to solving certain specific problems, and therefore were built to act on a narrow range of frequencies. They were in effect raising or lowering the level of a fixed-position frequency point. When EQ was beginning to be cast in the role of sonic savior, the narrow-band units that dealt only with rumble and noise weren't flexible enough. So someone came along with the idea of many different filters for different purposes. These filters had different **bandwidths** centered on different frequencies for different purposes. A bandwidth, simply put, is the region of frequencies an equalizer affects. For example, a unit might emphasize or deemphasize a region around 1 K, leaving all other frequencies outside its bandwidth alone. This simple type of equalizer is still very common. It is called the **tone control EQ**. You have one on your stereo, your TV, and in many cases your portable studio.

But what about when the center frequency won't solve the problem? You're stuck, unless you have another unit with a different center point. So someone came up with the idea of having a group of different center points on the same equalizer. You could now switch from a 1 K center point to a 3 K center point and raise or lower the volume of this frequency bandwidth to address a problem. This type of equalizer came to be known as a **click-stop EQ** because you would turn a knob and click to the next selection like an old-fashioned channel knob on a TV. This new innovation required two controls for the equalizer — one to select the frequency, and one to change its volume. Click-stops are also still around on some great old pro consoles as well as on guitar amps.

The next development in the search for ultimate equalizer flexibility was the ability to move the center point to frequencies that lay between the click stops. The idea was to have a continuous area of selectability between the lowest center point on the EQ and the highest. This became known as the **sweepable EQ**, meaning that you could "sweep" back and forth in order to zero in on the most suitable frequency. Sweepable EQs are usually found in upper-end recording mixers, often in combination with tone controls or shelving equalizers.

Another approach to flexibility was the development of the **graphic EQ**. This clever device is actually a whole bunch of tone control equalizers with different center points all housed in one unit. These EQs typically have a series of vertical slots on the face of the device, each corresponding to a fixed frequency. Within each of these slots there is a slider control to boost or cut the level of the desig-nated fixed frequency. Graphic EQs are usually configured as outboard gear to be added on to a mixer or amplifier.

Fixed Bandwidth Equalizer

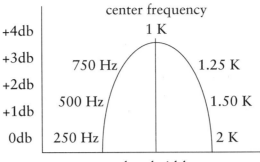

boost 1 K @ +4db

Even though the frequency is centered on 1K, the bandwidth will still affect a range of frequencies. Frequencies are affected in diminishing amounts the farther away they are from the center frequency.

At the end of the EQ unit good-better-best, the search for the ultimate in equalizing bliss has so far resulted in the creation of the **parametric EQ**. This is an equalizer that not only lets you continuously adjust the center point of the bandwidth, but the dimensions of the bandwidth as well. It's not as confusing as it sounds. With a parametric EQ you are able to affect a narrow region of frequencies or a broad one as you choose. This function is controlled by a knob labeled "cue." So a parametric has three controls: frequency, bandwidth (cue), and volume. The good thing about a parametric EQ is that you can be more precise about what area of sound you are shaping.

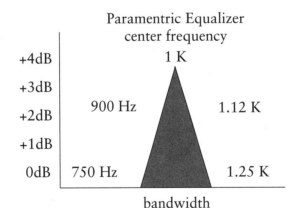

boost 1 K @ +4dB

The bandwidth of the parametric is variable, so it can be set to affect a narrow or broad range of frequencies around the center point; in this case a narrow bandwidth.

Here's how the flexibility of various types of EQs would affect a real-world situation.

You have a great rhythm guitar performance, but the sound is a little harsh. You want to smooth it out. The harshness comes from an overabundance of a certain frequency. For our sample EQ problem let's say it's 1 K (a frequent-offender frequency, by the way).

Least flexible solution: tone control. Portable studio with high-frequency tone control and low-frequency tone control

Look in the owner's manual to see where the manufacturer has located the center point of the equalizer. As this EQ is a fixed-position one with no user choice as to what frequencies are affected, the equipment designer has put the equalizer into a sort of "most useful" range. This will also mean that the EQ is probably quite broad in bandwidth and will affect a number of frequencies on either side of the center point. Let's say that the EQ is specced out at 1 K. Your guitar problem would be improved by reducing (cutting) the amount of high-frequency EQ.

If, however, the center point of the EQ is at 3 K, you will be less able to affect the offending frequency without cutting desirable frequncies as well. In that case you will have to decide if the cure is worse than the disease.

More flexible solution: click-stop EQ with a variable center point at 750 Hz, 1 K, 1.25 K, and 2 K

In this case the click-stop EQ will allow you a choice of center points. These settings will be displayed on the control to tell you which frequency you're affecting. If you wish to fix the guitar, you locate the click stop to 1 K and cut the volume of that frequency. Aside from the obvious advantage of being able to affect a number of different frequencies to address different instrument problems, you can also change the EQ at different points in the song. For example, if the guitar has a 1 K problem in the verse but a 3 K problem in the solo you can change the EQ as the song is rolling (but beware of the possibility of electronic "pops" whenever you're changing settings during recording).

More flexible solution yet: sweepable EQ with continuously variable center point

Using this type of EQ you can fine-tune which frequency you're going after. For instance, instead of being able to affect either 1 K or 1.25 K you can select a frequency between the two that may be a more accurate cure for the problem. This is an advantage when you're trying to be precise in EQing, like if an unpleasantness occurs in the guitar only on certain notes. By using a sweepable EQ you can zero in on the area that's causing the problem and leave the rest alone. With a click-stop EQ you would have to approximate the EQ setting based on what the manufacturer had preset, and you might inadvertently affect frequencies that you wanted to leave alone.

A different approach to flexibility: graphic equalizer with multiple center points

The graphic EQ is set up to offer a graphic shape to a sound. The assumption is that the complexity of sound is such that there may be several problems to be solved as well as characteristics to be brought out simultaneously. In our guitar problem you could use a graphic EQ to cut 1 K and 1.25 K to get rid of the harshness, and you could compensate by boosting 2 K and 500 Hz at the same time to add other characteristics that are more pleasing. After you set the slider controls you will see that they create a sort of graph of the shape of the frequencies affected.

Most flexible solution: parametric equalizer

This unit will really let you alter a sound with surgical precision. To fix our guitar we may want to remove 1 K but not 1.5 K or 900 Hz. With a parametric EQ we could target not only the center frequency but also how much of the surrounding sonic landscape we want to excavate. By altering the cue control we can narrow the bandwidth to give a rather acute filtering, or use a broad band to smoothly contour the sound.

Which to get? For my money it's a toss-up between the parametric EQ (my personal favorite) and the graphic EQ, which is usually cheaper and more of a utility player that's useful in a variety of roles. More on this in "The Studio Kit Chapter," where we talk about how to part with your money as painlessly as possible.

Compressor/Limiter

Imagine you have a large trash bin full of paper. Some of it is overflowing the top of the container. What to do? Easy. Jump in and stomp on it and mash it down. Well, a compressor is the audio equivalent of trash compaction.

What a compressor does is lower the level of the loudest of the sound and in effect raise the level of the quietest of the sound. In other words it artificially creates dynamic range parameters that the sound cannot exceed.

To describe this idea graphically; you're in the studio, it's two in the morning, and you're working with a guitar player who is somewhat prone to mood swings. In one section of the piece the playing is whisper-quiet, then a millisecond later it sounds like dueling chainsaws. You don't want to inhibit the person's enthusiasm, but the porta meters are being bashed to within a nanoweber of their little LEDs. Situations like this are what the compressor was invented for. By sending the signal through a compressor before it gets to the tape machine, you can reduce the difference in level between the quietest and loudest signals. This allows for all of the performance to be heard effectively instead of some of it being lost and other parts being too loud.

As an example let's say our manic-depressive guitarist friend uses levels that go from -5 dB to +12 dB. The tape machine may be able to handle those kinds of dynamic swings, but what's going to happen when you have to mix this track with the other instruments? You will have to be moving the guitar track fader up and down in the mix like a madman in order for the dynamics to be manageably mixable. A compressor simulates your moving the fader but does it electronically and automatically.

To go back to our challenging relationship with the guitarist, by using a compressor we can allow him to play as he chooses, but what gets to tape is modified by our compressor settings. Let's say we want the signal to be no louder than +6 dB. We set the compressor so that anything over 6 dB is reduced in volume automatically to just 6 dB. This would be an example of what's called **limiting**. In effect the sound hits a wall and can get no louder.

But if you set the compressor so that it reduces the signal some *proportion* when it goes over +6 dB — rather than limiting it to not exceed +6 dB — you would get a gentler effect. This is what's usually referred to as **compression**. The proportion of sound reduction is determined by the **compression ratio**, which you set with the controls on the unit.

Compressor Controls

Compression ratio: This allows a certain proportional dB increase in output for every amount of dB increase in input. If sound out equals sound in, the ratio would be 1:1, so it follows that a 2:1 ratio would mean that for every 2 dBs that come into the unit 1 dB of level will get out. A 4:1 ratio would mean that for every 4 dBs of input only 1 dB will get out and so on. The higher the first number in the ratio, the smaller the percentage of input level that will get out. So if the ratio is 20:1 it means that for every 20 dB of level in only 1 dB gets out. Think of that as hitting a wall and you see that the higher the compression ratio the more severe the limiting of the sound. When you get into "The Recipe Section" you will find some guidelines for compressor use.

Threshold: Think of the threshold of a compressor as the height of an overpass on the freeway. There is a sign that says no vehicles over a certain height will fit under the bridge. So when a sound hits the overpass only some of it goes under — the compressor lowers the dimensions of the vehicle. (I once had some roadies who forgot how tall our equipment truck was and nearly got it compressed at about a 4:1 ratio in Ohio, but I digress.) The threshold setting is the point of loudness at which the compressor starts to operate. Any sound below the threshold will be allowed through unaffected. So our 2:1 compression ratio will only affect sound above a certain level. Below that threshold the the ratio is 1:1.

Attack and release: These controls allow you to vary how quickly a sound is grabbed to be compressed once it exceeds the threshold and how quickly it's released after it's been affected. As a general rule, the quicker the attack the more dynamic control, and the longer the release the more smoothness in the sound. The converse can also be true. Sometimes you want the compressor to let a transient go by before grabbing the sound so that the rhythm is emphasized, and you might want to use a quick release to punctuate a phrase. Experimentation and experience are the keys.

Input/output: These controls do about what you would guess; however, in the case of compression, which is activated by volume (gain, level), the amount of sound into the unit will determine the amount that gets compression. In other words, if the unit is set to a threshold of +6 dB but the input to the unit is so low that the threshold is never reached, then compression doesn't take place. Follow me around a few curves here. What happens when the signal going in is too low? We have a tendency to turn up the output in order to be able to hear it. But what are you turning up? The combination of the unit's noise and the signal. Not only that, but in this case you aren't even compressing anything because the signal is below the threshold. So you're adding noise for nothing. As a general rule the compression should be set to lower the loudest sounds about 3 dB or so (unless of course the recording is very dynamic, in which case the gain reduction may be even greater).

Setting the Knobs — Coöperation

Using a compressor well is a balancing act between bringing unruly dynamics under control and still having a natural sound. The goal is to have the audience unaware that compression is used at all. This is called "transparency." The controls are usually tweaked so that each is optimized to serve its purpose. For instance, you may want the attack and release set a certain way, which may result in having to raise the threshold so less of the program is compressed. This in turn may mean adjusting the input level in order to maintain a good signal-to-noise ratio and so on. The best advice I can think of when it comes to using a compressor as transparently as possible is to remember that if you change one thing you have to listen for balance with all the other parameters.

Sound Colorers

Reverbs

First, a couple of terms to bandy about. **Ambience** is the sound of the environment. The more the sound of the environment interacts with a source sound the more ambient it is. The less ambient the sound the more **present** it is. The most present sound is one without any ambience, and the least present sound is one that is all ambience.

Reverb is the sound of multiple-reflection ambience. All that really means is that reverberation occurs when a sound repeatedly bounces off different surfaces in the environment at different times. Reverb is the most frequently used of the sound colorers. It adds body, smoothness, and sustain to a sound while placing it in a environmental relationship with other instruments. It gives us an important reference point in visualizing the imaginary room where the music is being played.

To the human brain reverb provides a menu of clues about the environment we're in. Without even realizing we're doing it we can determine roughly the size of a room, how high the ceilings are, what the walls and floors are made of, and how loud or softly we need to speak to be heard. We can also tell how far a source of sound is from us by the amount of ambience we hear relative to the amount of the source.

Imagine for a moment that you are standing in a cave and someone is talking to you. If they are nearby you will hear their voice relatively louder than the reflection of their voice bouncing off the walls. The voice will be relatively present. But if you stand still and they keep walking away while talking the voice will become less present. The farther away they get from you the more you will hear the sound of the cave, until eventually if they are far enough away it will be difficult to understand what they're saying because most of what you will hear will be the reflection of the sound off the walls. So increased ambience equals increased distance. This perception of distance based on ambience will play a major role when we get to the Mixdown chapter.

Another way that ambience affects us is much more subjective and individual. We subconsciously form *emotional* judgments about our whereabouts based on reverb. For instance, for some people the sounds inside a cathedral will evoke a positive response related to comfort or spiritual mystery. So the wealth of reverb information we take in not only contributes to our perception of where we are but also how we feel about it. Great recordists are continually aware of how a reverb choice *feels* as well as how it sounds.

A Minor Digression

Just a brief mention to illustrate how important reverberation is to our understanding of the world. One of the strangest auditory experiences I ever had was touring the Shure electronics facility. They have a special room there called an *anechoic chamber,* which is used to test the specifications of the microphones they design. This room is completely sound-damped, with foam covering the walls, floor, and ceiling. When you're inside you walk on a catwalk suspended above the floor. It was eerie. I mean *no* sound bounces off the walls, floor, or ceiling. When I spoke it seemed as if the sound came out of my mouth, went about an inch, and immediately fell to the floor. Any sense of where I was was confused by the lack of auditory information. It was a sensory-deprivation experience that was really unnerving, and I found myself feeling very disoriented. When I went back out into the hall I was struck by how pleasant it was to hear sound on good old linoleum again.

Reverb Sound Characteristics

There are all sorts of ways to slice up the subject of reverbs, but to keep it simple I'm going to divide sound types into two categories — **bright** and **warm**.

Controlling the Reverb

Many reverb units allow you great control over the various sound characteristics that they produce. You can set not only the size of the reverberant space but also a lot of its sound-reflection qualities. Simpler units contain just a selection of useful presets with very little individual control. In either case, knowing something about the principal parameters of reverb units can go a long way toward knowing when to use them. (By the way, it is beyond the scope of this book to really get into outboard gear parameters such as first reflections and such — see your product manual for more information.)

Bright and Warm

As you know from the "What Is Sound?" chapter, the way you perceive a sound has to do with the frequencies that dominate it. You also know that low-end sound waves take longer to develop than high-end ones. This means that low-end frequencies require more physical space to develop. Therefore the bigger the room the more apparent the low end. There you have the basic idea behind modern reverb units. The size of an imaginary room is largely determined by manipulating the amount of low end in the frequency mix. This manipulation determines the brightness or warmth of a given reverb setting.

Brightness is a way of describing how much high-frequency information you're hearing. For instance, a small room with hard walls would be considered very bright because there would be relatively little room for low end to develop. Try the "clap test" in your shower to hear a bright room. (By the way, brightness can also be used to describe *any* sound that is upper-frequency dominant, a keyboard patch or guitar amp for instance.)

The principal control on the reverb unit that determines the size of the imaginary room is the **decay time**. The reverb designers have created certain *algorithms* (mathematical calculations) that tell the unit how to imitate the sound of a space. So when you tell the unit you want a two-second decay time it synthesizes what would happen if you sent a sound into a room that had a two-second reflection time.

This parameter is the key to how your audience perceives the "room" the music is emanating from. To take an example from the real world, a concert hall has a decay of somewhere between one and a half and two and a half seconds. A bathroom may have a reverb decay of well under a second. But in the world of recording we don't exactly parallel the real world. We take some sonic license to achieve a desired perception. For instance, for me personally a one-and-a-half-second decay time seems too short to represent a hall-like space. So in my imaginary space a three-second decay seems more appropriate to convey the warmth and richness of the large concert hall. I also feel that while two-tenths of a second may be an accurate decay for a tile bathroom in the real world, to my ear the reflections are too brief to be heard as reverb. So I lengthen the decay time to six-tenths of a second make the effect more obvious.

Here's where the notion of bright and warm comes into the picture. A warm reverb would be one that has a relatively greater amount of low end. Low end needs room to develop, so a warm reverb with more low end would represent a bigger room and thus would have a longer decay setting. The warmer the reverb the smoother the effect. Here are some free association adjectives I would associate with a longer decay time: rich, romantic, inspiring, mysterious, lush. The shorter the decay setting the brighter the sound. Some free association adjectives with short decay times: energetic, punchy, percussive, light.

In the studio you can mix these reverbs to create multiple effects in the same track (see "The Step-by-Step Mixdown Chapter" and "The Recipe Section"). In fact, in the Men at Work song "Down Under" I used seventeen different kinds of reverbs and echos for the mix in order to provide depth and clarity. Other examples of very effective echo mixing are Peter Gabriel's "Shock the Monkey" and Thomas Dolby's "Blinded by Science." Listen to the way the reverbs move the music back and forth.

A Brief Note on Setting Up Your Reverb

On most semipro reverb units there is a "mix" control. This is used to combine the original sound with the effect sound so that if you were using the reverb in-line to feed a guitar amp you could use the unit itself to determine how much of the effect you would hear. In the case of recording, however, as you will see, you will bring the original signal in at one place in the console and the reverbed signal in at another. In other words, you will balance the amount of reverb using the portable studio, not the reverb unit. Therefore in most cases you will want to set your reverb so that the output is all effect. This is what I mean when I say to treat the reverb as an instrument when using the portable studio.

Delayed Reverb

Reverb is perceived as sound occurring inside an enclosed space like our cave. The farther back in the cave the sound source is, the more of the ambience we hear relative to the amount of the source. As was noted above, the level of ambience affects the clarity of the source. So what do you do when you want the body that reverb adds to a sound but you also want absolute clarity? You shift the source of sound from inside the cave to outside it. In that way both clarity and body are achieved. It's not as confusing as it sounds. Think what would happen if you were standing outside the cave next to someone who proceeds to shout into the cave. You would hear their voice clearly, and a split-second later you would hear the reverberations of the sound coming off the cave walls. There would be a time lag between the source and the reverb. This is called **delayed reverb**, and it is very useful for combining the best of both worlds. The reverb provides the sustain and ambience while the delay allows for a few milliseconds of absolute presence. For this reason I often use it on lead vocals because understanding the lyrics is important.

Many units have a control for setting the delay (sometimes called "pre-delay") that is measured in milliseconds. Usually I'll set the delay to a quarter-note or eighth-note duration before the reverb receives the signal. More on this later in "The Vocal Chapter" and "The Mixdown Chapter."

Echo

I often hear the term *echo* used interchangeably with reverb (I sometimes hear myself using it that way — shame). They are not the same thing. Where reverb is multiple randomized reflections bearing different phase relationships with one another, echo is a discrete linear reflection or series of linear reflections. That is a long way of saying that with an echo if you say Hello it says Hello back. There are two principle types of echo, the **single-slap echo** and **multiple-slap echo**, the latter also referred to as a **multiple-delay echo**.

A slap, as you might guess, is a single audible return of the echo. A single slap is where the repeat is heard once and then dies abruptly. It was the echo treatment used in early rock and rockabilly music. It is very effective in evoking this era of music, which is both a good thing and a not-so-good thing. If you use it be aware that the audience may perceive the echo as a fifties fashion statement. Be sure of the effect you want to give.

The multiple-slap echo sounds like a shout across the Swiss Alps. The sound repeats several times, with each repeat quieter than the last. But through all of this bouncing around it still maintains its integrity as an understandable duplicate of the original. This effect has an arresting, dramatic quality that I've always liked. I've used the multiple-slap echo to great effect on lead vocals and lead guitars. It can also be useful for sustaining an explosive sound, or for calling attention to a particular musical part. Sometimes it can be used to create harmonies to the source sound in fast-moving passages. To do this you would play the first note, then when the echo of the first is audible you play the second note, creating a two-note chord. You can hear variations on these approaches on Steve Miller's "Fly like an Eagle," the Men at Work records, and Robert Plant's lead vocals with Led Zeppelin.

The control on the reverb/delay unit for the number of slaps is labeled "feedback," meaning that the sound is fed back into the unit to be heard again. For a single slap the feedback is set to some minimal setting (see your owner's manual). For multiple slaps the feedback is set higher. Setting the feedback is a matter of personal taste, but generally I set the tempo of repeat so it is in quarter-note triplets to the source sound. Then I set the feedback so that the repeats will die out over the course of about three beats.

Treating Reverb and Echo

One more note: I usually treat the echo and reverb much as I would any other instruments. By that I mean that when mixing I want to be able to equalize the reverb and echo and often even add reverb to the echo. In order to do this I will bring the reverb return back to console channel inputs if possible. This will mean a lot more when we get further along. For the moment just remember I mentioned it here.

Creating False Stereo and Electronic Doubling

Our goal here is to get a stereo guitar part. As you have already learned, the recording of an instrument in stereo requires two tracks, each having some amount of the instrument on each track. Here's at least one occasion when understanding this concept has real-world results. Remember, equal amounts of a signal recorded on both tracks (50% left and 50% right) results in a mono sound in the middle of the stereo spectrum. So how do you double or create a stereo pair of the same part?

You cannot create a stereo double by recording exactly the same signal to two different tracks and then panning them hard left and right! The instrument will just end up mono in the center. Why? Remember how a pan pot works to put something in the center. It places equal amounts of the same signal on either side. In order to create a stereo pair of parts you have to record two different signals that happen to be playing the same part. Same part, but a different signal; it's the differences between the two signals that our brain perceives as stereo.

Now, to go back to the question of creating a double or stereo part. There are two ways to do it. The first is to play the part a second time and record it to another track. This requires a steady, near-perfect performance and uses up a track, neither of which may be a great option in the home studio. While the musical result is truly the sound of two guitars, the cost in resources may not be worth the effect.

There is another method. You can electronically double the part using one of several different types of outboard devices. This approach has the advantage of being automatically correct (because it's the same part), and by using the device in the mixdown you won't have to use another portable studio track for the stereo reproduction.

A perfectly reasonable question to ask would be, "If it's the same part, how is that different from recording the same signal to two tracks?" It's different because when the signal goes through the device it is altered so it's no longer the same signal. Same part, different signal. In effect the device replays the part for you.

There are a boatload of devices you can use to accomplish this (including reverb), but I'm going to discuss the three I use the most: the **harmonizer**, the **delay line**, and the **chorus effect**. Once you have the principle you can substitute your own favorite device in the equation.

Harmonizer

A harmonizer is probably best known for doing what its name implies; that is, creating a harmony to a sound by manipulating the frequency of the pitch. There are all kinds of parameters on these devices with myriad effects worth investigating. (For more in-depth information read Craig Anderton's excellent book on the subject of outboard gear, *Multieffects for Musicians*). For the purposes of this discussion I'm going to deal only with a parameter called "pitch bend."

To simplify the way a harmonizer works, it delays a signal slightly and alters its frequency signature at a constant rate, thereby changing the pitch of the note. A tuba goes in and a flute comes out. The rate of pitch change is measured in *cents*. When you add or subtract cents you raise or lower the pitch of the sound (-6 cents would be 6 cents flat; +6 cents would sharp the pitch, and so on).

To use the harmonizer as a stereo generating device you would split the signal, recording the original signal to one track, with the harmonized signal going to the second track. By changing the settings on the harmonizer you create a slightly delayed and subtly detuned mirror of the first part. The effect you achieve is to "spread" the guitar so it sounds richer and bigger. (To find out exactly how to do this check out Recipe 18 in "The Recipe Section." For the moment let me just say that in all of these techniques you are using only one output side of the device to create the stereo double. Check your owner's manual for which is the proper output — you want the "effect" side.)

The setting I generally use on the harmonizer for stereo doubling is about +6 cents. You may want to change this setting to suit your needs. Remember, the more cents further away from the original you are, the more stereo effect (beacause the two signals are more different) — but this also adds more delay and dissonance in pitch bend.

Delay Line

A delay line (see the discussion of echo above) can be used to generate a stereo double in much the same way as a harmonizer, but with a slightly different effect. In the case of the delay line you will create the stereo differential with time rather than with pitch. The increments used to set the delay line are usually measured in milliseconds. After setting a very small amount of delay between the original and the double you can record them to different sides and then pan them to different sides, creating stereo.

The amount of delay you will want to use will vary widely depending on the type of musical part. But as a general rule the longer the delay time the more noticeable the gap between the original track and the delayed stereo track. This type of approach can also be very effective for creating what are called *mults* (multiples) of vocals to "stereoize" them.

Chorus Pedal

I like the chorus effect a lot because it can cover a multitude of sonic sins. It has a tendency to smooth out harshness and can be used to good effect to enrich a sound.

The chorus works in a fashion similar to the harmonizer. It alters the pitch of the input. But unlike the harmonizer, in which a pitch change is constant, the chorus moves the pitch around. It takes a pitch and alters the frequency up and down around a center point. This sound is derived from the natural variations that occur when a group of people are trying to play in unison. Think of a violin section. Not everyone is playing exactly the same pitch with exactly the same vibrato — there are variations. This is what the chorus device tries to simulate.

There are so many units out there with chorusing capabilities that any specific settings I give you won't mean much. But in general I will try to keep the chorusing fairly subtle because otherwise the pitch variance can make the other instruments and vocals sound out of tune.

Other Cool Toys

Simple. Try everything you can get your hands on, phasers flangers, wah-wah pedals, distorto-boxes. Experiment using them in novel ways. One of my favorites is to flange the output of the reverb. I haven't tried wah-wah on vocals yet, but I will. Recording's a playground. Try lots of stuff.

Summary Notes

Equalizer: A volume control for certain specific frequencies. There are five main configurations of EQ:
1. **Tone control:** Controls level up and down of one frequency (fixed by the manufacturer)
2. **Click-stop:** Several positions to select various fixed-frequencies
3. **Sweepable:** Continuous variation of center frequency
4. **Graphic:** Slider-controlled with multiple fixed-position frequency centers
5. **Parametric:** Most flexible — combines continuous frequency selection with variable bandwidth

Compressor: A device for dynamic control.
Limiter: A compressor with a severe compression ratio.
Reverb: Ambience. Created by multiple reflections of sound.
Echo: A single, coherent, linear reflection of sound.
Stereo parts: Can be created by rerecording the part or by splitting and electronically manipulating the signal.
Harmonizer: A pitch-bend device that can be used to create stereo doubling.
Delay line: Can be used to create an echo but also to create a stereo image. It accomplishes this by manipulating time.
Chorus: A pitch-bend device that cycles between two controllable extremes.

TASCAM Ministudio Porta-03MKII

The Recording Studio Kit

Creating a Recording Studio

In the first section of the book we talked about the portable studio you just spent a whole bunch of money on. You've gotten a tour of the various features and how they work and now you're ready and rarin' to go. Well... not quite. Now you have to equip the studio that goes around the portable studio. Welcome to the "bent credit card" club.

First there are all those accessories to purchase in order to complete the well-dressed portable studio ensemble. A lot of the gear you'll need to create a studio is pretty obvious, and in fact you probably have some of it already. But for our purposes let's say you're building a studio from scratch. What purchases should you make? The ideal that you should be shooting for is to have an integrated system where every tool provides maximum utility and not a dollar is wasted on something that you will outgrow.

This chapter is broken up into three topics. First is the essentials, second is the wish list, and finally there is a checklist of all the little stuff that you forget about until you really need it and it isn't there.

Note: Because equipment changes about every other heartbeat I'm reluctant to be too specific about model numbers. I mention brand names and models only to serve as examples of gear that I personally use. Some of this equipment has been superseded by newer models; if so you can use my recommendations as reference points.

The Essentials

Monitoring

In order to get the best recording quality you need to have a studio that will allow you to accurately hear what you're recording. This is no small matter. Speakers and headphones need to be chosen carefully.

Speakers

Speakers should be chosen based not on how they sound in the store but how they sound in your studio. Seems obvious, but on the showroom floor it's easy to get dazzled by sonic Cadillacs and forget that all you have room for is a Hyundai. The whole notion of "great-sounding speakers" is really a sales thing and very misleading. How good a speaker sounds is mostly a matter of matching it to the size and shape of the space it's in. In fact, in pro studio construction there's a whole complicated process for matching air and speakers. The reason why this choice is so important is actually physics. As you know by now, low-frequency sound waves take distance to develop. The bigger the speaker, the farther away you need to be from it in order to hear the bottom end accurately. Using this logic, having a set of huge speakers in a small room may impress your friends but is not going to help you when it comes to making EQ decisions. You can't get far enough away from them. What happens is this: if you can't get far enough away to hear the bottom end develop then it sounds as if you don't have enough bottom on tape, and you compensate by adding onto the low EQ until it sounds right to you. But when you take the tape out to your car it sounds like it was recorded in a bass drum. You see, the bottom end was on the tape all the time — your speakers just lied to you. What you want is an accurate *reference* speaker, not one that will hype you. So when you're in the store try to keep a picture of your recording space in mind.

For most home applications I'd recommend a two-way speaker like one made by Yamaha called the NS10M. These are roughly 6″ × 6″ × 18″ and are a convenient size for a near-field monitor. They are also very easy to get used to. There may be new and improved models (they always do that) but you can find used NS10s in publications with a decent audio gear classified section. I also like the JBL 4026 model, and Alesis makes some very nice monitors as well. The prices on these are in the $200–400 range new.

Headphones

I'll make it simple. If you're going to be wearing headphones for hours at a time you want them to be comfortable. Don't get cheapies. Check to make sure they're not so heavy as to be fatiguing, as it's hard to sing if your neck muscles are cramping up from the weight of the phones. Make sure they allow for sufficient isolation from outside noise. I tend to prefer a "closed" headphone. This means that the back of the earpiece is covered with a sound-opaque material. Open headphones have foam earpieces back and front, like a Walkman-type only bigger (by closed I don't mean the kind that helicopter pilots use — those weigh a ton). A closed headphone is better able to keep sound from spilling out and "leaking" into the mic. My favorites are AKG and Sony and sell for $70 to $90 at pro audio shops.

Amplifier

There are a million out there so I'll just give you some thoughts. In the portable studio environment it's probably easiest to use a home stereo–type amp with auxiliary inputs so you can easily switch sound sources for reference. In terms of power, a 75 to 100 watt per side rating is plenty.

Two-Track Tape Deck

Ah, now for the budget killer. Remember we're building from scratch here.... You need to have a machine to mix down to. It is the final step in your recording, and quality is of the essence. Therefore I would highly recommend the purchase of a DAT (digital audiotape) recorder. Why? Because you will get a dramatically better recording result with a DAT than with the analog cassette two-track machine you're probably using now.

The reason is that recording on a four-track format usually requires that you do what is called premixing in order to make more tracks available. This is done by sending the combination of four tracks from the portable studio to be recorded on a two-track machine. The resulting combination is then rerecorded back onto two tracks of the portable studio in order to open up tracks for more recording. This process is called *bouncing,* and, in case you're a little confused, it will be the subject of much discussion later on. For now, let me just say that every time this process is performed there is the danger of adding noise caused by generation loss. If you bounce several times using an analog machine this noise could mar an otherwise good result. However, by using a DAT to perform these bounces you eliminate this problem. The nature of digital recording is that there is no generation loss. (For a more detailed explanation of digital recording see *The Musician's Guide to Home Recording,* said he, shamelessly plugging his other book.) Therefore you can bounce a virtually unlimited number of times without losing recording quality. What this does in effect is make your four tracks a whole lot more tracks.

Most of the high quality manufacturers make a DAT machine — Tascam, Sony, Technics, Panasonic, Fostex. They are pricey but the prices are coming down. You also can find them used. Look for a machine with a remote control. You can expect to spend a minimum of about $700. If you see one used, it's a good idea to get the machine checked out by a service center before you buy it.

Now that you've gotten over that shock let's look at some other ways to spend some more of your hard-earned dough. The following is the wish list of gear that will definitely help make your recording more professional and satisfying.

The Wish List

In order to get the most out of your portable studio there are some purchases that you should consider making as your interest and career develop. At the end of this section I recommend some basic stuff that I think any working studio should have on hand in the form of a "studio kit." But before we get to that....

As you know, there is a whole section of recipes at the back of this book designed to adapt professional techniques to portable studio recording. The reality is, however, that a lot of them cannot be accomplished without the use of outboard gear. Therefore some additional equipment has to be purchased beyond the budget-bending you've already done. Sorry, but that's it. I will herewith suggest some gear that will definitely expand the portable studio's capability and consequently your recording horizons. I promise that this equipment was chosen based on its flexibility of use as well as what it adds to your recording quality for the dollars spent. Sort of a "bang for the buck" approach.

One of my major considerations here was to recommend things that would remain useful no matter how you upgrade your recording equipment in the future. These tools will be mainstays in your studio even if Great Uncle Angus passes on and wills you his twenty-four-track.

Where and How to Get the Gear You Can't Live Without

I know that money is always an issue so this section constitutes a sort of wish list of equipment that can be acquired over time as interest and dollars (or pounds, deutsche marks, yen, *etc.*) permit. You may already have some of this stuff sitting in your guitar or keyboard rig, in which case begin to think of it as part of your recording setup. That way you'll make future purchases with multiple use in mind.

Some Notes on Buying New Equipment

New! Newer! Newest! As most of you know (unless you've slept through the last fifteen years) the audio equipment industry is changing on an almost daily basis. Just about every time I pick up a music magazine there is some new breakthrough, some got-to-have-it electronic temptation. The industry develops new products at a shocking rate. It seems that there are new and improved versions of something even before you get the wrapper off the one you just bought.

There is a logical reason for this. Companies have to develop new products in order to stay competitive. Generally this is a pretty good thing, because the functionality of equipment goes up and the price keeps coming down. But it also means that you need to choose carefully. For most of us there has been at least one piece of gear that you just had to have last year, spent good money on, and that now sits in the corner holding up a plant. As you'll see, playing the game well and avoiding a bad buy is really a matter of "musician, know thyself."

In order to make a logical choice you need to decide what level of recording you aspire to. There are occasions when you have to choose whether spending an extra few bucks to get an optional product feature will be money well spent. If you have a clear idea of where you're headed as a recordist you're less likely to be tempted by gear with lots of extra-cost bells and whistles that you'll probably rarely use. Try making a checklist of what musical characteristics you most want to enhance in your recording. Is the music you're doing predominantly acoustic? Then spending more on a good mic might be an answer for you. Are you keyboard-oriented? Then good signal processing may be what you want. But which microphone and what signal processor, and how do you find out so you don't buy the audio equivalent of a '59 Edsel?

So Where Do You Get the Information?

The product you see pictured in all its glossy glory in a magazine ad is the result of long hours and great skill. No, I wasn't referring to the manufacturer, I was talking about the ad guy. These folks get paid lots of money to create advertisements that will leave us drooling.

Don't fall prey to the electronic flavor of the month. Be sure that the piece of gear you're considering is truly useful and will remain so long after you buy it.

Determine if the piece of gear is really what it seems in the ad. How do you do that? Ask around. Believe it or not, most audio equipment salesmen are a pretty reliable source of information, particularly if you're clear in letting them know your needs and you prepare your questions in advance. Don't forget, a lot of these people are musicians themselves and have direct experience with the products. Also, a good music equipment merchant doesn't want to sell you something that you'll just return a week later. One recommendation however — ask at more than one store to avoid the inevitable product bias. Information that seems to be common to all these people is bound to be pretty accurate. And while you're there don't be afraid to speak to fellow customers in a music store. Total strangers will often give you the benefit of their experience with a piece of gear. (Sometimes they'll also talk your ear off or try to borrow money.) This can provide you with a different perspective than you might get from your friends.

Call professional recording studios and recording engineering schools to ask for their advertising brochures. These pamphlets will list equipment that they're using and will give you some idea of what's reliable and professional. When you call, try and speak to a maintenance tech or second engineer. If you ask nicely they might take the time to recommend some gear in your price range.

Call repair shops that specialize in current audio equipment. Ask about the failure rate of the equipment you're interested in and what kind of product flaws they've encountered.

Read product reviews in magazines you trust and that address themselves to your recording needs. Make sure that the product features the reviewer goes gaga over are really ones you can use.

Check the classifieds. If there seems to be a sudden abundance of used Gadiddle-Harps flooding the market soon after release, chances are it's a turkey. You'll probably be better off waiting for Gadiddle-Harp the Sequel before you buy; by that time they might have the bugs worked out.

The rapidly changing marketplace also means the rise and fall of a lot of new companies. I am a great believer in innovation and the need for new voices in the industry. However, I also have to say that before you buy from a new manufacturer check out what the dealers and salespeople think about the company's future. When you need to have your gear serviced is not a good time to find out that the company went out of business last Tuesday.

I will usually buy brands of equipment that have an identity specific to the audio/recording business. Generally speaking, I stay away from electronics store, department store, and generic brands. These companies frequently farm out the manufacture of a product to an offshore company and then put their name on it. Don't get me wrong, the stuff could be perfectly okay, but the service and support will not be up to an audio company specialist. Plus you'll probably find fewer people familiar with the product to give you tips. So, as a rule, a K-Mart condenser mic wouldn't be my first choice.

I also buy from a local dealer I know is responsible for the product lines sold at their store. You can usually tell who has a good relationship with a given manufacturer by the level of knowledge of the salespeople and the amount of inventory of a particular brand. If I want a Tascam product I will seek out a dealer that I know carries a fairly substantial stock of Tascam products and therefore has an investment in seeing that the relationship between the customer and manufacturer remains positive. Another thing to be aware of is that a good retailer is a direct pipeline to the equipment builder. If you have service questions or suggestions regarding a product the dealer can frequently provide a shortcut or two in getting a response.

When to Buy Used

Now after considering all my suggestions you've decided that it's time to buy that brand new Whatsit. Unfortunately there's a painful fact that's none too pleasant to think about in the glow of an expensive purchase. That is, when you buy a piece of gear new, it will probably be worth about twenty percent less than you paid for it the second you leave the store. Just by crossing over the threshold onto the sidewalk you are now holding a piece of used gear. You know it's exactly the same as it was inside the store, but to another buyer it's *used*. What this means is that you may want to look at buying used yourself and let someone else take the twenty percent bath. Most of the gear that is available in stores is also available for resale within a year of release, so if you can wait a little you can get some amazing deals. For instance, some people want to have the latest cool dealie no matter what and will sell a perfectly good piece of gear because they feel they've outgrown it. This of course is good. It keeps the wheels of industry turning, and it's great for you because you can find nifty stuff cheap. The place to look for bargains in the classifieds is in the most recently "obsoleted" pieces of gear. For example, if you liked what a Dribble Box Series 1 does, wait until Dribble Box Series 2 comes out and watch the papers. There will undoubtedly be a bunch of people who upgrade not because Dribble 1 was bad but because Dribble 2 comes in a cool shade of lime green. For the most part buying pre-owned recording equipment is a reasonably safe bet. The types of gear I would recommend to consider purchasing used are microphones; signal processors such as reverbs, compressors, gates, and equalizers; and keyboards and keyboard modules. Also look for gear being sold off by defunct bands — you can get some great buys in cables, direct boxes, mic stands, *etc*. The gear I would be more careful about buying used is anything with mechanical components, such as tape decks. While these may represent a good deal, you need to have a reputable shop check them out for tape-head wear, worn switches, and controls and transport efficiency.

Finally, it may be worth the extra bucks to buy new in order to get the warranty and dealer service. The peace of mind of having someone to call for help when your new thingie blows up can be very pacifying.

Stuff to Buy

The following are some recommendations (strong recommendations) of good ways to exercise your bank account. To heck with the rent, and who needs to eat?

By the way, the prices I quote are ballpark figures and subject to whether you buy new or used.

Equalizer

Of all outboard gear purchases, I would buy a good equalizer first. You already know what an EQ does, so you can imagine how useful it is when you have an extra. An equalizer is a great problem-solver, and the greater the EQ flexibility you have to work with, the easier it is to give each instrument its own musical space.

My first choice would be to recommend a parametric EQ. Because of its variable bandwidth you can zero in on desired frequencies more precisely. The graphic equalizer is a pretty good second choice. Even though it has fixed bandwidth settings it has enough frequency points to give you quite a bit of room to maneuver.

Hate to say it, but ideally you should have a matched stereo pair of whichever EQ you choose. By having two channels of EQ not only can you EQ two instruments at once while recording, but you can further refine a whole mix by EQing the left and right outputs of the portable studio just before it goes to the two-track machine (see "The Recipe Section").

Tascam, Yamaha, Roland, and Samson all make equalizers that are reasonably priced. You can find them both new and used. Expect to pay $100 to $500 a pair depending on the usual variables.

Compressor

This is the other first thing I would buy. A good compressor can make your life a whole lot easier. Find one with as much flexibility in the control section as possible. Look for separate controls for input, output, attack, release, threshold, and ratio.

Try to get a compressor that is a rack-mounted rather than a foot pedal. Remember that a compressor will in and of itself bring up the noise floor, so the quieter the better. This means — you guessed it — the quieter the more expensive. DBX and Yamaha make good ones. Expect to pay $100 to $400.

Noise Gate

This is a handy little gizmo for getting rid of noise, the true enemy of home recording. Look for a unit that has as many parameter controls as possible: threshold, attack and release speed, input, *etc.* A gate is a waste of money if it can't be set to respond differently for each application. Some of the less expensive ones are used for grossly removing noise from guitar gear. Be careful with this foot-pedal type as it may cut off notes before they've fully died out. There are some compressor units that have a gate built in.

DBX makes a very good gate, and Roland also has a good one. There are pro-quality units that while great are quite expensive. Expect to pay $100 or less for guitar-type units, more for the more sophisticated ones.

Signal Processors (Reverb/Echo)

There are too many models out there to make meaningful recommendations, but Alesis, Lexicon, and Roland all have good reputations and have made gear I've enjoyed using.

Delay Line (DDL)

Having a delay separate from your reverb processor can be money well spent. You can use this to create stereo effects from mono signals, or, as the name would imply, to create controlled delayed reverb and echo effects by using the delay to feed signal to the reverb processor. You can also use it for doubling vocals electronically, *etc.*, thereby saving tracks (see "The Recipe Section" and "The Step-by-Step Mixdown Chapter"). Roland is a good source.

The Studio Kit Checklist: Basics for Musical First Aid

This next stuff is a lot cheaper and less glamorous but every bit as important to have on hand.

It's two in the morning, you've got to finish your demo so you can play it for the Record Company Gods at ten... then oops. You need something, you don't have one. Yikes!

Stuff to Always Have on Hand

- An assortment of guitar/bass picks of different thicknesses — lose your only pick in the shag carpet and you end up having to use an old folded-up matchbook to play a guitar solo. Drag.

- An extra set of guitar strings — with extra high E and B strings.

- An extra 9-volt battery — unless the Energizer Bunny lives next door.

- Wesson oil or Finger-Ease — to help with finger noise.

- Soft rags — for the Wesson oil or Finger-Ease.

- Pencils and paper — to write down important notes like EQ settings, reverb parameters, and pizza toppings.

- Grease pencils — black and white. Those strange pencils that you sharpen by unwrapping a paper spiral at the tip. Good for marking levels next to the faders on the portable studio. The stuff wipes off with a little Windex.

- A head-cleaning kit — the right one for each of your machines.

- Ground lifter — that funny plug that looks like a three-prong plug with the third prong cut off. Available at audio stores. Use to help eliminate 60-cycle ground hum.

- Power strip/surge protector — basically a fancy extension cord, but it can protect your gear should your house get struck by lightning. These are also useful because they usually have an on/off switch that can control everything plugged into it and you only have to use one "clapper." Just kidding. About the clapper, I mean — not a good idea to use one. You can imagine: "C'mon everybody, clap along... ." (on, off, on, off...)

- Microphone stand — a much more professional way to mount a microphone than a broomstick and tape.

- Playing stool — chair arms and back get in the way when you're playing guitar or bass.

- Music stand — oh, you mean like for sheet music? Yes.

- Pop filter — not a way to censor your father. See "The Vocal Chapter."

- Flashlight — drop anything small behind your recording gear and the need for a flashlight becomes evident. The way stuff disappears, I sometimes think that there's an open gateway to a parallel universe right behind the effects rack.

- Extra guitar cables — always a good idea. Saves time resoldering a tip. Speaking of which...

- Soldering gun and solder — connectors break all the time. Learning to solder is a good thing.

- Wire cutters and strippers — need I say more?

- Screwdrivers — Phillips and flathead.

- Guitar Allen wrenches

- Jackknife — useful for about what you'd expect to use it for — cutting things. Also good for whittlin' while the players tune up.

- Sound deadeners, Sonex, blankets, *etc.* — having as much flexibility as possible in your recording environment is a very good thing. Try to build up an assortment of this stuff: from small bits for damping buzzing speakers to large bits for deadening a recording space.

- Y-splitter — this is special connector you plug something into — guitar, bass, *etc.* — that sends the same signal two different ways (scientific, huh?). Imagine an upside-down Y. The single "leg" is a female input you plug your guitar cord into, and each of the "arms" are outputs that you can plug into two separate places, *e.g.*, a console and a chorus pedal. Sometimes the splitter is a box rather than a connector, but it does the same thing; it takes one signal and routes it to two places.

- A good electronic tuner — I make a big deal out of this in "The Guitar Chapter."

- Metronome — it's generally good for everyone to play at the same tempo. Use it for count-offs.

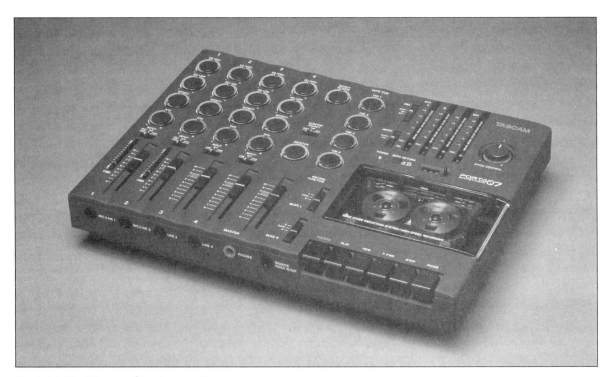

TASCAM Ministudio Porta-07

SECTION THREE

How You're Going to Do It: Techniques

The Drum Chapter

Great drum sounds are among my favorite things. When I first started recording I used to listen to all kinds of records looking for the "ultimate" drum sound. I would try to analyze the components of the drum recordings I liked so that someday I could use what I learned to create my own ultimate drum sound. What I learned, of course, was that there is no one all-purpose sound. Nope. What's more, over time I learned that a big part of the art of drum recording was in knowing how to create the ultimate sound *for* each particular piece of music. Sometimes the sound you end up using may be nothing like what you had in mind when you started.

Realistically, since we're talking about home recording, and more specifically, getting the most out of a portable studio, I think it's beyond the scope of this book to deal with miking up a full drum kit in your living room. So for the purposes of this chapter I'm going to deal with squeezing as much performance out of a drum machine or sequencer as possible and seeing to it that it ends up on tape.

The Aesthetics of Choosing Drum Sounds

Hey hepcats, it's a crazy modern world we live in, isn't it? Why, you too can have an amazing assortment of hundreds of drum sounds right at your fingertips. And all in a magic box smaller than a bongo. Press button one of the magic machine for Led Zeppelin drums, button two for Stone Temple Pilots, *etc*. An embarrassment of riches. And with such a wide variety to choose from, now the trick is deciding which sound to use. In order to do that you need to step back and make some judgments about where the drums fit in the music production you're creating.

The Drum Machine/Sequencer

The drum machine and sequencer arguably have been the most empowering developments in the home-studio march of progress. With these inventions it is now possible to fully realize and record your music without having to have the wherewithal to record a whole band. (They also may have created a whole sub-class of really lonely musicians, but that's another story.)

As with most music electronics, drum machines have gotten cheaper and cheaper, all the while becoming more sophisticated. Machines that could only produce what sounded like cartoon drums have given way to those capable of playing actual samples of pro studio drum sounds. Not only are the drums themselves realistic, but the patches are frequently preprocessed with reverbs and echos, creating effects previously only dreamed of in a home studio. Today, for a relatively small investment you can buy any one of a bunch of drum devices that will let you dial up just about any percussion sound you can think of. However, in order to use these sounds properly you need to understand them all the way down to their components.

The Drum Kit

The drum kit is the most common form of percussion in Western popular music. As you no doubt know, the kit is a set consisting of several drums and cymbals that are all played as an ensemble by one musician. The kit itself usually consists of one or more kick (bass) drums, a snare drum, some number of tom-toms, a high-hat cymbal set, one or more crash cymbals, and one or more ride cymbals, and may also include assorted specialty percussion.

The drum machine was originally designed to mimic its acoustic cousin and so is also a "kit" of sorts. You can choose the composition of your electronic set in the same way you could assemble a real drum kit — by finding drums that sound good together. Also, just as you can tune a real drum, most machines or sound modules offer a practically infinite variety of sound modifications you can apply to each drum patch. With all this flexibility it's easy to have so much fun modifying that you lose sight of how these sounds fit into the musical "big picture" you're trying to create. The thing to keep in mind when searching out sounds is that each of these drums is a separate instrument and has its role to play in propelling the track rhythmically. I'm going to take each component of the drum kit individually and discuss some of the factors you want to be aware of when choosing a sound.

Choosing Drum Sounds and Building a Kit

The Kick (Bass) Drum

The kick drum is the lowest in pitch of the kit drums and unfortunately is often the one given the least consideration in the home studio. There's a temptation to focus on the snare drum or tom-toms because that's what we tend to think of when we talk about great drum sounds. Since the kick is at the bottom of the harmonic range, it often doesn't command our attention. However, I would argue that the lowly kick may in fact be the most important ingredient in a successful rhythm track.

In popular music the kick drum performs a yeoman's repetitive role; usually the job of punctuating the downbeat of each measure to propel the music along to the next measure. A great kick part is one that does this without intruding on the melodic elements that it supports. Conversely, a kick part that doesn't work is one that is distracting or overbusy. The function of a kick sound is to be there but not overly *there,* if you know what I mean. You want it to be unobtrusive, kind of like a good waiter. You don't notice him when he's around but you'd sure notice if he went missing.

The key to having a great kick sound actually may lie in not finding a great sound at all. The secret is in creating a sound that works best in the complementary relationship between the melodic bass part and the kick pattern. When I go for a kick sound I think of it as the rhythmic component of the bass guitar, highlighting with percussion the roots of the chords. That may mean that a kick sound by itself might have to be rather uninspiring to work well in combination with the bass. A great kick drum isn't so much heard as felt. So my judgment is based on being able to feel a pulse to the music that's almost subliminal.

How does that translate into specifics? Creating an efficient kick sound is a process of manipulating the balance between percussion and tone. To better understand, think about the physics of producing sound from a bass drum. The drummer steps on a pedal, which in turn propels a hard beater to smack against the drum head. As in all drums the smack causes a column of air inside the drum to vibrate. The pitch of the vibrating air is the result of the tension on the drum skin. The number and frequency of overtones, however, is related to the size of the drum, the wood it's made of, *etc*. The frequencies that are emphasized when you *record* depend on how far away from the beater's strike zone you place the microphone as well as the EQ you apply.

Now imagine you're miking the bass drum. You put the mic inside the drum, aiming it at the skin that will be struck by the beater. The closer the mic is to the beater, the more of the impact the mic will hear; the farther away, the more low tones. As you know from your sonic basics, bottom-end frequencies take more distance to develop. Therefore the kick drum balance is largely determined by how far the mic is from the beater. Just to add another variable, the beater itself has a good deal to do with the sound produced. Beaters can be made of a variety of materials and shapes. Some have a flat striking surface and are made of wood. These produce a healthy percussive smack. Another type is made of felt, resulting in a softer, rounder sound.

Yeah, great but we're talking drum machines here. Ain't no beater in a drum machine. True, but the sounds created for drum machines are modeled after recordings of the real thing. By learning to listen you can categorize kick sounds as percussive or tonal and know which sounds will work best as a starting point for your ultimate kick.

Types of Kick Sounds

As with all the drums in the kit, the choice of a kick drum sound is largely related to tempo. To go back to our basics of sound, the lower the frequency the longer it takes to develop. The greater the amount of low end the longer the beat lasts. What this means is that if you're not careful, the low-frequency tone will appear to lag behind the rhythm, carrying over to muddy the next beat. Therefore, the amount of tone you want depends on when the next beat falls. This goes back to our statement about the balance between the transient, or percussive attack, and the low-frequency overtones. One of the major components is the cyber-"beater" you choose.

Tip: Use a hard attack sound for fast tracks and a rounder attack for ballads and slow tracks.

Tuning the Kick

Most drum machines allow you to tune the component sounds, and tuning the kick drum is no less important than tuning the snare. Kick drum pitch requires some thought. Contrary to what seems logical, if you want to hear more apparent bottom end, tune the kick drum *higher*, not lower. Huh? The reason is that below a certain frequency point the bottom end seems to disappear. It's still there but is not as tonally active to the human ear. Therefore if you want to *hear* (as opposed to feel) the low tone you need to have it in a range that is reliably audible. This means tuning the drum to a pitch with faster vibrating overtones (that is, higher). This is an important method of tonal balance. If you want to emphasize the *attack* of the drum and diminish a tonal carryover, try lowering the tuning.

Tip: Tune up for bottom tone. Tune down for punch and attack.

The Kick Drum and the Bass Guitar

As I said earlier, the bass and kick drum are most successful when they operate in concert. Visualize a connect-the-dots puzzle with the kick as the dots and the bass as the lines between them. In this regard the kick functions as an accent to the notes struck on the bass; together the two create a picture. Neither the bass nor kick drum by themselves have the same effect as the two of them together.

This impacts on the issue of drum pitch because in a fast-moving track the pitch of the bass changes frequently. The pitch of the kick drum doesn't — it's a constant. What ends up happening is that the kick seems strong on notes where the pitch of the bass and drum are the same or complementary and then can all but disappear when the tones clash. This means that the tonal element of a kick drum can interfere with its role as support for the bass.

Tip: Try to tune the kick to a pitch consistent with the key of the song. Listen for tonal clashes between the kick and the bass guitar.

Consistency of Dynamics

In my experience the most effective dynamics for a bass drum part are very little dynamics at all. In other words, each stroke should be of roughly equal loudness. The reason for this is that the kick part is a principal component of the "feel" of the song and functions to carry the listener along with the rhythm. In this role the part is more felt than really heard. So when a dropout occurs in the kick drum because a note is too soft, its absence is immediately apparent and the momentum of the track seems to stop. The bottom line (no pun intended) is that if the recorded kick fluctuates in dynamic level, it contributes an unsettled feel to the track.

Tip: Smooth out velocity variations in the sequence when designing a kick part.

Equalizing the Kick Drum

There is an EQ guide at the end of this chapter, but it should be said that a kick drum may contain frequencies that you're not even hearing but still take up energy on tape. These frequencies may cause a rumble that masks the punch in the bottom end. So as a matter of course with a portable studio I will EQ out any frequencies below 50 Hz.

Panning and Effects on the Kick Drum

As you know by now, low frequencies are perceived as monophonic, so putting the kick drum anywhere but in the center of the stereo spectrum doesn't make a lot of sense. What will happen is that the higher-frequency components will appear where panned but the low frequency will "smear" to the center.

As you also know, applying reverb or echo adds ambience to the sound, moving it farther away from the listener. Since the function of a kick drum is to add punch and clearly enunciate the beat, adding reverb defeats the purpose by blurring the drum's attack and diminishing its presence. So I will use reverb on a kick drum only as a special effect when the track is "wide open" and I want to give the illusion of vastness.

The Snare Drum

The core of the drum kit is the snare. In rock or pop or R&B this is the drum that usually nails down the beat. In jazz it's used as an important tool for accent and coloration. The snare possesses the most complex sonic signature of the whole drum kit and as such requires great care in recording.

Creating a snare drum sound is a little like mixing shades of paint together. As I see it you have three principal colors to work with: the **bang** (attack or transient), the sound of the stick striking the head; the **boom**, the tone of the drum, the pitch produced by the vibrating column of air between the top and bottom heads; and finally, for lack of a more elegant word, the **buzz**, the sound of the snares vibrating against the bottom head. Each of these components is variable to a great degree. Each snare drum sounds unique because it combines these elements in different proportions. So the drum you get on tape is derived from how you choose to manipulate these colors.

How a Real Snare Works

Even though we're talking about drum machines here, it's not a bad idea to keep the mechanics of a real snare in mind. Aside from bashing away, there are some other things the drummer does to produce a good snare sound. There are adjustments the drummer makes to the snare that will determine the characteristics the drum will have.

First, the drummer can damp the drum by putting tape or padding or some other material on its head. This shortens the length of time the drum will vibrate and thereby shortens the duration of the note. This duration is called the **decay** of the note and refers to the length of time between when a note is struck and when it is no longer heard. Second, the drummer can alter the pitch of the drum by using lug bolt adjustments around the rim to loosen or tighten the heads. This also can affect the duration of a note. Third, the drummer can change the sound of the drum by adjusting the tension on the snares themselves. This will allow for a different balance between the sound of the drum and the sound of the snares. The looser the adjustment on the snares the more of the snares are heard; and as you would guess, tightening the snares diminishes their vibration.

Choosing a Snare Sound

Okay, so now you can impress your friends by talkin' snare drum specs like a pro — so what? As was said earlier, a good set of cyberdrums will offer you a zillion choices. You can adjust a snare patch to tap out a rhythm or knock your woofers in the dirt. Well, in order to choose which snare to use for your recording, you have to make the same kind of adjustments an experienced drummer would make.

What you need to focus on is not how great the snare sounds by itself but how it "sits" in the track. By this I mean how well the snare contributes to the groove without being obtrusive or distracting. There are four principal factors to consider in creating your sound: tempo, tuning, frequency range, and ambience.

Tempo

In my opinion, the most important determinant of which snare sound to use is the tempo of the song. You want the snare to clearly define the rhythm of the music. If its sound hangs on too long it runs over into the next beat and can make the track sound sloppy. For example, if you're playing in ¼ time and the snare is struck on beats 2 and 4, you want it to die out before beats 3 and 1; otherwise you get the snare stepping all over the other drum parts. The feel you're shooting for will dictate how much "air" there is between these beats and therefore how long each snare note should last. If you have an uptempo tune you may want the snare to die a little earlier so that the eighth notes of the high-hat are exposed. On a ballad you may want the "weight" of a powerful snare for emphasis, and so you extend the duration of the sound.

Tuning

Along with its percussive qualities the snare also has a definite pitch. I generally try to tune the snare to a note in the triad of the key of the song. I find that having the pitch of the drum relate to the key of the song allows the harmonics of all the instruments to blend. For instance, if the song is in the key of D I will try to tune the snare to a D, an F♯, or an A. Sounds simple, sort of. The problem is that tuning a snare also affects the duration of the note. Tune the drum low and the note will extend; tune it high and the note will decay more quickly. So the question is how do you tune it for both pitch and duration? What you do is find a snare with the approximate duration you're looking for. Then, using a keyboard for pitch, tune the drum to the next closest note in the triad. For instance, if the song is in the key of D I may find that when I tune to the actual note D the note is too long for the tempo of the song. I will then choose a higher note (F♯ or A), whichever is closer to the desired decay and still in the key of the song.

Frequency Range

We talked earlier about the bang, boom, and buzz of a snare drum, and that refers of course to frequency range. This is where a carefully thought out snare choice can save you some sanity come mix time. How is it that a snare drum can be banging away on a rock tune and still seem perfectly blended even in an avalanche of crashing guitars? How can a slow song have a snare that sounds as big as a house but still doesn't get in the way? How'd they do that? The answer is explained by the term **apparent loudness**. As you know from the "What Is Sound?" chapter, certain frequencies are psychoacoustically active. We humans are more sensitive to them so we hear them more immediately than others even at equal loudness. To place an instrument in its proper musical space the recordist manipulates this range of human hearing, emphasizing frequencies that allow the instrument to "cut through" the music without actually having to turn up the volume. This is where we can bring into play the three principal colors of the snare that we talked about above.

The bang: The type of snare sound you get and how it interacts with the track is a matter of proportion between the frequency ranges that compose the bang, boom, and buzz. The bang is the attack of the stick hitting the drum head. As such it is the first event in the sound of a snare drum. Therefore it is also the clearest indicator of the snare beat. If you want to emphasize rhythm you will equalize to enhance this range.

Tip: Emphasize the bang for fast-moving songs.

The boom: This is the tonal component of the drum. By emphasizing this frequency range you give the drum more dimension and size. However, to utilize this range you need to make more room in the track for the drum. Remember, simply making the drum louder if it is inappropriately EQed will just muddy the track and squeeze the other instruments.

Tip: Emphasize the boom for ballads.

The buzz: Finally we have the buzz of the snares. This component of the snare drum is in the upper frequency range, and enhancing the snares has a tendency to soften the blow, so to speak. I will emphasize this range when I'm going for a less definite feel or when I want the snare to be less intrusive.

There is a danger you need to be aware of when EQing this range. The upper harmonic register is also where you find a lot of the characteristics of instruments like violins, distorted power guitars, and synth parts. Over-EQing in the buzz range can result in an unpleasant buildup of these frequencies. When I EQ I do it with the other instrumental parts in mind; that way I know that I won't lose the clarity of individual instruments. I might emphasize the sound of the snares when I want the song to "cruise" along.

Tip: Emphasize the buzz for softer midtempo songs.

See the EQ section at the back of this chapter for more specifics.

Ambience

As you already know, the ambience of a sound is one of the chief determinants of the listener's perception of how close or far away it is. This means that the reverb, echo, delay, *etc.*, that accompanies the snare sound will affect how prominent the snare is to the listener. Most cyberdrums include ambient effects either built into the sounds themselves or as an option. As convenient as this is, you should be aware that the processing you do to an instrument at the time it is recorded is there permanently. You can't get rid of it. It becomes part of the track. So if you are going to choose an ambient snare sound you have to be clear about where it's going to sit in the track. Too much reverb and the snare can sound like it's in another room; too little and it's right in the listener's face. If I have to record the reverb with the snare drum I will usually set up the snare so that I can hear it at the tempo of the song and preferably accompanied by a principal melodic instrument. This will give me some idea of the blend of instruments and the relative prominence of the snare drum in the final mix.

Another tip is to use a delayed reverb on the snare (see "The Effects Chapter"). This allows for the attack of the drum to be heard clearly before the reverb kicks in. The delay setting will vary according to the tempo of the song, but as a general rule I will delay the reverb by about an eighth of a beat.

The Tom-Toms

The toms are sort of the drummer's version of the exclamation point. They are used to add excitement to a passage, to announce a musical change (for instance from the verse to the chorus), or to provide a break in the sonic quality of the rhythm.

In contrast to the snare, which serves a primarily percussive function, the toms are used more as the tonal component of the drum kit. This means that choosing a tom-tom sound is a matter of finding what suits the song best in terms of melodic quality. Yes friends, the drums are a melodic instrument too. Just listen to any well-constructed drum track and you will hear that the tom-tom fills usually have tonal variety that relates to the song.

As with the snare drum, your choice of the duration of the tom-tom note is determined by the tempo of the song. However, the pitch of the drums becomes more of an issue with the toms because you're treating them as a melodic instrument. This means that you need to choose a register that makes sense for combining both pitch and duration.

Perhaps the easiest way to explain this is with an example. Let's say you want your cyberkit to have three tom-toms — high, middle, and low. Let's also say the song is in the key of D. You want the toms to be reasonably close in interval; that is, all of them within the same octave. Having toms too far apart in pitch makes the drums sound weird (of course weird could be good too). Second, you want them to spell out a D triad when played in succession. Finally, you have to have them decay in a way that makes sense for the tempo of the track. So ... here's how to do it.

RECIPE FOR TUNING TOMS TO THE KEY OF D

(Note: use a pure tone — no effects — on a keyboard or guitar for a reference pitch. The drum note you wish to tune is the pitch the drum decays to, not the first attack.)

1. Tune the top tom to an A.
2. Tune the middle drum to an F♯ below that.
3. Tune the lowest drum to a D below that.
   Listen to the duration of the tones. If the drums hang on too long, then:
1. Take the interval of the drums up: tune to a D on top,
2. A in the middle, and
3. F♯ on the bottom.
4. Repeat the process upward if the notes are still too long.

Equalizing the Toms

As with all the drums, recording the toms is a matter of balance between the attack and the tone of the drum. For faster-moving tracks the transient is usually the more prominent feature, while for slower tracks the tone usually dominates. See the end of this chapter for an EQ guide.

Toms and Ambience

The tempo of a track and the type of tom-tom part will determine the amount of reverb you use on the toms. If the track is slow or if the part is sparse then the toms will benefit from a fair amount of processing. The faster the part, the less reverb should be used in order to avoid muddying the track.

The High-Hat and Cymbals

The high-hat is a set of two cymbals fitted together like a clamshell and opened and closed with a foot pedal. It is played with a stick and is often the metronome of the drum kit. In pop music it is used to keep the rhythm going between the kick and snare beats. Believe it or not, it is often the high-hat that is most important in giving a track its feel.

In the modern cyberdrum kit there is usually a choice of open and closed high-hat. Mixing these two together is one of the chief ways a drummer captures a feel. So you need to be aware that using only the closed high-hat will give a inhuman, machinelike quality to the track. A human drummer will characteristically open the high-hat for emphasis and expression. This is likely to happen in various song parts, such as before a drum fill or to set up a new section, or sometimes simply as a recurring part of the rhythm. In order to get away from the dreaded "robo-trak" sound you should consider the open high-hat as an important color on your palette and incorporate it when designing a drum part. It can serve to provide a rhythmic breath, a subtle drum fill, or anti-monotony protection.

Tip: Choose a high-hat sound based on the mood of the song. Ballads and R&B use a light touch, while rock often uses a greater attack and a deeper-toned high-hat with more open high-hat accents. Listening to records is very instructive for designing high-hat parts.

Choosing Cymbals

Since we're talking rhythm we're talking tempo, and you guessed it — the choice of cymbals relates to the tempo of the song. This is true for the crash, the ride, and the high-hat. But that's not all. A cymbal can contribute to or just as easily damage the mood that you're trying to create. Below are some generalities that will help guide your choices. The descriptions of sounds require a little imagination on your part but I think you'll get the general idea.

- A crash cymbal is effective for calling attention to a new musical section. Typically it is struck on the downbeat of a chorus or solo or simply to break up the rhythm in a long passage.

- At most tempos, a crash should last for roughly two full beats.

- When choosing a ride cymbal for rock, use a hard sound as if the drummer is hitting the bell, or top, of the cymbal (sort of a "clang").

- For softer, ballad, or jazzy numbers the ride cymbal works best with the sound of the tip of the stick lightly tapping the cymbal.

- For variety's sake use more than one crash cymbal sound during the course of a song.

- Slower songs generally call for deeper, richer cymbal tones.

Premixing and Panning the Drum Kit

There are a few conventions for the placement of the drum kit in the stereo spectrum that you need to be aware of. That doesn't mean you have to follow them. But like most conventions in recording, they're there because they work.

First, the kick and snare drum are usually panned in the center of the audio "screen," with the other drums arrayed around them. This wasn't always the case. Instrument placement was a matter of experiment and evolution. For instance, in the early days of stereo, some recordings had all the drums coming out of the left speaker and the singer and all the other instruments coming out of the right. While this stereo separation may have been vastly entertaining to stereophiles, it could be a real drag for the average Joe if he happened to get stuck sitting in front of the left speaker. All he got was a drum solo.

Another reason for the method of panning we now use is that the important and consistent elements of a track should be equally audible from anywhere in the stereo field. That way you can follow the plot no matter where you're standing.

Other little conventions have developed which have to do with the perspective from which the audience hears the drums. Some recordists tend to array the drums as if you the listener were sitting on the drummer's lap. This means that for a right-handed drummer the high-hat would be coming out of the left speaker and the high to low toms would be left to right. Others (like me) will place the drums in the stereo spectrum as if you were standing in front of the kit looking at the drummer, in which case the high-hat would be coming out of the right speaker and the high to low toms would go right to left. Both approaches have their champions and it really is a matter of taste which you choose. However, it *is* a little unsettling to swap them around from song to song and may cause the listener to run for the motion sickness pills.

Premixing

Having discoursed *ad nauseam* on the history of drum panning, let's talk about the premixing process and the various steps to creating an effective stereo drum mix. One of the axioms of recording seems to be that you never have enough inputs for everything you want to do. This is true whether you're using an eighty-input pro console or a six-input portable studio. I don't know why, I think it's just one of Murphy's laws. So early on in your recording career you need to learn how to get around this limitation. In the portable studio world it's particularly important to get the most out of every input you have. One way to do this is to **premix** synthesized sounds *inside* the drum machine and use the stereo outputs of the machine to send the signal to two channels of the portable studio. In this manner you can have a virtually unlimited drum kit without having to have an unlimited number of inputs to the portable studio. Here's how to do it.

Recipe for Premixing a Drum Machine Kit

(Note: All of this takes place inside the drum machine. The result is then output to two inputs of the portable studio.)

1. Choose kick and snare sounds.
2. If your drum machine has EQing capability, use it on each sound individually. Try the EQ suggestions at the end of this chapter. If you don't have this capability try to choose a snare and kick drum that are complementary enough that they will be enhanced by the same EQ when you input them to the portable studio (*e.g.*, both kick and snare can be EQed to enhance the attack).
3. Choose cymbals and high-hat.
4. EQ cymbals.
5. Choose tom-toms.
6. EQ tom-toms.
7. Choose reverb for snare, toms, and cymbals.
   a. Reverb should be in stereo
   b. Toms should have most reverb, snare a little less, and cymbals and high-hat the least.
8. Play the sequence and balance the levels of the drums.
   a. Kick and snare are approximately the same relative volume (kick is slightly louder in pop music and R&B, snare slightly louder in hard rock).
   b. Tom-toms are slightly lower.
   c. Cymbals and high-hat are lower still.
9. Pan the drums as follows:

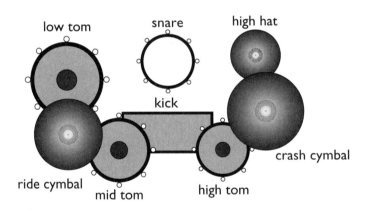

low tom   snare   high hat

kick

crash cymbal

ride cymbal   mid tom   high tom

left   center   right

10. Take the left output of the drum machine and plug it into line input 1 of the portable studio.
11. Take the right output of the drum machine and plug it into line input 2 of the portable studio.
12. EQ inputs 1 and 2 of the portable studio.
13. Record to tracks 1 and 2.

You now have an eight-piece drum kit recorded in stereo using only two tracks of the portable studio.

EQUALIZATION TIPS FOR THE CYBERDRUM KIT

Kick drum

For bottom	boost	80–100 Hz
For transient	boost	3 K
For top	boost	6 K

Snare drum

For boom (tone)	boost	125–250 Hz
For bang (transient)	boost	1–2 K
For buzz (snares)	boost	5 K

Tom-toms

For tone	boost	250–500 Hz
For attack	boost	7 K

Cymbals

For top	boost	10 K
If muddy	cut	200 Hz

High-hat

For heavy rock	boost	500 Hz
Light	boost	5 K
For top	boost	10 K

TIPS FROM THE PROS

Pat Mastelotto is one of the premier drummers recording today. He is known for his versatility, having played everything from straight-ahead rock and pop to the advanced challenges of King Crimson. His credits include the Rembrandts, Mr. Mister, Al Jarreau, and Cock Robin as well as numerous sessions and guest appearances. Following are some of his favorite tips on how to record a human feel with a drum machine.

Spill a beer on a drum machine and it won't work; spill a beer on a drummer, he'll work better. — *Levon Helm*

Drummers have suffered both a great advance and setback with this technology. I feel sorry for players coming up in the early 1980s. I began just a little bit before the birth of the "box" so I can remember songwriters coming in with a grooveless song. Shuffle? Ballad? Rocker? No one knew. The drummer and rhythm section made an interpretation based on an artist's solo performance on guitar or keyboards. The symphonic arrangement was in each individual's mind. Not so today. Every client's a drummer. The writers now bring a beat, tempo, feel, *etc.* Or in fact often use the box for everything (at the expense of young — or old — percussionists getting to develop their skills at this art form). Think of all the great drummers that may have missed their calling without being able to experiment on demos. I think there is a brotherhood in music and we owe something to the future. We learn as much from accidents as rudiments. This brings me to my first suggestion on humanizing drum programming — let a drummer do it! But if you can't, then...

• Think like a drummer: tap on a tabletop, stomp on the floor. See what your feet do during a groove. Do they stop when you play a fill? It is very amateur to keep the kick going in some wild pattern when your hands change up. Some drummers' feet stop, others play quarter notes. More advanced players will syncopate magic in between their hands, and the best do all of the above at just the right time.

- Don't pan the high-hat or the toms to the far outside of the stereo spectrum. Since every drum machine component is discrete it is possible to isolate things too much. In a real drum kit things bleed. A high-hat may be panned hard to one side but will change image because of bleed into other microphones.

- Try not to let the tones remain too static. A drum's timbre changes with volume (velocity) and sticking (the difference between the left and right hands). You can simulate this manually as most sound modules let you do this nowadays.

- Don't let volume remain too static. No human (besides John Robinson) plays completely even velocities. In the old days of Linndrum machines I would manually change these factors as we recorded the box to tape. And then (move faders) again when we mixed. For example, kick beats are usually harder on downbeats or when a crash cymbal is struck. Pickup, or "ghost notes," are softer — sometimes inaudible nonetheless contribute to the feel.

- Have all the parts of your kit sound the same; *i.e.*, don't mix a big-room kick (long reverb) with a "dry" snare.

- Quantizing: There's a lot you can do here. For some dance music, quantizing sixteenth notes is fine, but for a more rock feel try quantizing quarter notes on the kick and snare and then eighths on the downbeat high-hats with no quantizing on the upbeat high-hats.
  Try not quantizing the fills. Quantize the hat and kick but not the snare or use steptime entry to place certain beats back or ahead. For ballads try moving beat 4 of the measure back, or add a tom-tom to the snare. Or you can lengthen the snare note with a tambourine striking at the same time, making it seem "back."

- Make long patterns: Instead of looping a two- or four-bar pattern eight times for a verse or chorus, link them up as one pattern and add a high-hat "pea soup," or skip a kick beat, or double up a snare beat in gaps in the vocal or wherever you like to make each verse unique. Treat each verse, chorus, or solo as one pattern.

- Overdubs: Use real percussion or cymbals, snare drums, or whatever you have to to loosen or humanize the feel. Or leave the machine high-hat unquantized for that Charlie Watts feel.

- Pump it out: Send your box through a speaker to a room and mic it (see Recipe 17 in "The Recipe Section"). Put the speaker in a room with some real drums for rattle and hum overtones. Go on out into the room and shout along or grunt like an overpaid drummer might.

- Effects: A big blessing of a machine's perfect time is that you can add delays very consistently. Use this for boogaloos or swing. Use in-tempo repeats for fills (see "The Effects Chapter").

- Try different machines: I must have had fifteen or twenty machines and sequencers by now, and each one has something to offer. I'll try a Yamaha china cymbal with an Alesis high-hat and Roland crash cymbals. I'll put two snares from different machines together with MIDI delays and different velocity interpretations and strange randomish things will happen. Some of my personal favorites are the Linn 9000 high-hat sliders; the R&B feel of Emulator's early "beat box"; the old Roland Rhythm Ace (like a lounge lizard might use); or, the one box to take to a desert island, the Alesis SR-16, in my opinion the best value out there.

- Break all the rules: What if Zappa, Lennon, or Coltrane had beat boxes? I doubt they would have followed the owner's manual.

- Think of the genre of music: Every style allows for custon interpretations. So, again, blow all my ideas off. Prince will often put a huge ambient kick drum with a dry snare with grand impact. Check out Trevor Horn productions like Seal or Grace Jones — twelve arms all going at once in a fashion no drummer could dream of, much less play, and it swings to the max.

- Try to keep the box alive: It is not always necessary to print a drum machine to tape (see the discussion of virtual mixing in the chapter "Keyboards Part 2: Synths and MIDI"). By using virtual mixing you can save your tape tracks for realtime events (vocals, guitars, and percussion) and keep updating your machine around your real live human events (planned or not). You could set up all effects and internal balances and tweak until the bitter end.

- Save your data! This is a big deal. Save it often, perhaps in different formats, cassette dumps, floppies, or — although it doesn't tell you so in most manuals — almost any sequencer can take a MIDI system dump just as it would performance data. Practice safe sex and safe music.

Good Luck! Party! Have fun. Blow up the box at least once and you'll know you're onto something.

The Guitar Chapter

Here's a fairly obvious fact of musical life: there are as many different guitar sounds as there are guitar players. Every player's sound is as individual as a fingerprint. The combination of ability, touch, type of guitar and amp, outboard gear, and the interaction between all of the above are variables that taken together create a guitarist's sonic signature. Given the vast array of styles and sounds, it would be impossible for me to lay down any all-purpose hard-and-fast rules for recording guitars. A technique that sounds great with a jazz guitar probably wouldn't work for a wall of Marshall amps with the volume set on eleven. Therefore, I think the most useful method of dealing with the subject is to create certain categories of guitar sounds and then suggest ways to get good results in each situation. Once the player has a good basic recorded sound it's only a short step from there to modify and enhance it.

This next little bit is about the rudiments of guitars and how they produce sound. For those of you who are guitarists it may seem like a trip through familiar territory. Those of you who aren't guitarists may well wonder if this is just another hunk of useless info to slosh around in your brain pan. Trust me. It's good stuff for any recordist to be aware of, particularly when it comes to getting the most out of equalization.

Guitar: A Few Strings, Some Wood, and a Cigar Box

As you already know, the sound of a musical instrument is made up of three principal components: tone, overtone, and nontone. All of these are produced by doing something to set the instrument and the air around it vibrating. **Tone** has a specific pitch, the fundamental; **overtones** are a group of pitches different from but related to the fundamental. The series of overtones is determined by the characteristics of the particular instrument. (As was pointed out earlier, the actual character of an instrument lives in its timbre, and timbre is largely composed of overtones.) The **nontone** component has an irrelevant pitch and is a result of the mechanics of producing the sound.

How does all this come together in a guitar sound? A guitar creates sound by the vibration of a plucked string. This vibration in turn vibrates the air around the string, creating sound waves. Tone (pitch) is affected by the length of the string (changed by placing your fingers on a particular fret). Nontone is produced by the sound of the pick striking the string, finger noise, and the thump of your hand on the body of the guitar. The overtones are the result of sympathetic vibrations that are produced in relationship to the frequency of the tone. The most obvious of these are what are referred to as *harmonics*. These are octave-related overtones produced on a partially muted string. Knowing which of these components you want to emphasize is the key to recording great guitar sounds.

Creating a guitar sound is largely a matter of what you do before you start to record. The old saying "garbage in, garbage out" is particularly true when it comes to guitars. No amount of recording equipment can generate a great guitar sound if the fundamentals aren't there to begin with. So let's start with some basics: preparing the instrument and the player to record.

One of the axioms of recording is that what works in a live situation will probably not stand up to the scrutiny and repeated listening of the recording process. In a live gig the audience has only one chance to hear a particular performance of a piece of music. The music just flies by and you're on to the next song. In the few minutes it takes to play a song, things like amplifier noise and line hum are generally not a serious detriment to the audience's listening pleasure. But a recording will presumably be played over and over again, and any extraneous noise, however minor, will eventually become seriously annoying. The more often you hear the song the more obvious and distracting the noise becomes. Eventually it gets to be like watching a TV with poor reception. You can make out the picture and maybe follow the story but the static begins to drive you nuts. Part of the studio process is about eliminating anything that distracts from the music.

As I noted earlier, the human brain has the capability of censoring out unimportant information. What this means to the recordist is that often we get so hooked into the music that we literally don't pay any attention to anything else. But one of the characteristics of the recording process is that the microphone reports *everything* it hears, including the noise that a human brain may filter out in the heat of the musical moment. The mic doesn't censor anything, and as the recording process goes on, barely perceptible noises accumulate. What started as a little bit of noise from one instrument added to a little bit of noise from the next overdub, *etc.*, ends up sounding like a track recorded in a hailstorm. Remember, once noise is recorded it is very difficult to get rid of. The answer then is to make sure it doesn't get recorded in the first place. This requires a good deal of attention to detail and careful preparation before the red light goes on. Below are some tips that will help eliminate unwanted noise before you start recording.

Getting Ready to Record

One of the biggest time-wasters in the studio is an amplifier that wheezes, buzzes, and hums. Following are some different types of amp noises and ways to get rid of them.

If there is a constant hum coming from your amp it is probably related to the power in your studio. Try the following to fix the problem:

- Plug the amp into a power point on a different circuit from the other gear. Use an extension cord to another room perhaps.

- Make sure all connectors used by the amp are shielded (internal connections as well as cables).

- Try a "ground lifter" plug on the amplifier (see "The Recording Studio Kit Chapter").

- Sometimes these noises are related to a time of day when the municipal power grid is most active. The best procedure here is to sit down, have a nice bowl of Wheaties, and just wait it out.

Amp noises are often pitch-related and intermittent, appearing only when certain notes are played. Because these noises come and go, they're difficult to track down. Here is a method for hunting down an elusive buzz or rattle.

1. Plug guitar straight into the amp, no effects.
2. Put your ear to the speaker and turn up the volume to a point where the speakers are working fully (if you're lucky, this will be below the threshold of pain).
3. Start with the low E string and play up the string one fret at a time (most rattles are caused by low frequencies).
4. When you find the buzz, remember what note caused it.
5. Remove the grillcloth or speaker screen. Check for obvious tears in the speaker cone and check to see if the dust cap in the center of the speaker is secure. If that's okay, then play the offending note and see if the buzz has gone away. If so, leave the grillcloth off.
6. If that didn't fix it, tighten the screws holding in the speakers. Still buzzing?
7. If it's a tube amp, check to be sure the tubes are properly seated.
8. If that doesn't cure your problem, then it could be that the chassis is buzzing or something soldered or welded has come loose, You may have to get your amp serviced.

Another common type of amp noise is the GZZZT! (pronounced "son of a *@**#!") This is an intermittent blast of nastiness that usually means a bad connection or an overloaded circuit. If you have a GZZZT!, some possible places it may be coming from are:

- The most obvious, of course, a bad guitar cord.

- An effect that is in need of a new battery.

- A loose input or output connector on any of the devices (including the guitar) that you're using.

- Too much signal overloading the input of an outboard device (particularly with an active pickup on an instrument).

In addition to equipment problems, lack of preparation on the part of the guitar player can be cause for great frustration. It's difficult enough to get a good performance on tape; don't make it harder on yourself by not having it together before you start recording. There are a lot of potential problems that can be avoided by observing the following tips.

- Break in two sets of strings for about half an hour each on the night before a session. This will give them a chance to stretch and will make it easier to keep them in tune when recording. *Never* put on a new set just before you're going to record unless it's an emergency.

- If you have two guitars, set one up for rhythm using a heavier gauge string than you might use for lead. This will help maintain tuning and string life over many takes.

- Try to keep the temperature constant in the playing area even if it means sweating a little until you get the right performance recorded. Variations in temperature can cost you a lot of wasted time in spoiled takes because as the climate changes so does string tension. By the same token, don't put the guitar in another room between takes. While you're out taking your break your guitar is busily inventing a new tuning.

- Get your amp tubes tested before you record. This will ensure that you don't have a tube go south at a critical moment (say at two in the morning). This will also help avoid "microphonics" (usually high-pitched whines or yelps) that appear intermittently while you're playing.

- Check your outboard gear and pedals for noisy switches.

- Put in new batteries before they begin to fade. It is seriously frustrating to be in the middle of recording a great solo and have a battery fail.

- If you have multiple effects, balance the output level to the amplifier so the relative volume will remain the same no matter which sound you're using. This is particularly important if you are recording rhythm and lead parts on the same track and will save a lot of headaches in the mix.

- If a guitar sound is heavily compressed finger noise may become a problem. To remedy it, put a small amount of Wesson oil (or similar) on a rag and wipe it on the strings. It's as effective and certainly cheaper than some of the commercial guitar products (plus it comes in handy if you want a salad).

- To return to the subject of tuning, it's very important that all the players have the same reference to tune to. More often than not, each musician will have their own tuner hooked into their rig. The problem is that different tuners may have slight variations in sensitivity to overtones. In order to avoid tuning nightmares when you begin to stack on the overdubs, it's best to choose one tuner, calibrate it to a true A440, then use the same tuner for all instruments for all of the recording.

If you are producing the session you'll save a lot of time and needless aggravation if you can have your players follow the above guidelines. If you're the one playing it may be even more important because it'll be your time that doesn't get wasted on outtakes.

Deciding on a Sound

Now that the gear and the players are ready, you as the recordist have two basic jobs to do: decide on the right sound for the song, and get the right sound on tape.

Acoustic Guitar

The acoustic is one of those instruments that is either amazingly easy to record or a real nightmare. It all depends on the quality of the instrument and the expertise of the player. Unlike the amplified guitar there is precious little you can do to disguise a flaw. If the instrument sounds clunky in the room it's probably going to sound clunky on tape. There is, however, a closely guarded secret method that professionals use to deal with this problem... we borrow a good-sounding guitar from a buddy. In this case, the choice of the instrument itself goes a long way toward successful recording and lower blood pressure.

When recording an acoustic guitar you need to pay attention to the age of the strings and be ready to change them as needed. Over the course of many takes the strings will begin to lose elasticity. They will also pick up skin oils from your fingers which will darken the tone. A decline in the brilliance of the sound is the result. As the strings go dead, the EQ you so carefully dialed in will become less effective, and generally the sound will just start to fall in a hole. It's a judgment call as to when to change the strings, as doing so will undoubtedly cause a lengthy interruption, but the alternative is recording a great performance played on crummy-sounding strings.

Miking an Acoustic Guitar

The guitar, like any acoustic instrument, has a sonic sweet spot. This is the place where the mic picks up the most desirable sound qualities. Placing a mic is a matter of trial and error and individual to each instrument, but here are some guidelines.

ACOUSTIC GUITAR MIKING RECIPE

1. Have the player sit on a stool in playing position.
2. Place the mic 5 to 7 inches away and at a 30-degree angle from the instrument, aimed at the soundhole. Make sure the player's hand is clear of the mic.
3. Have the guitarist play while you listen to the monitors. If you are the player, you should record a little bit and then listen to a playback rather than try to make a judgment while playing.
4. Listen for a desirable balance of tone. Adjust as follows:
   a. **Too muddy:** aim the mic closer to the bridge, or where the pick stikes the strings.
   b. **Too bright:** move the mic slightly farther from the instrument to pick up the longer waves of the low frequencies.
   c. **Too "picky":** move the mic to pick up more of the neck away from where the string is struck.
5. Try to eliminate finger noise, loud foot-tapping, and thumps as the player's hand strikes the body of the guitar.
6. EQ (see below).

Direct In (D.I.) Electric Guitar

As an alternative to miking an acoustic, a "clean" electric guitar is often used. The basic principle behind D.I. recording is simple: Use the guitar pickup to send electric impulses directly to the console rather than to an amplifier and speaker. Not so long ago this was accomplished by plugging the guitar right into the input of the console and recording. A guitar sound recorded in this fashion had terrific clarity, but it was a skinny little thing — there was no "meat" to the sound. The result was for the most part pretty one-dimensional and generally not very exciting. However, as more guitar effects began to be developed, the results of D.I. recording got more interesting. In addition to effects like chorusing and flanging there are now dozens of preamps and speaker emulators on the market that can provide a good alternative to miking an amplifier. These work by using circuitry to synthesize the sound of speakers and may be plugged directly into the console. The D.I. approach is particularly useful for clarity, for overcoming space limitations, and for recording in a populated area in the wee hours of the morning. Other than the method of getting the sound to the console, all other considerations of recording (EQ, etc.) are the same as with a mic/amp configuration.

DIRECT IN RECORDING RECIPE

1. Plug the output of the device into the channel line in. (Or, if your gear is equipped with XLR connectors, plug into channel mic in.)
2. Set the fader to unity gain (zero, or whatever the manufacturer designates) and follow normal recording procedure.
3. When the track meter is responding, balance the output of the guitar device with the input of the console to get the best signal-to-noise ratio (see the discussion on signal-to-noise ratio at the beginning of "The Effects Chapter").
4. EQ.

Amplified Electric Guitar

You could make a good case that rock and roll speaks with the voice of the amplified guitar. Amp and guitar are the stuff of a nearly infinite spectrum of expression, from the crisp and precise to a peal of thunder louder than God's hammer. All's fair in love and guitar. Want it to sound like trash cans rolling down an alley? No problem, fire up the ol' Les Paul and let 'er rip. Pretty leads, crashing chords... all things are possible. That being said (and with advance apologies to those experimenting on the guitar frontier) let's for now just pretend there are only two types of amplified electric guitar sound, of which all others are variants: clean and distorted.

As was mentioned earlier, a major part of successful recording lies in keeping everything in perspective and understanding what role a particular instrument is going to play in the end product. This is especially true of guitars because the broad band of frequencies produced by a guitar can easily overwhelm another musical part, particularly a vocal. In order to avoid a mixdown meltdown between guitar and vocal it is important to have a clear idea of which guitar sound to use to fill the proper amount of musical space. Too much space and the vocal gets smothered; too little and the vocal is unsupported. This isn't as much a matter of guitar aesthetics as it is understanding the ensemble nature of the recording process. A major part of production is anticipating how each instrumental piece fits in the puzzle. What it may come down to is this: the guitar sound you're used to, worked on, sweated over, and is killer in a live situation, may have to be adjusted or even heavily modified to suit the needs of recording. Believe me, this is very often the case. Recording and live performance are two different art forms and require two different sets of techniques.

One of the first and most astonishing things I learned about recording is that a lot of those huge power-guitar sounds I so admired on records were produced in the studio by an amp about the size of a hamster cage. Little amps like an old Fender Princeton or the small Ampeg practice amp I often use distort easily and when miked properly sound like a concert stack. So the first thing to be aware of is that when recording you don't need a lot of amp to get a lot of sound. In fact, when it comes to power sounds, recording big amps at high volume is often less than satisfying, particularly when the physical space is limited (like in your bedroom). One advantage to overdriving a small amp is that you won't drown out the ambience of a small space that can add to the sound. You can scale down acoustic effects (sort of like using miniatures in a film) to get a kitchen hallway to stand in for an amphitheater. You can also use multiple mics with less danger of phase problems than when recording at high dBs. Another major advantage is that you don't have to move to another apartment immediately after your first power guitar session. So for distorto-power-thrash-metal sounds investigate pawn shops for little amps to try out.

For a clean guitar sound, a bigger amp is a better way to go. Something in the range of a Fender Twin or a Roland Jazz Chorus (my personal favorite clean amp) is likely to give you a warmer, richer sound than the small amps mentioned above when run at low volume. The bigger speakers move more air, which translates into warmth and body. Clean guitars are also a bit "spiky," and larger speakers can help round out pick attack and unpleasant transients.

Once you decide on the type of amp sound you're going for, you then have three major considerations: 1. the type of physical space you wish to record in (live or dead), 2. miking technique, and 3. equalization.

Out of the Closet, Into the John: Ambience

In the real world the ambience of a space contributes to the audience's perception of where the music is coming from. Lots of ambience and the audience perceives the music as far away; very little ambience and the listener thinks you're right in his ear. To be an effective recordist you need to be aware that ambience is a primary color on your sonic palette. Knowing how to manipulate it will play a major part in the expression of your music. That being the case it is important to choose your recording space wisely. Being creative about space is a art often overlooked in the home recording environment. There are a variety of resources available to you amid the comfort of your own stuff. Why, yessir, you can get a great guitar sound without ever having to change out of your pajamas if you are creative about how you look at space.

For example, you could put your amplifier in a tile bathroom, mic it up, and you've got a quasi-rockabilly sound. However, by choosing a "live" (reflective) ambience that will leak into the mic, you are committed to adding that color into the sound as it's recorded.

Another possibility would be to use a closetful of clothes as an isolation booth of sorts. By aiming the amplifier into the closet you limit the amount of ambient sound bouncing around. This is what's called a "dead" (nonreflective) space. If you choose a dead space to record in, you are opting for a more controlled sound to which you can later add ambience with electronic effects (like reverb). There is of course no right or wrong, only what's appropriate to your own musical vision.

There are a lot of nooks and crannies that make great recording spaces. Just a few to check out are:

"Live" spaces
- A garage with a concrete floor makes a good "concert hall" for power sounds.

- A kitchen with vinyl floors will sound "live" but less bright than tile.

- A hallway with a hardwood floor is good for distant miking.

- Various bathrooms.

- Your vast two-story polished marble entrance hall (butlers make great mic stands).

"Dead" spaces
- Closets.

- A "cave" built out of sofa cushions to surround an amp.

- A living room with carpeting and overstuffed furniture.

- The Oval Office.

There is no formula for when to use a live or dead space. What it comes down to is control in the mix. Remember, once ambience is recorded with the track it's there for good. You can't get rid of it unless you record the track over. So you need to have a good idea of what you want the overall track to sound like before you choose the space to record in. By the way, not only will mics pick up unwanted amplifier noise, but you can also get some pretty good recordings of airplanes, fire engines, and garbage trucks to go along with that guitar solo. Be sure when you record that the mic is as isolated from outside noise as possible. Like ambience, any noise that's recorded with the music is there for good.

Miking the Amp

Every recording engineer has favorite miking techniques. I'm no different. The techniques that follow are my favorites. They certainly aren't the only ways to do the job but they are the ones that I've had consistently good results with and that I know provide a good basis for departure and experimentation.

Choosing a Mic

In a previous chapter there was a discussion of the various types of microphones. There is a huge variety by different manufacturers in a wide range of prices. As with miking techniques, an engineer's choice of which microphone to use is a very individual thing. Over time and with experience, the engineer learns the different characteristics of particular products and knows how to apply them to their best advantage. There are a number of mics that will yield good results for recording guitars, and your choice is largely a matter of personal preference and pocketbook. That being said, and at the risk of starting a tavern brawl over the merits of some very fine products that I neglect to mention, let me make some personal recommendations for recording guitars. First, for a dynamic mic I would suggest the Shure SM 56, 57, or Beta 58. These are readily available and relatively inexpensive (especially if purchased used) and I have used them for years with good results. For condenser mics (remember, these require a power supply and perhaps a transformer, depending on the portable studio you have) I would suggest the AKG 1000 and the substantially more expensive Neumann U-89, or for brighter guitars the AKG 414. The purchase price is pretty steep for the last two but they may be rented on a daily basis in most metropolitan areas.

Mic Placement: Close Miking, Distant Miking, Multiple Mics

The position of the microphone relative to the sound source will determine to a large degree the emphasis placed on certain characteristics of what you record. As a general rule, the greater the distance between the mic and the amp the more bottom end appears. When the mic is closer more high-frequency information will be emphasized. This is because low-frequency sound waves require more distance to fully form. However, there is a point of diminishing returns when it comes to adding bottom end with mic distance. While doing so may improve the low end and perhaps add body, it will also give you less clarity. Remember that high end is what allows the human ear to figure out the direction a sound is coming from in our own personal stereo spectrum. Low frequency, on the other hand, is much less directional and is used by the brain to tell us how far something is from us. Too much unfocused low end has a tendency to muddy a sound, making its location in the mix less definite. When that happens to the guitar it will not be easily positioned in the stereo spectrum and will end up muddying the whole track.

The amount of recorded ambience is another factor affected by mic distance. The farther away the microphone is from the amp the more the ambience of the space will be added to the sound that goes onto tape. So you can see that there's more to the process than just sticking a mic up in front of the amp. Choosing the miking distance from the amp deserves some serious consideration and is dependent on how much space you want the instrument to take up in the final mix. The more lows and ambience, the more musical space the sound needs. As a result there is less room available for other instruments.

Here is one way to help train your ear to tell how much low end the mic is hearing.

1. With nothing plugged into the amp raise the volume so it is hissing audibly.
2. Position the microphone about six inches away from the amp, then go to the portable studio to listen to the monitors.
3. After you've gotten used to that sound, move the mic to two feet away from the amp, return to the portable studio, and listen for the differences in sound, particularly the bottom end and the reflections of the sound off the walls.

Then move the mic two feet farther still and so on. By repeating this process and with a little practice you will get an idea of how different distances determine which frequencies become dominant. It's also a good way to determine the characteristics of the space in which you're recording.

Electric Guitar Miking Recipes

Whether I'm using a live or dead space, the following are the methods I generally use for miking an amplifier. When using any of these techniques have the guitarist play the part to be recorded. Don't make mic position choices while he's tuning or noodling around.

SINGLE CLOSE MIKING RECIPE

Application: To enhance clarity of guitar sound.
Requirement: One mic
1. Elevate the amplifier off the floor using a chair, stool, etc. But never use an enclosed box or speaker cabinet. These resonate and may add mud.
2. Choose *one* speaker of the amp to mic.
3. Position the mic so it is equal in elevation to the center of the speaker to be recorded.
4. Do not place the mic directly perpendicular to the speaker but rather at about a 30-degree angle off axis and pointing at the center. This will help diffuse unwanted blasts of air caused by speaker movement.
5. The distance between the mic and the speaker is a matter of personal choice (see above). But I generally begin with the mic about six inches away from the center cap, listen through the monitors, and adjust the mic accordingly.
6. EQ.

SINGLE DISTANT MIKING RECIPE

Application: To add ambience to a guitar sound. Also useful for adding power to chords, etc., or to provide a short echo.
Requirements: One mic, live space
1. Elevate the amplifier as in above recipe.
2. Place the mic stand on a blanket or rug (this is to avoid reflections into the mic directly off the floor).
3. Position the mic three feet away from the amp to begin.
4. Position the mic so it is pointing directly at the speaker.
5. Listen through the monitors and adjust according to taste.
6. EQ.

MULTIPLE MIKING RECIPE

Application: Mixing a combination of near and distant mics to create a sound is a good way to maintain clarity and still add a controlled amount of ambience. Particularly good for recording power guitars and solos in very live spaces.
Requirements: two or more mics, live space
1. Determine the number of mics you wish to use and plug each into a se parate channel mic in on the portable studio. Assign them all to the same record track and monitor that track.
2. Follow the procedure outlined in the Single Close Miking Recipe above.
3. Place the first distant mic three to four feet away from the amp and at least a foot above the height of the close mic. (Be sure to place the mic stand on a blanket or rug as before.)

4. Listen through the monitors to the combination of mics for any phase-cancellation problems.

5. If a problem is detected, move the distant mic to the right or left. Repeat listening. Solving acoustic phase-cancellation problems is often a matter of trial and error, requiring several adjustments in mic position.

6. Mix the ambient and close mic sounds to taste.

7. EQ each channel. When using combination miking I generally EQ the distant mic to emphasize the high end and take out a little bottom end to prevent unwanted rumble.

Equalization

Because of the wide variety of guitar sounds it's virtually impossible to formalize any kind of magic guitar EQ. However, there are certain broad categories of sounds that in some combination are the components of all guitar sounds. The trick to successfully EQing a guitar is in recognizing which of these elements you want to bring out and which you want to diminish. By now you know that the equalizer is really another volume control. The difference is that it is frequency-dependent. The guitar, particularly the distorted power guitar, is a mother lode of frequencies. That being the case, the process of EQing a guitar is not just a matter of boosting frequencies to enhance the guitar but also one of omitting frequencies from the guitar sound that will interfere with other instruments (see "The Mixdown Chapter").

GUITAR EQ GUIDE

Electric Guitar

For bottom	boost	100 Hz
For warmth	boost	250 Hz
For body	boost	500 Hz
For pick or percussion	boost	1–2 K
For "cut" (solos, lines, etc.)	boost	3–4 K
For "presence"	boost	5 K
For "buzz" (distortion, etc.)	boost	7 K
For clarity and string decay	boost	10 K and up
To remove muddiness	cut	200 Hz
To remove harshness	cut	1–3 K

Acoustic Guitar

For warmth	boost	250 Hz
For body	boost	500–700 Hz
For pick	boost	1 K
For lines	boost	3 K
For brilliance	boost	5 K
For sparkle	boost	10 K and up
To remove rumble	cut	100 Hz and down
To remove finger noise	cut	7 K

To Squish or Not to Squish: Using a Compressor

As you have seen in "The Effects Chapter" (and will see again in "The Mixdown Chapter"), the compressor is very useful for smoothing out dynamics. In effect what a compressor does is make the quiet stuff louder and the loud stuff quieter. This makes it a particularly useful tool for recording guitars. Aside from the obvious uses (like keeping that one really loud note in the solo from ripping your sinuses out) there is another very useful function; a compressor can lend additional sustain. The reason why this is so is inherent in the way the compressor works. The compressor is trying to limit dynamic range so that every note can be heard. As a note dies the compressor automatically raises its volume, keeping it audible longer and thereby artificially adding sustain. This feature is particularly nice to have when recording solos or acoustic guitars. However, as usually happens, along with the benefit comes the tradeoff. As the compressor raises the level of the note it also raises the "noise floor" (read hiss). You need to be careful. There comes a point when that lovely sustained note gets drowned in the sound of electronic surf. So by *judicious* use of compressor settings you can get that last singing note to sing a little longer. Here's how to do it.

COMPRESSING FOR SUSTAIN RECIPE

1. Set up the compressor (for example, see Recipe 8 in "The Recipe Section").
2. Set the compressor at 4:1 ratio to begin.
3. Set the "threshold" control so that the signal level is reduced by 1 to 3 dB.
4. Set for fast attack and slow release.
5. Play guitar notes where the sustain is desired.
6. Increase the ratio until the desired effect is achieved.
7. Lower the threshold for desired effect.

For further information check out "The Effects Chapter" and "The Mixdown Chapter."

The Bass Chapter

In nearly all Western popular music, the bass is the core of tonality. It is not a bad idea to occasionally remind ourselves of that. Typically, the bass is responsible for sounding the lowest root note upon which the chord is built. In addition, as any bass player will gladly tell you, what he or she plays is the principal melodic element of the rhythm section. It is through the bass that chordal movement is felt as well as heard. In this regard the bass is the force that propels the listener along the musical track. So why then is something as important as the bass often treated by the recordist as a poor cousin to the guitar?

That being said, I herewith present a chapter disclaimer. Lest anyone think that I omit their instrument from this chapter due to poor cousinhood I offer this statement: While I certainly recognize the beauty of the acoustic bass viol and admire what a *guitarrón* can do, as a practical matter most home portable studio recording is done either with an electric bass guitar or some form of keyboard bass, and so with apologies to those left out, that's what this chapter is about.

Bass Parts (No, I Don't Mean Fish Anatomy)

If you do a bit of critical listening, your favorite CDs will give you some idea of how the bass is treated and used in different kinds of music. In fact, you can almost define a style of music by the type of bass sound used and where and how it sits in the track.

In some recordings, notably dance, urban, hip-hop, and R & B, the bass is very prominently featured, often sharing the spotlight with the vocals. Frequently a whole song is built around the bass part. Guitars, horns, and keyboards are not much more than punctuation marks clarifying the groove. In this case the bass is the backbone that gives the song its shape.

For slow songs or ballads the bass often serves a dual role. It is both melodic and rhythmic, adding phrases and counterpoint between the beats. The purpose of the bass here is to provide warm support for the song to float on.

In rock and roll the bass usually acts as a platform for the chordal instruments. Frequently the bass is less musically obvious, being used primarily to carry the weight of chord changes in rhythmic partnership with the drums. Here the bass is often treated almost as the tonal component of the kick drum.

In hard rock, thrash, metal, and similar aggressive music the bass takes on a slightly different role. It is frequently used to double a rhythm guitar riff to add power, sort of like the bigger older brother you go get when you want to kick serious butt.

In each of the above examples the bass plays a different musical role, and for each one the bass sound needs to be treated differently. Choices, choices, choices. Is it a straight-ahead electric bass guitar or a funk keyboard bass that best suits what you hear in your head? In this chapter I'll give you some useful techniques for recording each style.

The Electric Bass Guitar

The electric bass, as we all know, is exactly the same as an electric guitar except it's got just four really big strings. Right? Well, that's a bit like saying that because a gorilla and your uncle Lem both have hair on their backs they're pretty much the same, except of course the gorilla could squish Uncle Lem's head like a grape. The point is that while the bass bears a superficial resemblance to its six-string sibling, and even operates on basically the same transduction principle as the electric guitar, it's a very different animal to record. This is mainly because the frequency range and musical function of the bass and guitar are so different. Just for illustration's sake let's assume that the drums and guitars are musical opposites (insert your own joke here). For the purpose of our example, the drums are strictly rhythmic and the guitar is only melodic. In a well-constructed track the bass is the glue that holds the drums and the guitars together. It is neither strictly rhythmic nor strictly melodic, so from the standpoint of sound the bass must be a little of each in order to bind the drums and guitar together. There is of course a collection of elements that go into creating the right electric bass sound for the track and then getting it on tape. Let's start with the need for having gear that's studio ready.

Preparation

As with the guitar there are some classic gear-related time-wasters that can be avoided by a little preproduction foreplay and player awareness.

Tips for Recording the Amplified Electric Bass

- Use only one speaker cabinet to record. This will allow you more control of the bottom end and will help prevent useless rumble that may be caused by reflections off the walls or floor.

- Record at a reasonable volume. When it comes to bass, loud doesn't add excitement, only mud.

- As with the guitar, get the speaker cabinet off the floor with a chair, stool, or perforated milk crate. Do not use a spare speaker cabinet. You're trying hard to get rid of bogus low-end resonance, and an extra bass cabinet, plugged or unplugged, is definitely going to act like an bass bin and give you heaps of rumble.

- Use the same procedure as described in "The Guitar Chapter" to eliminate speaker buzzes and rattles. As was noted, the low frequencies are usually the culprits in generating the little intermittent noises that drive recordists nuts. The bass has lots of low frequencies, so take a few minutes to check out the speakers and avoid the sudden migraine that comes with saying, "Geez, I didn't hear that buzz when the bass was recorded."

• Tighten the screws around the speakers periodically.

• As with the guitar, check for noisy switches on your effects.

• Replace batteries about three days before you think you need to. If you have an active bass pickup, put in new batteries before an important session.

• Get the bass professionally intonated and the pickups set so the output level from string to string is balanced. An instrument that is correctly set up will go a long way toward preventing tuning problems as well as stabilizing recording levels that from string to string are leaping all over the VU meter.

Some Player Tips

• If you play bass, develop an equal ability with a variety of techniques. Work on being able to use a pick, your fingers, the thumb hammer, etc. If you are recording a bass player, choose someone whose technique works comfortably with the song. Square pegs and round holes make for mixing nightmares.

• As sets of bass strings go dead don't throw them away. Start a string file. Boil strings to put life back in them. (See the "Strings and Things" section.)

• Check bass tuning frequently when recording — at least every third take. Check to make sure that octaves are in tune as well as first position.

• When designing a bass part I've found it to be almost always true that less is more. Learn to listen to how well your part suits its job of supporting the track. Oftentimes you'll find that it's the notes that you leave out that contribute the most to the groove.

• A player's consistency of touch can make a huge difference in keeping bass dynamics under control. The more controlled the player's technique, the less artificial electronic compression is needed. One technique for greatly improving touch skills is practicing like this:

  1. Plug the bass into the portable studio so you can monitor your playing level on the VU meter.
  2. Use a metronome to set your practice tempo. Start practicing the part you're going to record at a slow tempo.
  3. Watch the VU meter on the portable studio as you play and try to keep the volume of every note within a -2 dB range.
  4. After you've successfully played the part a couple of times in the target dB zone, move the tempo up a notch or two and try again.
  5. Keep at it until you can play the part with consistency at the desired tempo.

I guarantee that in a very short period of time your recording technique (and your sense of tempo) will improve dramatically.

Recording the Electric Bass

Just as with the electric guitar, there are two basic techniques for getting a bass on tape: miking an amplifier or recording directly (D.I.) into the portable studio. Each approach has a distinct sound and is useful for different things.

Miking the Bass Amplifier

Typically, the amplified bass is used for recording a more live-sounding track. Every bass player has a favorite amp combination. But as I've said *ad nauseam,* what works for a live gig doesn't necessarily sound so great in the studio. The successful studio amp formula is one that is set up for tonality and control of bass frequencies and not just for blowing people through the back wall.

For example, bass bins (large speakers for extreme lows) work well live because they push a lot of lows at high sound pressure levels out to the audience. In a live setting the bass really is as much a physical force as a musical one, and it takes a lot of volume to get the speakers moving. (By the way, it was rumored that the Italian government developed an extreme low-frequency system for riot control, loud enough and low enough that suddenly everyone in the crowd needed to go to the bathroom in a hurry.)

But when music is recorded, a lot of the lows get lost or are not reproduced by the stereo speakers, and so in order to get any musical muscle the recordist can't rely on brute force and must go after "apparent bass"; that is, a bottom end that makes up for the lost low oomph by adding a focused punch. One way of describing it would be to call it a "pulse" of the music. This is all a way of saying that large bass speakers need high volume and are therefore a nightmare to record. In addition to the fact that most of the low lows won't get effectively recorded at all, that loud bass bouncing around will appear on tape as unmusical rumble. So a smaller speaker running at lower volume is a more desirable choice.

The Space

While a guitar sound can benefit from a "live" environment, I've found that recording a bass that way can be problematic. As we all know from our brief sound wave theory lesson (in the "What Is Sound?" chapter), standing waves are something to avoid. Low-frequency standing wave problems are more likely to develop where the sound is ricocheting off the tile. Therefore I tend to use moderately dead spaces for recording bass amps. If I want a live sound I've found that it's easier to control if I simulate a live environment with reverb. Around the house I would suggest that a closetful of clothes is perhaps the easiest space to record a bass amp in.

When you're choosing the space, another thing to be aware of is extraneous noises. One particular pain in the neck in the home studio is wall and floor rumble. This can be caused by all sorts of stuff, from jets overhead to Aunt Bertha's step aerobics, and you need to be vigilant about listening for this stuff if you want avoid ruining a good track.

First of all look for a suitable space that is naturally isolated from the rest of the house and farthest from traffic — a back bedroom for instance. Low-frequency information from passing vehicles travels amazingly effectively through floors and walls, and since you will be equalizing to bring out the lows it's best to get as far away from the street as possible (unless of course you want a pinch of dumptruck to go with your bass sound). Extraneous noises are a pain to track down and eliminate, but it's way better than recording them.

A Brief Digression — Mystery Noise #1

While in Australia working on an album, I was recording a bass amp and decided that for the sake of isolation I would put it and the mic in a storage room some distance away. Later that afternoon when the band started tracking I was puzzled by a metallic rhythmic sound coming faintly through the monitors. It would appear and disappear but was related somehow to the music. After frantically soloing every instrument on the console I figured out where the problem was coming from but had no idea what was causing it. I went back to the storage room, opened the door, and discovered a guy in coveralls hunkered down over a six-inch pipe that ran through the wall next to the amp. He had a pipe wrench in his hand and had apparently been keeping time on the pipe while he worked on the plumbing. When I came in he just looked up at me and said, "I like a good bass. Bit loud in here though, reckon you could you turn it down?"

MIKING THE BASS AMP RECIPE

1. Choose a dead space to record in (faced into a closet, *etc.*)
2. Elevate the speaker and put some sound-absorbing material on the floor in front (cushions, Sonex, blanket, *etc.*). This will help eliminate unwanted bass reflections from bouncing off the floor into the mic.
3. Place some padding under the base of the mic stand to damp vibrations that may come through the floor.
4. Choose one speaker in the cabinet and elevate the mic so it is at the same height as the center of the speaker.
5. Position the mic aimed at the center of the speaker but at a 30-degree angle off axis.
6. Begin with the mic for to six inches away from the speaker and adjust accordingly. The correct position of the mic is the one that gives you a suitable balance between the bottom end and the rhythmic attack of the note. The closer the mic is to the center of the speaker, the more the percussiveness will be brought out; the farther from the speaker the mic gets or the more it is pointed at the speaker cone, the more the bottom will be emphasized.
7. Set the compressor.
8. EQ.

DIRECT IN (D.I.) BASS RECIPE

1. Plug the bass into a compressor if desired (see Recipe 7 in "The Recipe Section").
2. Plug the output into a channel line in.
3. If the bass has active electronics, you may have to pad down (reduce) the signal to avoid distortion. Use the pad on the portable studio. If you don't have one, *line pads* are available at pro audio stores.

4. Set the compressor to eliminate "spikes." The bass signal should not be recorded overly hot, peaking at about +2 dB on the meter.
5. On the other hand, too low a level will contribute a constant hissing noise (see the discussion of signal-to-noise ratio in the chapter "How a Tape Recorder Does What It Does"). Try to keep the bass above -4 dB on the meter.
6. EQ.

After You've Plugged It In: The Playing Technique

As has been mentioned many times before you got to this page, the art of production is the art of making balanced choices (and of course in some cases the art of knowing when to pretend you planned something that was really just a cool accident).

To continue in this semiphilosophical vein, shaping music is a matter of choosing parts. Shaping a musical *mood* is a matter of choosing sounds. With the bass guitar, the player's technique for producing the sound is an important element in complementing the musical part and thereby enhancing the mood. There are three basic techniques for producing sound from the bass: the **pick**, the **thumb hammer**, and **fingerstyle** playing, and all color the sound in dramatically different ways. While there are certainly no commandments from on high about when to use what technique, each seems to have its logical place in suiting different types of songs. The choice of how the string is struck will have a lot to do with whether you wish to emphasize the percussive (rhythmic) component of the bass sound or the tonal (melodic) component.

Fingerstyle Playing

This is probably the most common technique for playing bass guitar. The player plucks the strings with either the finger pads or nails. It is a versatile sound for this reason. With the soft pads of the fingers a round warm sound particularly suited to ballads is produced. Plucking with the fingernails produces more of an attack and can be used in conjunction with the drums to provide additional rhythmic support. By mediating the touch between the two a wide variety of intensities can be accomplished. Oftentimes a player will mix various touches in the same song. While this certainly creates musical interest, it may also present some recording problems. For one thing, the dynamic range of the part may be hard to control. This can result in dropouts at some points of the song and boominess in others. A compressor can help smooth out these level variations, but a compressor is an artificial device for controlling the dynamics of the player. A better solution is to have the player be aware of his dynamics and modify his playing accordingly.

Another problem arises when the player gets a little overenthusiastic and plucks the strings too hard. This can result in fret buzz or string rattle, problems that are virtually impossible to get rid of once they're recorded. If you desire more attack try playing closer to the bridge rather than thrashing the string.

Finally, when combining finger techniques you may find that the EQ you set up beforehand only works for parts of the song. If this happens you'll need to compromise and EQ in two stages. Equalize for the tone of the bass as it's being recorded and wait for the mixdown to EQ for the rhythmic parts.

Playing with a Pick

Personally I prefer recording a bass played with a pick for most applications simply because the dynamics are more controlled. This is particularly true when I do rock and roll. In these songs the bass and the kick drum are the heartbeat of the song, and therefore the attack of the bass note needs to be clear. The pick striking the string has a sort of percussive quality that is useful in defining the beat. I also find that the tonality of the bass is in better balance with the transient and as a result is easier to EQ for the entire song.

Playing with the Thumb Hammer

The thumb hammer is a way of producing a bass sound by tapping the side of the thumb percussively against the string. It's often used in conjunction with the "burp," which is a sharp pluck of the string with one of the fingers, usually an octave above the thumb-hammered note. This technique is great for fast-moving parts, and from an EQ standpoint is quite easy because essentially you are treating the bass as a rhythm instrument. A compressor is useful for controlling spikes, but must be set on a very fast release in order to prevent muddiness. Remember, a compressor can be used to add sustain, and sustain is probably not what you're looking for in a thumb-hammer part.

The Keyboard Bass

I know that you know that there is a separate chapter that deals with the general world of synths and goes into a fair amount of detail, but I thought, what the heck, I'm here talking about low notes so let's talk about recording synthesized bass sounds.

In the dark ages of the early seventies when people first started using the synth bass there really weren't a lot of different sounds to choose from. Basically you could use the froggy-sounding Moog thing or the froggy-sounding ARP thing. Don't get me wrong, those sounds were and are very cool. It's just that that was it, dueling frogs with an occasional pitch bend. Now with the advent of sophisticated and easily modifiable sound synthesis and the evolution of sampling technology virtually anyone with even a modest budget can have a whole bunch of basses in a box.

What this means of course is that most of the sounds available on an electric (or acoustic, for that matter) bass are available in cyber form. This also means that the basic recording techniques described in this chapter can be applied almost without exception to the synth bass. There are some differences, however. For the most part the synth bass is much more controlled in terms of dynamics than a bass guitar. Also, and perhaps most telling, is that each note of the keyboard bass sound is optimized, leveling out the subtle variations of a human hand striking a string. This can translate into a sameness that is perceived as unexciting. In the case of sampled sounds, the transient (or front end of the attack of the note) has often been "de-edged" by the sampling process. This contributes to a smoothness that can sound unnatural. So if the keyboard sound you're going for is a stand-in for a bass guitar the real challenge you face in recording is providing the expression and variation associated with a bass guitar. Here are some tricks that will help you.

- Use an amplifier. The speaker has to move physically in response to the electric signal from the synth. The speaker will provide some variations, because in the physical world it cannot be a perfect mirror of a cybersound. Using a speaker will add in a few little imperfect colorations (in other words, sonic warts) that will make the bass sound more natural.

- Vary the dynamics slightly. (I know, I know I'm contradicting what I said earlier about dynamics making it harder to record a bass, but I'm writing this thing so I can bend the rules a little.) By "vary" I mean have the choruses a little louder or more aggressive than the verses, for instance, or have the downbeat of each measure more pronounced, almost as if the "bass player" got excited. You can even give the "bass player" a dose of Jolt Cola ("twice the caffeine and all of the sugar") by taking the bass part up a little in tempo in the chorus so it is just a hair on the front of the beat.

- Be sure to EQ in a manner appropriate to the playing technique you wish to emulate — fingerstyle, pick, or thumb hammer.

- Combine synth sounds for the same part. Use one for its tonal qualities and another for its attack and balance the two (or more). One nice combination is a muted picked bass and a fretless.

- Use portamento effects to simulate slides.

Using Effects on Bass Sounds

There is a technique that I use regularly to fatten up a bass sound. I've found that by splitting a bass signal and sending one side to an effect and then to a channel input and the other side to another channel input as a "straight" sound, the combination of the two adds great definition to a bass part. The effect I use most often to accomplish this is a flanger adjusted so the flanging is subtle. A chorus pedal also works well. I EQ the two sounds differently, emphasizing the upper mids (3 to 5 K) of the effect channel and the lows of the straight channel. I then balance the two channels for the desired effect and send them both to be recorded on the same track. This technique is diagrammed in detail in Recipe 15 of "The Recipe Section."

Compression

The bass is certainly a candidate for the "most likely to be compressed" award. As I said earlier, controlling the dynamics of the bass plays a major role in how punchy a track will be (in this context punchy is a good thing). The compressor can solve the dilemma of the dreaded vanishing bass note or control the ego of the note that would be king, but great care should be taken to ensure that the cure isn't worse than the disease. An improperly used compressor can add unwanted sustain by not releasing notes quickly enough, which can make a track sound lifeless and muddy.

BASS COMPRESSOR RECIPE

1. Set the compressor at a 4:1 ratio.
2. Set the threshold control so only the notes desired activate the compressor circuit.
3. Set the attack and release controls to fast.
4. Play the part and adjust the gain reduction so it reduces no more than 3 dB.

EQ TIPS FOR THE BASS

The equalization tips that follow are designed to allow you to make the rhythm-versus-tonal decision discussed at the beginning of the chapter. By balancing the various components of the sound you can arrive at the one that most complements the tempo and mood of the song.

For lows	boost	80–100 Hz
For tonality	boost	800 Hz
For rhythmic attack	boost	1 K
For string sound	boost	3 K
For clarity	boost	6 K
To reduce muddiness	cut	200 Hz

STRINGS AND THINGS: ERIK SCOTT ON STUDIO BASS

Erik Scott is a highly respected bass guitarist who has recorded with such acts as Kim Carnes, Alice Cooper, Bill Conti, Jack Douglas (producer), Peter McIan, and Carl Palmer (of Emerson, Lake, and Palmer), to name but a few.

In the studio, the sound of the bass guitar is most affected by three things: the strings, the pickups, and the player. Yet at home the effect the strings have is too often overlooked.

The type, gauge, and age of a string will make a vast difference in its tonal quality. For instance, there are three types of strings, and each sound quite different. Round-wounds are the brightest and have the most high end. Half-wounds have less brightness, and flat-wounds, even less. Sustain will also vary, though only slightly, with round-wounds having the most and flat-wounds having the least. So when picking the type of string to use, make sure the sound fits well with the style and instrumentation of the music.

The gauge of the strings will also make a difference in the tonal quality of the instrument, and they, too, should be chosen carefully. You may want to avoid prepackaged sets so that you can hand-pick the gauge of each string. For instance, you may want the E and A strings to be a medium-light gauge, while using slightly heavier-gauged strings for the D and G. Yet, since each instrument and each song is different, you should experiment with the gauges to see which work best.

The age of a string is something that is often oversimplified. Bass strings are not merely "live" or "dead." They go through three distinctly different sonic stages before they finally die and have to be buried. When brand new, they sound very bright and have a great deal of sustain. They also produce a wealth of harmonic overtones, which gives the sound a transparency that keeps it from obscuring other instruments in the track.

This first stage, which lasts for one or two days of regular playing, is followed by a period during which the strings are, according to some bass players, at their best. They still have all the sustain you can use, and though they've lost some of their metallic brittleness, they still have calmed down, so you can get more of the punch that complements the kick drum. Unfortunately, however, this stage only lasts two or three days, after which the strings lose sustain and brightness and tend to just thud along.

Some players can do wonderful things with dead strings, particularly in fatback R&B, but they make the bass sound too dull for most other applications. One way to bring dead strings back to life is to boil them in water for about three minutes. Then, once you take them out of the pot, you dry them off with a hand towel and carefully blow-dry each of the ends, which should keep them from breaking prematurely. When you put them back on the bass, they'll sound as good as new, although they will go through each stage of aging again a bit more rapidly.

As you can see, with so many different variables involved, it's important to keep track of your strings. However, that doesn't mean just being aware of the strings you're using at the time, because if you do enough recording work, you'll have numerous sets of strings around, and each will have been subjected to a slightly different amount of wear.

For example, I might be working a session with strings that are in the second stage of wear, but the producer wants to hear a brighter sound from the instrument. That means putting on a new set of strings. But instead of just throwing the old set, which is still in an ideal condition for certain sounds, into the garbage, I'll label them and put them away, so that the next time a track calls for the punchier sound of slightly used strings, I can just put these strings back on.

Another reason I catalog strings according to age is that this makes it easier to replace a broken string in the middle of a session. For example, if I'm using a three-day-old set of strings, and one of them breaks, I can't just stick on a brand-new string, because there would be a noticeable difference every time I played a note on it. However, by cataloging my strings, I'm usually able to pull out a replacement string that is as old or as new as the rest of the set.

Another useful aspect of studio technique is muting, or "choking," the strings as you play. This can be done either with the heel of the right hand, which allows you to vary the amount of muting you give to each note in a pattern, or with a piece of foam, placed under the strings by the bridge, which mutes each note evenly.

The muting technique you chose should depend upon the style of music being played. For instance, when recording the power-type rock of Alice Cooper, I choked the strings with the heel of my right hand while attacking the notes with a fair degree of force. By doing so, I was able to create a punchy rock rhythm while avoiding the sustained rumble of unmuted strings. When recording for Kim Carnes, whose music is more open and less influenced by guitar, a track would occasionally call for the slight but even muting produced by placing foam under the strings.

Of course, the other alternative is to play with a wide-open, totally unmuted string sound, which offers an unlimited amount of sustain. You should be careful when applying this technique, however, because the recording will need to have plenty of room for the expanded bottom-end response.

The Vocal Chapter

There are a lot of professionals who think that the most complex and difficult instrument to record is the human voice. I tend to agree. In most cases the vocal is the emotional centerpiece of a song so it's important to get it right. A moving vocal performance is created by a rich language of subtle nuance, dynamics, and inflection, all shaded with the singer's unique vocal color. Even when we can't understand the lyrics, the sound of the voice can tell us the story. All this is my quiet, simple way of saying that there's a lot more to this than just sticking a mic in the general vicinity of the singer's face and punching the record button.

In this chapter we're going to explore the key elements of recording good vocals — the interactions between the recording space, singing technique, and electronic technique.

The Voice

The human voice is a marvel of engineering. With apologies to you medical students out there, I'm going to endeavor to totally oversimplify how it works. The sound of vocalization starts when we use the diaphragm, a muscle just below our ribcage, to push air up a windpipe to vibrate the vocal cords in the larynx, a little box in your throat. When we're just breathing the vocal cords are slack, which lets the air pass through a wide slit. This causes no vibration other than your normal wheezing. However, when you want to say (or sing) something, the muscles of the voice box get flexed. The tighter the vocal muscles contract the cords, the higher the pitch. We vary pitch by manipulating these muscles to "tune" the vocal cords. (By the way, in men the vocal cords are generally longer than in women, which is why men generally have lower voices.) Once the pitch is generated in the larynx it is sent to rattle around the sinus and oral cavities, where it is amplified. Then the lips, teeth, tongue, and the shape of the mouth are used to conform the sound into mostly recognizable words. Each step in this process adds its own colors to the sound and the combination of all these is what gives each of us a unique voice. This is what makes Rod Stewart sound different from Rod Steiger. The art of recording a human voice lies in the act of choosing how much of each of these tonal qualities you want to have end up on the tape.

The Recording Environment

The first thing you need to decide before you start recording is where you're going to sing. One important step to good vocals is to allow yourself as much control as possible over what reaches the microphone. This involves having as controlled a recording space as you can. The idea is to spend your time getting the *performance* on tape instead of outside noises. If the vocal isn't carefully recorded you'll waste time in the mix tapdancing around a minefield of unwanted noise problems. So should you do your vocals in a room that is live or dead, big or small? Well, for the home studio, my answer is: A small dead one is better than a big live one. Here are some things to consider before you set up the mic.

Wanted: Dead or Live

The most immediate factor in choosing a space is whether or not you're the one doing the singing, producing, and engineering. If the singer doesn't need to be the engineer then you're able to move him or her around and find an ideal combination of acoustics for the vocal. If, however, your solo album is really a *solo* album and you're the whole recording enchilada, you need to be physically close enough to the portable studio to reach the record button and sing at practically the same moment. This means that since the machine is only an arm's length away there is a danger that the mic will pick up any mechanical noise the machine might make. Since your job is to keep each track as pristine as possible, you want to minimize any extraneous noise. Therefore it is probably best that you don't record in a big, live, marble bathroom where any stray sound will bounce around the walls for a while before inevitably leaking onto your best vocal track.

The main reason why I usually feel that recording vocals in a live space is problematic is the issue of controlling ambience leakage. In a dead space, what ends up on tape is almost exclusively the voice. In a live environment you're likely to get some of the room sound on tape along with the vocal. What this means, as you know by now, is that the ambience is on the tape to stay. You can't get rid of it later should you discover that the treatment doesn't suit the song.

Aside from the problems of noise and ambience that recording in a live setting presents, there is also the simple fact that if you're belting your lungs out in a live room you will hear the sound of your voice off the walls as loud as you hear it in your headphones. It can be very disconcerting to still hear your voice careening around the room after you've stopped singing. It plays havoc with your timing.

And finally, just to put the icing on my case, so to speak, even when you think you hear a "live" vocal sound on a CD that you want to emulate, you may discover that it's not live at all. For instance, live concert vocals are frequently not live concert vocals. Sometimes a singer hits a few of what we politely call "clams" when performing, so — and I know it's supposed to be a secret — live vocals are often fixed; rerecorded in the controlled environment of the studio. Reverb is added to make the new vocal blend with the "concert" sound. In other words, sometimes even live is dead. So except for special circumstances — unless you need the ambient leakage and extra noises for atmosphere — you're better off dead.

Creating the Dead Zone

For this next little bit I'm going to assume that you are the proverbial one-man (or one-woman) band as well as the whole staff at your studio. Since you have to record yourself and you probably have the portable studio semipermanently affixed to the rest of your studio setup, it's inconvenient to move everything to an ideal vocal recording environment. Instead you'll probably want to create a sort of "vocal booth zone" that's handy for doing your vocals. This would be an area that is reasonably dead and where you can still reach the portable studio controls. What you're trying to do is to keep the sound from rebounding off the wall and getting into the mic. You don't need a ripsaw and nail gun to create a controlled space, just a little ingenuity.

Here's how you do it. Pick a spot near your setup and dedicate a hunk of wall about four feet wide and as tall as possible to get the sound-deadening treatment. There are several materials you can use to accomplish the purpose. For instance, stack some cushions against the wall from floor to ceiling, or suspend blankets from ceiling hooks, or tack some cardboard egg cartons or Sonex to an area of the wall. Now place the mic stand four or five feet away so that you are facing the treated wall. Place a tall stool to the side and between the back of the mic and the wall to act as a portable studio stand. This will help the microphone reject any noise from the portable studio while still keeping the portable studio within comfortable reaching distance. By singing toward a treated surface you eliminate any sound reflections leaking into the mic. *Voilà,* instant vocal booth.

Noise

Environmental Noise

As you already know, the enemy of good recording is noise. In the chapter "How a Tape Recorder Does What It Does" you read about signal-to-noise ratio. This is a description of the amount of electronic noise relative to the sound you want to record. But obviously noise also comes in other shapes and sizes. These are the garden-variety environmental kind; things like garbage trucks, squalling babies, rocket launches, and so on. Sometimes this background noise is so omnipresent that you become accustomed to it and even cease to hear it. I have a friend who lives near an airport and at this point in time he doesn't even notice a 747 passing twelve feet over his living room. The point is, don't take for granted that you're hearing what you think you're hearing — check it out.

When you're choosing your recording location you need to be able to identify potential problems. One way to do this is to place the mic in a likely spot and record the environment for fifteen minutes. Then listen back. What you'll hear are the sounds the mic will hear as a background to your vocals. Can you hear the refrigerator kick on? The air conditioning whistling through the vents? The sound of enthusiastic birds? Your dog scratching on the door to be let out immediately, or else? You need to be aware of all these little problems so that you can go about fixing them. The refrigerator? Unplug it while you're doing vocals. The air conditioning? Turn it off, go ahead sweat a little, suffer for your art. Birds? Cover the window or move to where there is no window. Try to record at a time of day when they're not picking up the garbage. Remember, if you can hear it the mic can too. You'll have to figure out the dog situation for yourself.

Headphone Noise: Volume and High Frequencies

For recording vocals, or anything involving an open mic, you're going to want to record with headphones. This presents another potential source of noise. While overdubbing with phones is vastly preferable to using speakers, there is still likely to be a certain amount of leakage from the headphones into the mic. This is principally due to two things: the volume at which you're listening and the amount of high-frequency information in the headphone mix.

The trick is to find a headphone mix that is exciting to sing with but controlled enough so it doesn't show up later as noise. To do this you just have to know what to listen for.

About Headphone Volume

Part of the job of singing for the microphone is having a little discipline when it comes to what you want in the headphones. Being a singer myself, I know that when I record I want to be surrounded by the music. I want the headphone mix to sound as much like a record as possible; I want it as big as Cinerama. It motivates me to really perform when the headphones sound great. So sometimes over the course of a vocal session I find myself turning up the gain to get "into it" a little better. Headphone volume is kind of like a sonic drug: as you get used to one volume it's no longer enough, you want more, more, more! Unfortunately this is a slow march toward disaster, because it is written in Murphy's law that somehow the best vocal take will also be the one where you turned the phones up just a little too much and let in the most leakage. And when it comes time to mix and you clarify everything, this leakage has a nasty way of sticking out like a hit man at a baby shower. There is a way to defeat Murphy, however.

Determining Headphone Leakage Level

1. Start with a volume in the headphones that seems comfortable.
2. Record a guide vocal.
3. Listen to a playback of the vocal track soloed (with the other instrumental tracks and all effects turned off). Note how much headphone leakage you can hear.
4. Keep trying until you find a good volume balance between inspiration and unwanted leakage.
5. Check periodically during the course of recording to make sure you maintain your reference balance.

High Frequencies in the Phones

High-frequency leakage is a little more problematic than simple loudness. The real leakage villains are often the instruments that you want to hear a lot of for pitch or rhythm. For example, in the rhythm world the high-hat is a good reference. Unfortunately, it is also one of the worst leakage offenders. If possible I try to eliminate the crash cymbal from the headphones altogether. Then I will lower the level of the high-hat so it is about two-thirds of its normal mix volume. If the drum kit is already premixed and recorded I will EQ the playback of the whole kit to diminish the high frequencies while I am recording vocals.

With regard to pitch, some singers feel that they need a lot of keyboards or guitar to find their vocal notes. Sometimes it almost gets comical. On one take the singer asks for more guitar and on the next asks for more vocal because he can't hear himself cause the guitar's too loud, and back and forth. Guitars and keyboards have a lot of high-end energy and what's really happening is that the highs of the instruments are conflicting with the high end of the vocal, causing a lack of clarity in the singer's phones.

I have found that it's actually easier to get pitch from the bass than from guitars. There are a couple of reasons for this. For one thing, the bass is usually playing a simple part centered on the fundamentals of the chords. Vocalizing to the root note and its harmonics is comfortable for most singers. Also, the bass is most often playing an octave or more below the range of the vocal performance and is thus less likely to interfere with the singer's being able to hear herself or himself. Finally, the bass is in all likelihood going to have a minimum of effects or bent notes, so a pure pitch is easier to pick out and refer to. Oh, there is one other benefit to using the bass as a reference. Listening to high-frequency instruments for an extended period of time causes ear fatigue. Simply put, after a while you just don't hear so good anymore. And what do you do when you don't hear so good? You turn it up! You try to solve a frequency-related problem with volume. What you end up with is more leakage. It may take a little practice to zero in on the bass for tonality, but it's worth it because then you can turn down the guitars and keyboards and minimize leakage.

The Headphone Mix for Vocal Overdubs

So what is the ideal headphone mix? Well, it varies with personal taste of course, and there is a good deal of trial and error, but in the home studio here's how I go about it.

1. Create a good, dry (without reverb) instrumental balance in the headphones. If your portable studio has the capability, spread the instruments out in the stereo spectrum so that they are easily distinguishable.
2. Pan the vocal being recorded to the center of the stereo spectrum.
3. Apply enough reverb or echo to the singer's voice to allow vocal notes to sound rich and full, but not so much that sustain interferes with hearing the beat clearly. Add a small amount of reverb to the instruments — except the bass.
4. Raise the level of the bass to be the dominant instrument.
5. If the bass is premixed with the drums, reduce the high-frequency EQ of these tracks on playback to help eliminate high-end leakage.

Ideally the headphone mix should be balanced in such a way that all instruments can be heard clearly but are subordinate to the bass and the track you're overdubbing. The final headphone mix should have the vocal and bass the loudest, the rhythm instruments next, and all the other instruments providing color put more in the background. Remember that in order to sing the song you don't need to hear everything you've recorded. Try to eliminate anything from the phones that is not essential to your vocal performance.

Of course there are no hard-and-fast rules for something as personal as a headphone mix and I realize that different singers like hearing different instruments for inspiration, but... it is self-defeating to crank the power guitars for excitement in the headphones only to have the singer screaming just to hear himself. The result is going to be a not-so-great vocal on tape.

Mystery Noises #2: A Cautionary Tale

I was working with a very attractive female artist and for one high-energy song we decided that it would be a good idea to record her vocal with a "live room" sound. This particular studio had a space that was mirrored and marbled and sounded like a low-rent Taj Mahal. Any sound went rocketing around the walls and ceiling, so it was perfect for what we had in mind. I stuck a mic in the middle of the room and went back to the control room to listen to her sing some practice takes. While she was singing I began to hear some odd unplanned noises. Kind of a whoosh-tap-jingle just below the level of the vocal. I walked into the room to take a look and realized she was wearing a bunch of bangle bracelets. I suggested either she take them off or clamp her hands between her knees to keep the jingling down. She took the bracelets off. We chuckled, oh my, yes. Fun in the studio. I started to walk away and then for good measure asked her to take off her hard-soled shoes to prevent tapping. She took her shoes off, we chuckled a little more, and I went back to the console. She started singing again. Everything was fine except that the peculiar whoosh-whoosh sound was still there. Puzzled, I walked back in while she was singing and discovered the problem. She was moving her legs in time to the music. She was wearing leather pants. Whoosh-whoosh. What did I do? You guessed it: I suggested she sit on a stool. The moral of the story is don't wear anything you don't want recorded.

Another little habit to break — don't hum along with the guitar solo. Unless you're singing be quiet, breathe quietly, don't tap or grunt or slap your thighs in time. Don't say anything. This is particularly true of background singers, who often seem to feel that the best time to discuss a part is just before they're about to sing.

Singing Technique

This little section is not meant to be a tutorial on vocal technique. But I think there are a few little things that can make your vocal recording life a mite easier. By now you know that singing for the studio microphone exposes the vocal in microscopic detail. Things that you wouldn't notice in a million years on stage show up on tape like major blemishes. The principal culprits are pitch problems, vocal quality, and dynamic problems. There are some slightly quirky things you can do to help.

Problem: The singer goes flat

Solution: Have the singer smile on the offending note. This ain't a happy-talk thing, it is actually manipulating the mechanics of sound production. A smile tends to make the facial muscles and oral cavity squeeze the note slightly sharper. If the singer is going flat during a held note, smile longer.

Problem: The singer goes sharp

Solution: Have the singer open their mouth a little more on the note. Often a singer knows there's a difficult note coming up. They get so wound up psychologically that they overshoot the mark. Kind of like slam-dunking into the second balcony — impressive but wrong. Opening the mouth a little more will help to keep the singer from squeezing the note too hard and going sharp.

Problem: The vocal sounds unpleasantly edgy 1

Solution: Turn the head slightly sideways to the mic on the offending notes. This kind of sound happens for several reasons. The singer may be straining for a note or singing too hard. What's happening may be that on particular notes certain frequencies in the voice are actually distorting the microphone. Or perhaps the overtone series in the singer's voice is unpleasantly accentuated. By turning the head slightly, the sound pressure level will be lessened at the capsule of the microphone.

Problem: The vocal sounds unpleasantly edgy 2

Solution: Open the mouth a little more on the vowel *E*. *E*s are the usual culprit in the "needle through the ear" vocal sound. By opening the mouth a little more the sound becomes more rounded.

Problem: The vocal sounds unpleasantly edgy 3

Solution: Stand up straight and sing. Believe it or not, straight posture makes it a whole lot easier to sing. The body doesn't need to fight itself to get air through the passageways, and the diaphragm muscles are freer to do their job. Standing up straight can literally add whole tones to usable singing range as well as increase dynamic control.

Problem: Loud thumps on certain syllables (popping *P*s 1)

Solution: Turn the head slightly sideways on the offending syllable. This is the dreaded *P* pop. A pop is caused by a blast of air hitting the microphone capsule as a by-product of pronouncing a sound. For all intents and purposes you might as well hit the mic with your forehead. One answer might be to never sing a song with the letter *P* in it. But even that won't get it, because *WH* and *B* and other syllables will also whack your woofers. The experienced singer will do one of two things when coming to a dangerous letter: either deliberately de-emphasize the pronounciation (difficult), or turn the head momentarily so the exhalation of air doesn't hit the microphone capsule directly.

Problem: Loud thumps on certain syllables (popping *P*s 2)

Solution: Get a pop filter. This is a simple device that is placed between the sound source and the microphone. Its purpose is to disperse any concentrated blast of air before it hits the microphone capsule. There are a variety of pop filters available for microphones. Some are foam balls that you put on the end of the mic like a hat. Personally I prefer another type that is a screen made of thin material suspended in front of the microphone. My feeling is that there should be as little obstruction as possible between a sound source and the mic capsule. Some of the foam balls are a little too thick for my taste. I want to eliminate pops, not smother the sound. At the end of this chapter there is a recipe on how to make your own pop filter for about zero cents, zip, nada.

Problem: The vocal sounds muddy (unclear)
Solution: Have the singer back off the mic. In the first part of this book we talked about proximity effect, which can appear as a buildup of low end that obscures the upper frequencies. This is a common problem when recording vocals. The reason is that the singer gets too close to the mic when recording. This may be because he or she 1) is used to practically eating the mic for live gigs, 2) can't hear enough of the vocal in the phones, or 3) gets to a soft passage and thinks that no one will hear unless the mic is against the tonsils.

Here are some recommended distances for singing into a mic to help with muddiness.

Condenser: Stay about eight to ten inches away the mic.
Dynamic: Stay one or two inches away from the mic.

By the way, if the vocal sounds too thin it may be because the singer isn't close enough. Go ahead, experiment. Mic distance may very well vary slightly from song to song depending on vocal register and power of the vocal.

Equalizing the Vocal

To think of the human voice as an instrument is useful as far as it goes, but the truth is that the instant you include words in the melodic construction you get a whole different animal from other instruments. The inclusion of words creates some interesting recording problems that you wouldn't have if the singer was just singing "la la la." Obviously real words are different from one to the next. The thing that makes them different of course is the way they sound. Unlike other instruments that sound essentially the same from note to note, the human voice can sound radically different depending on what syllable is being sung. The equalization of a vocal has to be constructed so as to sound good when *any* syllable is sung.

When recording vocals I'm mindful of three distinct ranges of frequencies and the balance between them. As with all instruments, the high frequencies of the vocal are largely responsible for timbre and the characteristics that distinguish one voice from another. The midrange is responsible for the pronounciation of consonants that have an attack —the letter *T* for instance. The lower frequencies produce what we perceive as tone, body, and warmth. The right combination of these elements is what good vocal recording is all about. Imbalance can result in a lack of clarity or wimpiness or unpleasant harshness, any of which can ruin all the hard work you put in on the other elements of the song. Perhaps for the vocal more than any other sound the key words are *EQ balance* between the frequencies.

The Upper Frequencies

For the purposes of this entry I'm going to define the upper range as those frequencies that lie between 3 K and 12 K. This, as I said, is where individuality and vocal distinctiveness live. First of all, a word of caution: don't confuse pitch with EQ range. The uniqueness of even a bass voice is determined by the upper harmonic range of frequencies. Low notes don't exempt the voice from high frequencies. As a listening exercise put on some Rod Stewart and try to pick out the higher frequencies. They are in fact what gives Rod that distinct vocal sound, and they are clearly audible even when he's singing lowish (not that he sings all that low). His trademark raspy quality is the sound of nontone (air pushed across his vocal cords) and is accentuated by boosting the EQ somewhere around 10 K. In other words, that rasp is a very high-frequency component of a low note. With Men at Work's Colin Hay the same area of frequencies was accentuated but the result was a completely different sound. So low pitch or not, vocal quality is up in the uppers.

This frequency range is also the neighborhood of lyric intelligibility. Clarity of words is often greatly enhanced by accentuating around 10 K. It is here that we sound the subtle stuff that makes syllables crisp and the breathy quality that lends intimacy to a vocal. Okay, cool, so let's boost the heck out of 10 K and everyone will sound great. Unfortunately it's just not quite that easy. Here's why. When you accentuate one set of frequencies another set recedes into the background. If all we did was boost 10 K the voice would sound thin because the highs would overwhelm the lower-frequency elements.

Another problem with accenting the highs too much is the hiss of over-sibilance. Sibilance is the sound of the letter *S*. The range where the letter *S* is produced is about 7 K. You have to be very careful when you boost 10 K that you're not inadvertently also boosting 7 K. If you hear something that sounds like steam escaping from a radiator every time the singer says "Susie" you need to back off the high-end EQ.

There is another favorite vocal frequency boost that is a double-edged sword. As you already know from the Effects chapter, one way to retain presence is the absence of ambience. There is another way to fool the ear into thinking the vocal is very present. When someone whispers they sound very close. The frequency range that comprises a whisper is around 5 to 7 K. If you boost this range you will give the voice the impression of closeness. While 5 K is a very good and frequently used vocal enhancer, you have to be careful to check for edginess and excessive sibilance and not overdo it.

The Midrange Frequencies

This is a region that I define as between 1 K and 3 K. It is a critical area because it's where the attack of a syllable lives. It is these frequencies that give clarity to the enunciation of words. When you pronounce certain sounds you use your tongue to create a transient much like a stick hitting a snare drum. That's how we sound the letter *T* for instance. Go ahead, pronounce a *T* and check out what your mouth is doing. Your tongue is hitting the back of your teeth as it begins to form the letter. There is very little tone to a transient consonant. It is as instantaneous as a handclap. In order to accentuate a transient this 1 to 3 K range is where you would boost. Terrific, no problem. Unfortunately, like most things in the recording world, understanding the tradeoff is the essence of success. The area that you are boosting for lyric clarity is also an area of the vocal that can result in some very unpleasant sounds. In fact, I've found that when the vocal is cutting my ears to shreds the offending frequencies are likely to be somewhere around this range.

There is a little trick to isolating the midrange to listen for problems. Face the speakers and cup your hands just behind your ears. You will in effect eliminate lows and highs, creating your very own midrange resonator. You may be in for a shock. Listen to each word for problem syllables, then reduce the amount of mid boost so that the clarity is accomplished but the vocal doesn't sound harsh.

The Low Frequencies

The richness of a voice is determined by the emphasis placed on the low midrange. These frequencies of the voice are really where the melodic center of the performance lies. When talking about a vocal I define this as the area between 100 Hz and 1 K (sound in this region is frequently referred to as "warmth"). The body of the male human voice is around 250 to 500 Hz. A female voice is a little higher. What I'm referring to here is the true pitch of the voice, the foundation upon which all the overtones and harmonics are built.

When treated carefully these low midrange frequencies lend body not just to the vocal but also to the whole track. However, they can be a little tricky to deal with. They fill a lot of musical space, they can really muddy the track if you're not careful, and they can appear to drag the tempo.

Bigger May Not Be Better: Space

Musical space, as I use the term, was defined earlier as the space an instrument occupies in the stereo spectrum. This refers to, among other things, the apparent "size" of the instrument. This size is created by the amount of low-end energy applied to the sound. Ever since we were cave people we have instinctively interpreted a low rumble as, "Uh-oh, run away! Something really big is coming!" Our ancestors' psychoacoustic space was easily filled by low sound. To this day we interpret low frequencies as powerful (think of thunder for instance). But with the power comes volume (I don't mean loudness but bigness). And this means that where the vocal is concerned the tradeoff goes like this: Boost the lows on the voice and you gain power but take up a lot of room. Be prepared to lose musical space for other instruments in the mix.

Big Muddy: Clarity

Because the low-end frequencies are in the form of very long waves it takes a long time to for them to resolve, and this can blur the transition from one note to the next. In moderation this is what gives the vocal its continuity and smoothness. But when overdone the vocal becomes muddy and indistinct. Sometimes the voice will mix with other low-end instruments and sound unclear. What's happening is that the low end is masking definition. With regard to a vocal, the tradeoff goes like this: Boost the lows and gain warmth but lose clarity.

Too Big Too Slow: Tempo

The time that low-end frequencies take to resolve can also interfere with the tempo of the song. Bottom end gives the impression of ponderous weight. Because of this it generally is not a good idea to slather too much low end on a vocal when the song is rocketing along. It's like lugging a sonic boulder around — it's hard to keep up. Often simply boosting the low in a vocal can make the singer appear to be singing behind the beat.

So how do you know when to boost the low end of a vocal? Generally speaking, the slower the tempo, the sparser the instrumentation, and the more distinct the enunciation of the voice, the more lows you can add. The amount of low end you can apply is also related to the sound of the singer's voice. The higher the vocal pitch, the more lows will be appropriate. Remember, the low end of the voice is what ties notes together; boost to help reduce choppiness, cut to help reduce mud.

A Final Note on Vocal EQ

The way to go about EQing is to be continually aware of the balance between the frequencies. Unfortunately there is no easy EQ formula. You find the right balance by sculpting the EQ a little bit here, a little bit there.

Using Effects on the Vocal

I covered the uses of signal-processing gear earlier, but I think vocals present a special case and warrant some additional words. In "The Mixdown Chapter" there is a discussion about the front-to-back element in stereo space. It is ambience that creates the depth of the imaginary room that contains all the instruments. The amount of ambience you add determines how far into that room the instrument is placed. Another way to look at it is to say that ambience tells the listener how far away something is from him. There is an important by-product of this depth perception: how far away something is also determines how much attention the listener pays to it. As you'll see in "The Mixdown Chapter," this perception is vitally important to a successful mix.

That being said, I normally would suggest that you shouldn't record ambient effects on the same track with the instrument, particularly the vocal. It's dangerous. The reason, as I've said elsewhere, is that once you've recorded a reverb or echo with the track you can't unrecord it without redoing the whole track. If the ambient effect you've created doesn't work in the mix then you got big trouble. However, the limitations of the portable studio and the realities of the process of bouncing tracks sometimes make it necessary to apply effects to the vocal track before the final mix. Here are some guidelines that will help keep you safe from unfixable mistakes. (First, go back and read "The Effects Chapter" again. Make sure you're clear on the various parameters of the effects you're about to use.)

For the most part you'll be using one (or a combination) of three signal treatments for vocals. The **straight reverb**, the **delayed reverb**, and/or the **echo**.

Straight Vocal Reverb

I'm using the term **straight reverb** to mean that the vocal directly triggers the reverb without any processing interruption. This is the simplest type of reverb setup. The function of any reverb is to act as a sort of sonic glue that holds the walls of the musical space together. When ambient effects are applied to the vocal the object is to make the singer sound like he/she's singing in the same room as the rest of the band, and make the vocal notes also to sound connected to one another. If you listen to a vocal "dry" (without reverb) the notes and phrases seem to be choppy, lacking sustain and melodic continuity. Applying reverb smooths out the gaps between where one note ends and the next begins. However, just as when applying EQ, achieving the best result is a matter of balance. If you crank the reverb too much, the vocal sounds like it's coming from the bottom of a well. Not enough and the vocal is uncomfortably separated from the music, like someone yelling in your ear.

Here are some other things to think about when applying straight reverb to a vocal. Reverb has an impact on the intelligibility of the vocal. An overabundance of reverb and the words are tumbling all over one another, making them hard to understand. And last but not least is how reverb relates to a song's tempo. This is chiefly a function of the decay time. Set the decay time too long and the reverb doesn't die out soon enough, making the rhythm of the vocal mushy and indistinct.

Tips on Using Straight Reverb

When you have to record reverb with the vocal:

- Be conservative. Add a little less than you add to the other instruments so that the vocal will remain in the front of the stereo spectrum.

- Make sure that you can understand the lyrics clearly. No matter how good the reverb on the vocal sounds, if the audience has to strain to understand the singer, it's too much.

- Check the tempo with the decay time of the reverb. For ballads and slower songs a decay around 2.5 to 3 seconds is appropriate. For faster songs the decay time should be shorter. There is no formula — it is a matter of ear — but if the vocal seems to drag, try shortening the reverb decay time.

Delayed Vocal Reverb

The delayed reverb has a user-defined "interrupt" between when the source sound begins and when it is sent to the reverb. You can control the size of this gap to allow for a brief instant of dry clarity before the reverb is triggered.

This is my preference for vocals. It's especially useful if you have to commit to recording the reverb. The delay allows the vocal to be heard clearly before the reverb kicks in. The reverb is then used primarily to fatten up and sustain the note. This type of treatment is more forgiving if you make a mistake when recording it with the vocal. The vocal will always have some presence because for a matter of milliseconds it is heard dry, which is as upfront as you can get. The drawback is that you have to have the signal-processing capability to do it (see "The Effects Chapter" or "The Recipe section").

Tips on Using a Delayed Reverb

- Set the delay time of the gap so that the reverb kicks in at a logical point related to the tempo, usually an eighth or a quarter of a beat after the note is struck. Make sure that your delay time doesn't interfere with other rhythm instruments.

- When you set the volume of reverb remember that in this case the ambience is being treated like an instrument with a definite need for musical space. You need to be sure you have enough room in the track for the delayed reverb to be heard, but not so much that other instruments get crowded out.

Echo (echo echo...)

Ever since I first heard Led Zeppelin, one of my favorite sounds is the **echo or slap echo**. I used it on the Men at Work albums, and I feel Colin's unique vocal sound combined with the echo treatment created a memorable musical atmosphere. A carefully applied echo can add an arresting dramatic element to a vocal. In other circumstances it's also particularly useful for strengthening a less than stellar vocal performance, disguising a multitude of sins.

Tips on Using a Repeat Echo

- Use a single repeat to create a rockabilly vocal sound. Turn the echo feedback control very low until only one repeat can be heard.

- Use repeat echo to lengthen a sound by making the repeats audible. Turn the feedback control up until the repeats die out at the desired point.

- Set the repeat echo in quarter-note or half-note triplets (see "The Effects Chapter") so the repeats don't get lost by landing on a beat. For example, if the snare drum is struck at the same time as the repeat, the echo will be covered by the snare.

COLIN HAY ON VOCALS

I asked Colin Hay, lead singer of Men at Work and a brilliant solo artist, to fax me a few words to share with you on the process of being a spontaneous singer when you have to push buttons and remember overdub points.

I believe that finding one's voice either literally or metaphorically is one of life's great challenges. It is also essentially joyful.

It is one thing to stand atop a hill, wind in the hair and bursting into song; it is another, however, to sing freely amidst a sea of wires and blinking machines. (They could be "winking" at you.) Yet essentially it is the same thing. It is simply the environment that differs.

Let us dive straight in and set up a scenario. The bed tracks are down, an acoustic guitar and the somewhat annoying keyboard line is there which you'll get rid of later. You're alone in your recording room and you feel like singing. By the way, I'm assuming you know your way around your equipment, otherwise you'll get upset and probably start drinking. I feel the ideal situation is to minimize the degree to which you have to think about what you're doing. It is important therefore to make sure you are not going to go into distortion when you let fly and you can comfortably reach your punch in/punch out button. I find a foot pedal to be the most satisfactory. I also like to stand up when I sing as it is less restricting and you can clutch various parts of your body as you get more excited. In other words, set up your environment so that the technology enhances yet does not encroach on your freedom.

So, here we are, the mic is set up, the machines are bracing themselves in anticipation, the track is good, you sort of know the words but you feel a bit tense. So here's what you would do: Stay in the room, sit quietly for about ten minutes and don't think about anything; most importantly, don't do anything. After a few minutes you'll feel calmer; yes you'll feel almost ready, and you know what they say, don't you? That the best things you do in your life you do when you're almost ready.

Virtually yours,
COLIN HAY

Getting Down to It: Recording the Vocal

After you've gotten your EQ happening and your reverb set up, the time has come to get the vocal on tape. In my opinion, the foremost consideration in successful vocals is controlling the dynamics. The object is to have every syllable clearly audible yet still in balance with the rest of the music. This can be a little tricky. The success of a vocal relies on a combination of production skill and electronic savvy.

Putting On the Producer's Hat

Here's a common scenario: you get to the mix and realize that the only way to hear the vocal is to keep turning it up. But then it sounds unnatural and separate from the band, so you turn up the guitar a little and now you can't hear the vocal so you turn the vocal up a little and then you can't hear the... how come?

Without going into a long discussion about the aesthetic techniques of record production, I will say that a big part of the producer's job is to make sure that there is room for the vocal amongst all the music in the track. In a song (as opposed to an instrumental) the vocal is the center of the universe; all those great guitar, keyboard, and bassoon parts exist to support it. So make sure to keep that in mind when you're recording. Reserve cool instrumental parts for places in the music where the vocal isn't. Otherwise, at mixdown time you will definitely be pulling your hair out as you realize that the guitar and the vocal can't occupy the same space. Principle Number One is to "lay" for the vocal. If you leave room you won't be fighting a battle with vocal dynamics.

That being said, let's talk about recording vocal dynamics.

Putting On the Engineer's Hat

As usual, nothing is quite as simple as it seems. The electronic part of recording vocals is no exception. A well-recorded signal is a balancing act between the input to the console, the processing that you do to color and shape the sound, and the output of the signal from the console to the tape. A vocal is just a little more so, a more delicate operation. You have to guard against distortion when the signal comes in and unnatural processing — like over-equalizing, compression, and distortion — when the signal goes to tape.

The Input

When you are bringing the signal into the console from the microphone you need to be aware of any distortion occurring from the miking process. Mic and mic preamp distortion are usually pretty easy to spot. They usually occur when the singer gets to the hard notes. Then you hear an awful blast of buzzy sound that's the aural equivalent of a dentist drilling a nerve. When you hear that sound it means that either the mic is overloaded (usually only happens with a sensitive condenser mic) or more likely you need to turn down the trim on the mic preamp. So what's the big deal — when it happens you'll turn it down, right? Well sometimes the distortion can sneak through without it being so obvious. This usually happens when the singer is going for it but at the same time the guitar is hammering a power chord. What happens is that the distortion buzz on the vocal gets masked by the upper midrange of the guitar. So you go on with your life thinking everything's great until you get to the mix and notice that some of the vocal sounds downright unpleasant. A word to the wise: As soon as you get one complete take of the vocal on tape play it back without accompaniment and listen for trouble spots. It's a drag to have a great lead vocal performance ruined by preventable distortion.

The vocal is arguably the most dynamically erratic instrument there is. Singers will go from a whisper to a scream in the blink of a nanoweber and this can play havoc with your carefully set record levels. The object is to get the vocal on tape consistently within a 6 dB range or so. For example, if you set up the vocal levels to reflect a soft part of the vocal you will probably end up in distortion when the singer cuts loose on the louder parts. If you set the level so the loud parts don't distort then the soft parts may end up inaudible. If it sounds like a major problem, that's because it is. Fortunately there are a couple of solutions.

Compression and Limiting

Compression and limiting used with a vocal allow the track to stay at a consistent level on tape no matter how hard or soft the singer is singing. The obvious advantage is that come mix time the vocal can remain the constant centerpiece around which the rest of the track is built. There are a couple of ways to achieve dynamic control: **hand limiting**, and using an **electronic compressor/limiter**.

Hand Limiting

You already know what an electronic compressor/limiter does (see "The Effects Chapter") but there is another type of limiting that is actually preferable for recording vocals. This is called hand limiting and is about as low-tech as you can get. What it means is that the engineer manually raises and lowers the gain of the output signal (fader) as the vocal is being recorded to keep a balance between audibility and dynamic control. In other words, the engineer "rides" the faders up and down with his hand.

Here's how it works. The engineer gets to know the vocal and during a period of rehearsal learns the dynamics the singer wishes to put in. The job is to protect the track from distortion at one extreme and muddiness at the other. During the actual taping the engineer will lower the fader when the vocal is too loud and raise it for softer passages, keeping the recorded vocal track inside a range of a few decibels. This is often done phrase by phrase. The recordist gets to know where trouble spots are and can dip or raise them in level as they're happening and return to the base level in a natural-sounding way. In effect the engineer is performing with the singer.

There are a couple of reasons why I prefer hand limiting to electronic compression. First, there is greater control, so vocal nuance is better captured. Second, the fewer the electronics the quieter the signal. An electronic compressor will definitely add noise and so great care has to be taken in setting the compressor, With hand limiting there is no additional electronic noise.

You've probably spotted the major problem with hand limiting in the portable studio environment: it's practically impossible if you're the one doing the engineering and trying to sing at the same time. It will probably cause a heck of a left brain–right brain collision. So what to do?

Electronic Compression

You already know all about compressors, but there are some special-case factoids that you need to keep in mind for vocals. The more a compressor has to work, the worse it's going to sound. Therefore it's best to set the threshold so that the compressor is activated as little as possible. You want most of the signal to get through the compressor and have it activated only by unacceptable dynamic surges in the vocal performance. The compressor is trying to respond to dynamic changes by raising the soft bits and lowering the loud bits. The more frequently it has to do this, the more audible the sound of the compressor itself will be. Experience will tell you when this is happening. Where vocals are concerned the idea is to have the compressor be "transparent"; that is, not to hear it at all. If you're trying to solve a dynamics problem with radical settings, the compressor will start to "pump" each time it's activated. Here's what I mean. Say you set the compressor at a 20:1 ratio with a low threshold. When the compressor is activated by a loud signal it slams the sound, allowing only 1 dB of sound increase for every 20 dB of signal gain. This brings the apparent level of the noise floor up. (Picture a car getting flattened at a wrecking yard — the floor pan ends up at almost the same height as the roof.) When the compressor lets go of the note the noise floor returns to normal and the result is a sort of "waves crashing on the beach" sound each time the compressor cycles.

Another thing that happens when the compression ratio is too severe is that the sound can become muddy. This happens because the frequency structure of the sound is compressed too, thereby bringing out some characteristics that might not be desirable. For instance, the lows may come up and the sparkle of the voice may be diminished. Logically you would think that this can be overcome by equalizing the vocal — boosting the highs, for instance. Well, yes and no. Remember that the equalizer is really just a frequency-selective volume control. When you boost a frequency, you're making it louder. What happens when you send a louder signal to the compressor? It compresses more. By EQing and sending more high end all you're doing is making the compressor work harder.

One way around this is to use an equalizer after the sound has gone through the compressor to reattain some of the frequencies lost in the compression process (see "The Recipe Section").

COMPRESSOR RECIPE FOR VOCALS

1. Set the threshold control so that only the the loudest notes activate the compressor. The gain reduction when the compressor is active should be no more than 3 dB.
2. Set the attack control to fast.
3. Set the release control to medium slow by ear. Each note should decay naturally.
4. Set the compression ratio at 4:1.
5. Send enough output level out of the compressor to achieve a good signal-to-noise ratio.

The Output

The final consideration in recording is the actual level of vocal signal to tape. Here's where the proof is in the pudding. If all goes well and you've been able to correctly balance the input, EQ, and compression, the vocal should record in about a 6dB range. The vocal should not exceed +3 dB at any point, because you don't want to lose transient response or go into tape compression by hitting the tape too hard.

USING A CONDENSER WITH YOUR PORTABLE STUDIO RECIPE

Application: For higher quality recording
Requirements: Direct box, condenser mic, power supply for mic

1. Place microphone on stand.
2. Plug microphone into power supply. (Note: Some condensers have internal batteries and do not require external power.)
3. Plug XLR connector from microphone into the XLR connector of the direct box.
4. Plug a ¼″ phono cable from the output of the direct box into a channel of the portable studio.
5. Use trim pots to bring mic input to desired level. (Remember, a condenser is more sensitive than a dynamic; adjust your levels accordingly.)
6. Proceed with recording as usual.

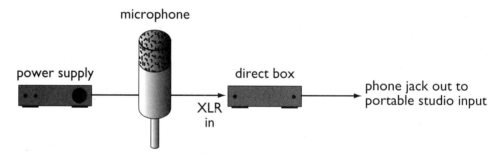

VOCAL EQ RECIPE

- In general, EQ vocals as gently as possible.
- If the singer's high notes are piercing:
      Cut at 900 Hz for male vocalist.
      Cut at 3 K for female vocalist.
- If there is too much sibilance ("ssss"), cut at 7 K.
- Boost at 10 K to add sparkle and air.
- Boost at 5 K for presence.
- Boost at 250–500 Hz for body.
- Cut at 200 Hz to clean up muddiness or proximity effects.

COAT HANGER POP FILTER RECIPE

Application: Placed between the singer and the mic, it disperses blasts of air that cause pops.

Requirements: Coat hanger, scissors, pantyhose (color optional)

1. Straighten out a coat hanger, then bend it into a circle approximately eight inches in diameter.
2. Twist wire to close circle, leaving the two ends of the wire sticking straight out.
3. Cut the foot off of a pair of pantyhose.
4. Pull the nylon over the coat-hanger circle.
5. Twist the ends of the wire around the microphone stand.
6. Position the pop filter about one to two inches from the capsule of the mic.

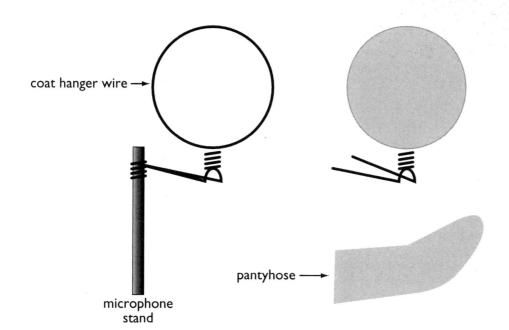

coat hanger wire →

microphone stand

pantyhose →

Keyboards Part 1: Recording the Piano

I am a keyboard player. I started my career as a singer/songwriter accompanying myself on piano. I spent half my early touring days lugging and moving and tuning and miking pianos, most of the time fervently wishing I was a flute player. As synths became more sophisticated and accessible I began to rely on them to supply a great deal of the color in my recording work. I love really good keyboard sounds. In this chapter I'm going to disuss how you can go about getting them.

Keys to the Keys

There are a number of characteristics inherent in keyboards that present some recording challenges. For one thing, you can play separate notes with all ten fingers (and one with your nose for that matter). For those who have more fingers than sense, or more enthusiasm than skill, this can be a real chunk of sound to have to manage on tape. Another feature of the keyboard species is the rich variety of sounds available. This is of course true of the synthesizer, but it is also true of the acoustic piano with the complex overtones it generates. Also, a keyboard usually has a wide capability for sustain from one note event to another. Preceding notes can be made to hang over through the playing of an entire passage, thus further complicating the overtone picture.

In this chapter I will discuss how to mic and record an acoustic piano as either a stereo or a mono instrument. In the next chapter I will deal with synthesizers and establish a set of guidelines for recording various shades in the spectrum of synthesizer sounds.

The Acoustic Piano

When I was a kid I once saw a piano-smashing contest on TV. Apparently, the object was to break the piano up into little pieces with a sledgehammer and pass the bits through a car window. The team with the best time won. All this took place to the cheers of a few dozen alchohol-powered onlookers. I don't know why I just thought of that, except to say that there are some things that you can do with a piano that just don't work as well with a synth. One of those things is that for my money a piano still makes the best piano sound.

Piano Mechanics and Recording

When you push down on a piano key, the sound of the piano is produced by a hammer (usually covered in felt) striking a tuned string. This sound resonates through a wooden soundboard that amplifies it and directs it out into the room. The soundboard functions in much the same way as an acoustic guitar body. The sound bounces around and picks up much of its tonality from the contained airspace and the resonance of the wood itself. This makes the piano somewhat unusual in that it is an instrument that is part percussion and part big acoustic guitar, creating some interesting EQ and miking challenges.

The complex tonality of the piano is a function of its mechanics and construction, and the decisions that you make about mic placement and EQ will emphasize or diminish different characteristics of the particular instrument you're recording and the environment it's in.

Deciding on the Piano Environment

The "Size" of the Piano

When I'm referring here to the "size" of the piano I'm not talking about whether it's a studio upright or a Yamaha grand but rather the amount of musical space it takes up in the recording. Perhaps more than with any other instrument the treatment of space is critical in the recording of a piano. You need to be very clear with regard to the placement of the piano in the final mix. As I noted above, a piano can take up a lot of musical room. You have to decide how much is warranted based on the role the piano occupies. For example, a classical piano piece will have the piano occupying center stage in terms of musical space, whereas a rock piano may be more of a rhythm instrument placed in an ensemble setting. In either case, the recordist has to decide on the appropriate placement and which techniques will best serve the purpose.

The Piano Player

Before we get to the specifics of piano recording I need to mention a few things about the piano player. As in the case of the vocal, performing technique is particularly important to success when recording piano. I'm not talking about piano-teacher technique *per se* — fingers up, hands flat, *etc.* — but about playing piano for recording. Being aware of techniques unique to recording can head off some potential headaches.

There are certain habits that players often develop for live performance that are not really suitable for recording. The two most common concerns are the sustain pedal and the temptation to play every note in a chord (particularly if you wrote the song and are used to accompanying your solo vocal.... Who, me?)

The Pedal

When you strike a note on the piano, a piece of felt called a damper is lifted as the hammer hits the string. This allows the note to ring for as long as you have your finger on the key. When you take the pressure off the key the damper returns to its normal position. This stops the vibration and deadens the note. The sustain pedal works by lifting all of the dampers, allowing the strings to ring even after you've let go of the key.

The sustain pedal on a piano is a great ally when you're playing live. If you're pounding away trying to be heard over the rest of the band, the pedal helps greatly with expression. The problem is, as I have noted, recording ain't live. The mic hears with acute clarity, sometimes more than you'd like it to. Where the sustain pedal is concerned, the amount of sustain that sounded just right for playing in a club or accompanying your solo vocal may very well sound like mud when recorded. When one note hangs over into another it can present some recording problems.

If we go back to our basics of sound you'll remember that overtones make up the timbre of a sound. When you hold down the sustain pedal, not only are the fundamental pitches of the notes carried over, but the harmonic overtone series of each note is drawn out as well. These upper harmonics are bouncing around clashing with one another, canceling each other out, and after a few sustained notes generally sounding unrelated to the music you're trying to make. In a live situation that doesn't seem to be a problem — the overtones seem to decay pretty quickly. In reality this is simply because your ear is somewhat removed from the sound so only the louder harmonics reach you. But if you were to stick your ear in the soundhole you'd be amazed at how much stuff keeps rattling around. Well of course that's exactly what's happening with the mic; you are sticking the recorder's ear right into the piano. So what comes out of the speakers can sound pretty dense.

I mention (or should I say belabor) this because sustain abuse is one of the less obvious yet very common causes of muddy piano recordings. It's something that's usually not immediately apparent unless you solo the piano, but it affects not only the piano but also the clarity of other instruments. Remember, the microphone reports the harmonics of the ringing notes. The overtones from the sustaining piano mingle and clash with the overtones of the other instruments. This is a subtle event often hidden in the track. But come mix time you'll have to battle to get the clarity you know should be there.

So as a rule of thumb, when you're recording try not to use the sustain pedal at all unless the piano is exposed or is the solo instrument. The one exception might be at the end of a song or some other place where you want the notes to ring over.

For piano players this can be a hard habit to break. One thing that helps is to have the player monitor some reverb in the headphones when recording to augment the sustain of the sound.

I Can't Be Out of Notes! I've Still Got Fingers Left!

As Ray Charles once said, "It isn't the notes you play that count, it's the ones you don't." This is by way of pointing out that a frequent minor sin of the keyboard player is playing too many notes, particularly when filling in a chord. Sometimes the most effective piano parts are those that are simple lines or two-note chords. Obviously, the way you approach a piano part is related to the type of song you're playing. For the moment I'm going to leave aside the solo ballad or jazz piece and talk about the piano in an ensemble role.

Just Another Piece of the Band

If you are a singer/songwriter/keyboardist chances are you are used to writing in isolation. You design a keyboard part that supports the melody, creates a groove, and inspires you. You also probably require the keyboard part to at least hint at every part every other instrument is going to play in the final version of the song. So you try to make the accompaniment as full as possible. For the process of writing you are a one-man band, and that's good thing. But what happens when it comes time to record? There isn't room for all those notes if you intend to add any other instruments.

The most frequent culprit in creating the recording traffic jam is the bottom end. The bottom end of a piano is the wandering semi on the highway of music: It takes up a lot of room, and it's hard to get by. From years of playing, we keyboard folks are in the habit of adding bass notes to the chords we play. It usually gives the chord a root note to rest on. The problem is that when you're recording you will have other instruments to fill that supporting role — like the bass, for instance (or a tuba, if you're so inclined).

Having a lot of bottom-end energy coming from the keyboard can really muddy the waters. You have less control over the amount of bottom because it's part of the overall keyboard part, so lowering the piano bottom in the mix means lowering the entire piano part. So when it comes to ensemble playing, let the bass do its job by you playing as little bass keyboard as possible.

I State My Case Redundantly

Now imagine what happens when you add a heavy bottom-end part with a sustain pedal. You get a sound so thick you have to cut it with a cleaver. What you're faced with come mix time is two choices: fighting the piano, or lowering its level to near extinction.

The Recording Environment for the Piano

Different types of music call for different types of ambient treatment of the piano. In some cases you want the ambient sound of the room in with the piano sound, while in others you want to make the piano very present by excluding the sound of any acoustic space. These ambient ingredients can be controlled by a combination of piano placement, miking technique, and equalization. A crucial thing to keep in mind is that combining the natural room sound with the instrument when recording is in effect adding reverb to the track. You have to be careful not to overdo it. Too much of the room sound will make the piano appear distant and also will limit your ability to use other reverbs and still retain presence.

To Room or Not to Room

Deciding how much "room" to add to the piano sound is a function of how much musical space you want to fill up. The more important the nuances of the piano, the more space it occupies, and that leaves less space for other instruments. To use yet another metaphor, picture a good bar on a weekend night. In order to be heard over the drunken throng you pretty much have to scream. This is okay and in fact quite effective when conveying a message like, "Hey buddy, your pants are on fire!" You don't need subtlety, screaming gets the point across. But if you want to convey another message, like, "Hey baby, you look really nifty, will you be my special friend?" then sonic competition is not a good thing. You want to be in a nice quiet corner where there is limited sonic competition and all the subtleties of your voice can go into maximum seduction mode. Too many nuances are lost in a room full of competing sounds. This is all by way of saying that if a piano sound is to be detail-rich and very "roomy" you will have to provide the space and subordinate other instruments in order to be able to hear it.

If you're recording a classical or jazz piece or if the piano is to be the central focus of vocal accompaniment you might want to include some of the room sound to give the piano some extra size, because the other instruments will be subordinate. Adding a room sound is a function of the interaction between the mic and the sound of the environment the piano is sitting in. If you are going to include the sound of the ambience of the piano you have to consider it to be as much a part of the piano sound as the hammer and strings. In other words, the environment you include in the piano sound has to be suited to the mood you're trying to achieve. This means that you have to be aware of the sound of the room. To do this you can use the clap test to determine what kind of space the microphone will hear and how much of it to include in the recorded piano sound.

For instance, if you are doing a sensitive quiet ballad, a hard bright surface such as a tile floor might not be what you're looking for to reinforce the mood. In that case you might want to deaden the space a little by strategically scattering sound-absorbing materials around.

The reverse may also be true. If you want to add some bright accents to the piano sound you might find that a roomful of furniture and drapes doesn't give you what you want. You can help remedy this by adding some reflective panels to create artificial "walls."

In other cases you may not want the sound of the room to leak into the microphones at all. This can be accomplished with close baffling.

Just a mention — if you don't want to alter the room you can always move the piano.

A Guide to Space

Here are some guidelines for including room sound with the piano sound. Since every song and piano is different and I've never been to your house, these are necessarily very general. With a little practice you'll be able to hear how well your environment integrates with your needs.

- For uptempo rock and roll, very little or no room sound.

- For midtempo rock or dance music, no room sound.

- For uptempo solo vocal accompaniment, limited bright room.

- For mid to ballad tempo, some warm room.

- For classical or solo piano, more warm room.

Miking and EQing

Okay, you've determined how you're going to feature the piano, and the overall sound you want it to have. Now we get to the nitty-gritty: miking and EQing.

Miking Technique

Piano miking is a lot like drum miking in that there are as many approaches as there are engineers. The techniques I'm going to outline here work very well for me. But be aware that these are general guidelines only. Miking a piano is a complex project because there are so many individual decisions to make. Basically it all comes down to trial and error and a lot of mic-moving until you find the positions that optimize the sound of your particular piano for each song.

Mic Placement: Knowing Where to Stick It

Picture a piano, or better yet look at the one you'll be recording. Whether it's an upright, a baby grand, or a console, this is a pretty big piece of furniture. Its sound surface covers several square feet. Obviously a mic isn't big enough to capture all of the sound equally, so where you put the mic will have a lot to do with what characteristics of the sound get emphasized.

The sound of an acoustic piano is enormously elastic. You can use it to fill a variety of roles. This is largely determined by where you put the microphone. And where you put the mic will have an enormous impact on what you have to work with when it comes time to EQ.

The relationship between the mic and the instrument can radically alter the perception of the instrument's job and the environment it's reflecting. For example, if you need a hard rock sound you might want to position the mic very close to where the hammer hits the string so you can get the percussive quality of the attack to dominate. If you need a soft quality for a ballad, you might want to move the mic away from the hammers so that there is less attack and more soundboard tone.

Mic Placement and Acoustic Equalization

In addition to the specific elemental characteristics of the piano that you can emphasize with mic positioning, you can also use the mic to control the instrument's frequency balance. In effect, by moving the microphone you are equalizing the signal acoustically. While this is true of every miking situation, it is particularly obvious in the case of the piano.

The Long and the Short of It

You know from the previous discussions in this book that waveform development is a function of sound frequency moving some distance through air. You know that low-end waveforms need more distance to develop than high-frequency wave forms. So it makes sense that the farther away the mic is from the piano strings, the more bottom end will enter the frequency blend. The closer the microphone, the more top end will be heard. So it would also seem to make sense that if you want the piano to sound big and bass-heavy you should move the mic some distance away. If you want it to sound tinkly and sweet, mic it close up. Good idea as far as it goes. Unfortunately it's not quite that simple. There isn't any one-size-fits-all miking formula. That's why piano miking is more art than science and can get a little tricky.

As you already know, the presence, or nearness, of an instrument is determined by the amount of top-end emphasis. Top end tells us direction, timbre, and nuance, while bottom end tells us distance, size, and power. Given that, you can see why the position of the piano mic has to be such that there's a suitable balance between top and bottom end. To determine what's suitable you need to know where you want the piano to fit into the track. In other words, you have to be aware of what the location of your piano mic is telling you and shift its position according to your estimate of the final ensemble needs. Knowing this, you can now see why one stock miking position isn't the answer to all situations.

Mono and Stereo Miking

There are three basic architectures when it comes to miking a piano. The simplest is the **single mic to single track (mono)** technique. The next is the **multiple mic to single track (mono)** technique ("multiple mic" means two or more). Finally there is the **multiple mic to multiple track (stereo)** technique. Each of these methods has its place, depending on what role you envision for the piano.

For instance, if you want to use the piano in a chiefly supporting or rhythmic function then the single mic mono treatment might be all you need. If the part is more complex but you have a shortage of tracks, the mono multiple mic process could be the best answer. If, however, the piano is the central support or focus to your music, you will want to consider a stereo approach.

I have used as many as seven mics to record a solo piano and room ambience. The results were awesome, but keep in mind that there was no other instrumental competition in the track. I more often will use one or two mics when there are other instruments to think of. The bottom line is that mics and tracks are resources that you don't want to waste where they're not needed. The moral of the story is, know where you want the piano to fit and how much attention you want the piano to get from the audience. Let this perception, not some Holy Grail of the ultimate "perfect" piano sound, guide you.

Mono Recording

Mono, as you know by now, means that the signal is recorded onto one track of the tape. This does not mean that only one mic can be used to record. Even when recorded in mono, a piano sound can benefit from having more than one placement point. So I'm going to outline two methods of recording a piano in mono: the single mic technique and the multiple mic technique.

The Single Mic Technique

This method is technically the simplest and arguably requires the best ears, but it is also the cheapest (remember, substitute talent for bucks). The principle seems straightforward. Position the mic so that it picks up as much of the piano sound as possible, EQ it, and record.

The problem is that not all of the characteristics of the piano are equally attractive. This is related to the construction of the instrument. The strings are laid out in such a fashion that it would appear that there is a separation between the low strings and the high strings, but really there isn't because all the strings use the same soundboard to reverberate. What this means is that you have a certain amount of sympathetic vibration rattling around in the piano that may include sounds you don't want to hear.

For example, let's say you want the piano to sound thick and rich. Logic would seem to indicate that you should probably opt for pointing the mic at the low strings. The problem is that the whole piano will resonate every time you hit any key. Therefore if you point the mic at the wrong spot you may get more resonance than string tone, thereby making the sound muddy and unfocused.

The same problem can occur when you place the mic too far from the strings. You will start to get more low-end ambience than tone. If you mic the piano from a distance of more than two feet you will get lots of non-tone noise, pedal and chair squeak, and ambient noise, as well as a real lack of presence.

Finally, there is the issue of dynamic balance between the registers of the instrument itself. Like all acoustic instruments each piano has a unique signature. The volume balance between the bottom and the top is important to note for mic placement. The object is to find a spot to mic where one end of the piano doesn't drown out the other. So where do you place the mic?

SINGLE MIC PIANO RECIPE

1. Use a wide-pattern mic (see "The Microphone Chapter").
2. Use a floor-base mic stand. Do not allow the mic stand to touch the piano (the stand will resonate). If the mic stand is on a hard floor place a foam pad or the like under the stand.
3. Begin by placing the mic five to six inches from the strings and pointed at the center of the visible strings.
4. Record a little of the un-EQed piano as a reference to determine mic placement.
5. Move the mic according to these indicators.
   If you want the sound balance to emphasize
   Mostly high strings: Position the mic so that it is aimed at the high strings and turned to reject the low strings.
   More high strings than low: Center the mic closer to the upper section of the visible strings. (Note: maintain a distance of five to six inches from the strings, however.)
   More attack: Place the mic closer to where the hammer strikes the string.
   More bottom end: Move the mic farther away from the strings or closer to the soundboard hole.
6. Plug the mic into a channel input of the portable studio.
7. Assign the input to a track.
8. EQ.
9. Check the record level.
10. Record.

The Multiple Mic Technique

The multiple mic technique is essentially the same as the single mic technique except for the obvious (more than one mic, more than one channel is required), and something that isn't so obvious — the effect of the phase relationship between the microphones.

Just a brief recap: The phase relationship, as you already know, is the way in which two signals from the same source interact when combined. It's a situation where the sum of the parts is less than the whole if the parts are out of phase with each other. If the same signal is arriving at two different receivers at slightly different times these signals will not be in phase with one another. The degree to which they are out of phase will determine whether they reinforce or weaken each other. For example, if two signals are perfectly ($180°$) out of phase with one another and are combined at the same volume, they will cancel each other out and you'll get a beautifully recorded nothing. But then again, nothing's perfect, so what you're more likely to get is something that sounds like it came through a drainpipe. This generally is not a good sound for an acoustic piano.

So when placing the multiple mics you need to compare what they sound like individually with what they sound like in combination. If you hear a negative discrepancy (lack of bottom end or an odd-sounding top) that sounds like neither mic alone then chances are you have to move one mic a little to get rid of the problem. With a simple two-mic setup you can usually avoid the problem by following the mic scheme in the following recipe.

Multiple Mic Mono or Stereo Piano Recipe

1. Use cartioid-pattern mics if possible (see "The Microphone Chapter").
2. Use floor-base mic stands. Do not allow the mic stands to touch the piano or each other (the stands will resonate). If the mic stands are on a hard floor place foam pads or the like under them.
3. Place the high-string mic five to six inches from the strings and pointed at the treble section and away from the bass strings.
4. Place the low-string mic five to six inches from strings, pointed at the bass section and away from the treble strings.
5. Assuming the phase relationship is suitable, move the mics according to the following indicators singly or in combination: (*e.g.,* more attack from the treble strings and more bottom end from the bass strings).
   If you want in the balance
   More attack: Place the mic closer to where the hammer strikes the string.
   More bottom end: Move the mic farther away from the strings or closer to the soundboard hole.
6. Plug mic 1 into the channel 1 input of the portable studio.
7. Plug mic 2 into the channel 2 input of the portable studio.

For mono:
1. Assign the inputs to combine to a single track.
2. Monitor the single track.
3. Balance the combination of both channels to the track.
4. EQ.
5. Check record level.
6. Record.

For stereo:
1. Assign each mic to a separate track.
2. Monitor both tracks (pan them left and right for monitoring if possible).
3. EQ.
4. Check record levels.
5. Record.

An important note: Listen to each mic separately, then combined. If the combination is "richer" than each mic alone, cool. If, however, this combination is "smaller," then you need to physically reposition the mics to remove phase cancellation.

The Grand Piano

Miking a grand is the same as miking an upright except that the piano's lying down. If you were to lay the upright on its back and then place the mics according to the above recipes you'd be pretty close to miking a grand. The only real difference is the greater ambient sound you get with a grand. The lid of the piano acts to reflect sound out to the listener, but it will also reflect it back to the mics. This reflection will become a component of the sound. So if you are recording a grand piano experiment with the position of the lid. Pro studios will often take the lid off. Other engineers will record with the lid closed to create greater isolation. Trial and error is the best answer here.

Tweaking Your Piano for Recording

I don't know about you, but most of the pianos I've had have been "previously owned." Some of them have been "previously, previously owned." They've all been wonderful, but in each case a little TLC was required to get them back into recording shape.

When a piano comes from the factory it is a marvel of musical mechanics. The strings are shiny and brilliant-sounding, the hammers and dampers are perfectly aligned, and the action (the amount of pressure it takes to push down a key) is evenly balanced across the keyboard. But after sitting around in Aunt Gertie's rec room for a few generations, the instrument you inherit tends to have a few signs of decrepitude. Aside from the doily marks and the whiskey rings on the finish, the piano will probably sound dull, with an indistinct tone and wheezy pedals. There are some remedies you can use to improve the sound of the instrument for recording. Some of them are of a fairly permanent nature and should not be performed on anyone else's piano without their permission (unless of course you never plan to see them again).

The thing to do when you're getting ready to record is to have a qualified piano technician come out and check out the piano. The first order of business is to tune it. Most pro studios will have the piano tuned before every session or, at minimum, every day. Obviously that gets expensive, but a good tuning every month or so or when you're about to record an important demo may be worth the money. (Also, while he's at it you can calibrate your tuner to his reference pitch.) While he's tuning have him look at the alignment of the dampers and hammers to make sure you're only hitting or damping the strings you want to. Ask him to check the pedal mechanism to make sure the dampers are engaging properly.

Resuscitating the Sound

The biggest problem I've found with old pianos is that the felt on the hammers has become grooved and soft. One way to fix this is to call a piano rebuilder and spend a small fortune refelting all the hammers. If you have a Steinway grand that you expect to pass on to future generations yet unborn that may be a good idea; if not, here are some less financially ruinous things you can try.

The following are modifications that will have some effect on the felt surface of the hammer. The first two suggestions are relatively temporary and easy to undo, while the last two are permanent, so you should be very sure that the solution is right for your situation. You should also test any method first on a key that is very seldom used (extreme upper for instance) to make sure you like the effect.

- Tack piano: Push a small flathead tack into the hammer where it meets the string. Remember that this leaves small holes in the felt, so try not to miss your spot too often. The result is a very distinctive hard sound associated with the saloons of the Old West.

- Place a small strip of gaffer's (duct) tape over the striking surface of each hammer. This will help eliminate the grooves and give the hammers a firmer hitting face. Bear in mind that repeatedly removing the tape may leave an adhesive residue on the felt.

- Use clear nail polish to "paint" the hammers. The varnish will be absorbed into and coat the surface of the hammer, thereby hardening it. You can use more than one coat to add hardness. Be sure to allow the polish to dry thoroughly — you don't want any on the strings.

- Take a small file and file down the felt a little bit (less than an eighth of an inch at most for really old hammers) to try and find fresh firmer felt. This is a time-consuming job but really is the most permanent solution. However, be sure to go slow and test the sound frequently. If you take too much off you might not get good contact with the string. Be very gentle so you don't knock the hammers out of alignment.

Compressors and the Piano

Generally speaking, when you're dealing with limited equipment circumstances I would recommend against using a compressor on the piano. The reason is that the compressor will bring up the level of any overringing notes, which will have a tendency to make the piano sound muddy.

Chorus Piano Recipe (Mono)

One of my favorite effects is to use a chorus on the acoustic piano. This is particularly effective if the track is fairly open and you want to add some special color to the piano but you can't afford the tracks to record the piano in stereo.

1. Plug mic into channel 1 mic input.
2. Check input level.
3. Plug portable studio effect output into chorus device in.
4. Plug mono out of chorus device into channel 2 line in.
5. Assign chorus and microphone channels to record on track 3.
6. Monitor track 3 (only).
7. EQ microphone channel.
8. EQ chorus channel.
9. Balance the two channels to track 3.
10. Check level to track 3.
11. Record on track 3.

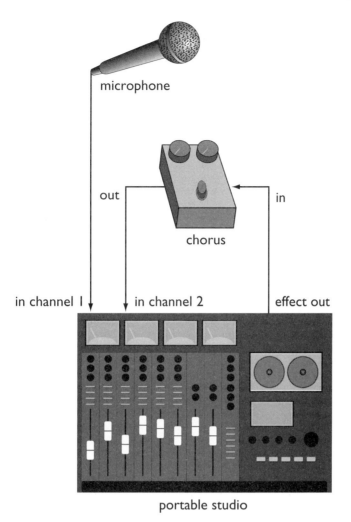

microphone

out — chorus — in

in channel 1   in channel 2   effect out

portable studio

use effect send channel 1
assign channel 3
record track ❸

Acoustic Piano EQ Guide

Every piano is different, so EQ is largely a matter of mic placement and trial and error. The following are just guidelines to give you indicators of likely frequency ranges.

If your piano sounds muddy

Boost	10 K
Cut	200 Hz

If you want a rock or ensemble piano

Boost	10 K
Boost	3 K
Boost	100 Hz

If you want a solo piano or vocal accompaniment

Boost	10 K
Boost	5 K
Boost	250 Hz

Keyboards Part 2: Synths and Midi

There are scores of good books out there on MIDI and MIDI management, so I'm going to adopt an approach specific to the process of recording synths with a portable studio. In the next few pages I'm going to focus on two main areas: the concept of virtual recording and mixing, and some tricks for "qualitizing" synthesizer sounds to suit your musical vision.

Virtual Recording and Mixing

With the advent of practical and increasingly inexpensive sequencers and synthesizers, virtual recording and mixing has become one of the most powerful tools available to the portable studio user. With it you can record a practically unlimited palette of instruments even though the number of actual tape tracks you have is limited.

So Virtual, It's Virtually Virtual

In the computer world the word "virtual" means not really real. Huh? (Good thing we're not in the computer world.) It means that the essential *quality* of something exists without the thing itself. Huh, Huh? You know, like a virtual-reality game world it looks real and acts kinda real but it's not a real world, it's just the projected characteristics of a real world (without door-to-door salesmen, mosquitoes, or lint). Glad we got that cleared up. Well, **virtual recording** is recording done without a tape recorder. It is the functional essence of recording without the hardware.

This semantic difference is probably not very important but I'll amuse myself with it anyway. Tape recording involves storage of complete electronic analog "pictures" of a sound, everything that's needed to reproduce the sound. Virtual recording, on the other hand, records a list of instructions that are then used by the instruments to recreate the sound. Kind of like sheet music for synthesizers. No sound exists until some instrument follows the instructions. This is the basis of virtual instrumentation in the recording process. If these instructions can be synchronized with the sound "pictures" of conventional tape recording then the sequencer can act as a virtual tape recorder, providing you with more "tracks" of instrumentation.

Virtual mixing is the process of combining sequenced, synthesized sound that plays "live" along with standard taped recordings when you mix to two-track. A simple analogy is any karaoke recorder you'd find at a drunken luau. This machine works by letting you sing along with a prerecorded music cassette. Then as you sing into the mic both you (singing live or thereabouts) and the tape of a fake Nancy Sinatra's band are combined and recorded into a final mixed rendition of "These Boots Are Made for Walkin'" onto cassette for you to cherish forever.

In the non-luau recording world, virtual mixing is a very useful tool for adding a whole raft of instruments to a limited number of tracks. In short, it's great for portable studio recording.

The way it works is that one track of the portable studio is used to record a MIDI Time Code signal — usually generated by a sequencer — to the tape. This signal is recorded as if it were an instrument. Then the signal is fed out of the portable studio and plugged back into the sequencer, which in turn controls all of the synthesized sounds. As the portable studio plays back the taped MIDI Time Code track the sequencer is told to tell the synthesizers to play the "sheet music" at a certain tempo.

This process requires that your music be recorded in two places, with the MIDI Time Code acting as a translator to get both sources to play together. You record music in the normal way to the tracks of the portable studio, and you also record synthesizer MIDI events to the sequencer memory. You can alter the order of the events or the parameters of each event within the recording and editing capability of the sequencer. This information is fed out of a MIDI cable to whichever synths are hooked up. The MIDI Time Code recorded on the portable studio tape then tells the sequencer how fast to make these events take place. The MIDI Time Code is the electronic equivalent of a pace car at the Indy 500. It makes all those cars move at the same speed so they stay in their same relative places.

The MIDI Time Code then, is a synchronizing reference point, sent out by the tape recorder to control the sequencer. (There are other situations where the sequencer controls the tape recorder speed, but that's one of those things for a MIDI book.) If you didn't have the reference code, the only way to synchronize the stuff that's on tape with the stuff the synths are playing would be to start both machines at exactly the same time and hope that they would continue to run at a constant speed (which I can tell you from bitter experience when I've had a code dropout, they don't).

The machine sending the controlling code (the portable studio) is called the *master,* and the machine that is being controlled is called the *slave.* Kinky, huh?

Okay, now you've got a track of the portable studio controlling the sequencer, which is in turn controlling the synthesizers so they're all playing nicely together. How then do you hear what all those synths are playing? How do all those sounds get to the two-track for the mix? All you have to do is input the synths into the console section of the portable studio and away you go. Two thousand instruments and a brain hemorrhage later you'd be happy as a clam. But there is one fly in the head-cleaning fluid: How do you input two thousand instruments into only a six-channel portable studio?

One answer is a thing called submixing. Submixing is the process of taking the output of the various synths and using a separate small mixing console to combine the signals and send them to two channels of the portable studio for input. After that the process is the same as for any instrument or vocal. In essence the submix is just another instrument.

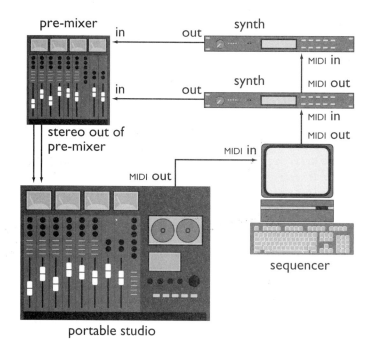

In addition to the extended number of tracks the virtual approach affords, there is another advantage that has to do with maintaining flexibility up until the last possible minute. You see, you can change the synth sounds without having to re-record a track. All you have to so is give the sequencer a new set of instructions and a new sound joins the fun. If, for instance, you don't like the tuba anymore, go ahead, change the sound to a fuzz laser, no one gets hurt. You can change sounds right up to the final take of your final mix.

Recording Midi to Tape

Before you do much of anything with a sequencer and a portable studio you need to "stripe" one track of the tape with the Midi Time Code signal. This will act as the timekeeper for synchronizing events between the conventional and virtual instruments. I refer you to your portable studio manual for how to handle the input and output of the Midi signal, because different machines handle the situation in various ways. In the world of the portable studio the last track (either track 4 or 8) is usually normalled for "code" (see the chapter "Anatomy of a Portable Studio: The Tape Machine").

Checking if the Code Is Readable

Record the Midi signal to whichever track the manual recommends. Record it at a level between -5 dB and -7 dB to start with. Record it (and nothing else) for the whole duration of however long you expect the song to run. Then, before you go any further, record a Midi-controlled reference click track to the tape (use very low level to avoid print-through of this highly transient sound). In other words, let the taped Midi stripe drive the sequencer to record the click. That being done, play back the taped click track while you let the Midi stripe control a new sequencer click track. Monitor both of these: The two should be playing simultaneously all the way through the song (pan the clicks to opposite sides if you can to compare). If this seems like a boring exercise, that's because it is, but pay attention. If your Midi Time Code is corrupt you can waste a whole lot of work when the sequencer won't synchronize with the stuff you recorded onto tape.

If for some reason the two signals cease to synchronize with each other, then you may have a dropout on the MIDI stripe. This could be because the level of the signal is too low or the tape itself is missing some oxide (see why I said don't use old tape?). If this happens, raise the level to tape of the MIDI signal from the sequencer and rerecord. (In no event should you need to record MIDI signal above -3 dB. Anything louder may result in crosstalk and leakage.) If you still get dropouts, try changing to a new cassette, and if that doesn't fix it then take your portable studio to the shop for an azimuth check.

This is probably a silly thing to mention (of course that never stopped me before), but don't listen to the track of the MIDI tone itself. It sounds like an atomic spit valve and will not contribute to your sense of well-being if listened to for very long.

Zounds! Sounds Abound

To do some of the tricks I propose you'll need to be fairly familiar with the workings of sequencers and synth parameters. For instance, the more parameter control your sequencer program allows you, the better able you will be to change dynamics and coloration on the fly. You will be able to modify vibratos and note bends even after you've performed the part without having to perform the actual notes again. In this manner you can add nuance and emotion to the machine-generated sound.

There are a number of good cost-effective sequencers and computer-based sequencer programs out there and I would consider it a very good investment to get the best you can afford if you plan to use a lot of synths in your recordings. That being said, your ability to implement the suggestions I make here will be determined by the type and amount of gear you have available to you.

A Note about Quantizing

Quantizing, as you may know, is a method of correcting human error when recording into a sequencer. Quantizing will fix the sequenced note so that it is played perfectly in time. In other words, it makes your sixteenth notes fall right where they should no matter how long you've been up partying.

Quantizing is a nifty thing to be able to do, but it's also an easy thing to overdo. It is usually better to play a part correctly than to play it and correct it with quantizing. This is particularly true of any part that is exposed in the track. If your fingers seem to have a mind of their own, try quantizing only the most offensive part of the track and leaving the other parts alone. This will lend a more "human" feel. In the case of section sounds (like strings or brass), quantizing may be necessary but can be humanized in the same way by turning the quantizing on and off during the part so it is not entirely quantized.

Copying Parts versus Doubling Parts

Copying a part is the process of cloning it electronically to add it to some other area of the song. *Doubling* is cloning a part to be played by a different instrument in the same part of the song. When you copy parts to replay at different points in the song, try to vary each copy of the part slightly so you don't get a "cookie cutter" sameness. For instance, if you copy the first chorus string part to use in all the other choruses, try changing the vibrato rate for each chorus copy or swapping some voices or patches. The same part over and over, no matter how cool it is, causes a certain amount of attention fatigue in the audience. You can avoid this by giving them something subtly new to listen to, plus you can build dynamics in the song at the same time.

P.S.'s

P.S.: I'm going use the common term "patch" to refer to a particular set of synth parameters that compose a particular sound.

P.P.S.: I'm going to use the term "double" a lot. As you probably know, a double is an exact copy of a part, in this case a sequencer-controlled synth part. Remember that if you use a double to create stereo it must be treated differently or it will just end up in mono when you split the two signals left and right. So you need to change it in some way. I've found slight variations in pitch, timing, or vibrato to be the answers I go with the most.

DAVID WILLS ON VIRTUAL MIXING

David Wills is in great demand as a MIDI *consultant to such megastars as Michael Jackson, Whitney Houston, and Phil Collins — to name but a few, He is also the creator of two excellent videotapes,* Mind over MIDI *and* Understanding Samplers and Sampling, *available from* **Mind over** MIDI, *12312 Willow Way, Los Angeles, California 91331-1471.*

A lot of people talk about the limitations of portable studios. I like to prove them wrong by producing something that sounds like it has been recorded in a huge studio. That is getting easier to achieve nowadays because a lot of people have drum machines and sequencers which can add the equivalent of a lot of extra drum tracks to their productions.

Now, once you have gotten over the fact that you will lose a track to lay sync down, you can look at all the advantages of the extra MIDI, or virtual, tracks that will come along for the ride. The only trouble some of you will have is that you need extra channels to bring these MIDI instruments into your mixer. Of course if you have a great number of keyboards, modules, and drum machines you will need to get an extra submixer. But if you have perhaps only one workstation-type keyboard like a Korg 01-W or an Ensoniq SQ-1 you can learn to do a great deal of mixing inside the keyboard, and thereby save the need for a submixer.

Typically you want to be able to change the level, pan, and effect level of each sequencer part. All workstations I know of have the ability to change the level and pan. You need to look in your manuals under the Effects section to see if there are ways you can change the effects levels to different parts. This way you only need to use up two channels of your mixer to bring your workstation in — and in fact if you are running out of input channels and can do without EQ, you could bring them in on two effect returns.

If you have the luxury of using a computer-based software sequencer, quite often they have virtual mixers in there. In Opcode's Vision and Mark of the Unicorn's Performer you can set up sliders for each sequencer part and send out MIDI Volume (controller 7), MIDI Pan (controller 10), and, depending on whether your keyboard responds to it or not, Effects Level (controllers 91 through 95).

The great thing about getting your keyboard to respond to all of these messages is that if they are in your sequencer chances are you can record them and have a budget automated studio.

Qualitizing: Sound Reasoning

To "qualitize" (that's my own word by the way) means "to bring out the unique qualities of an instrument." (Or maybe it means some kind of dry-cleaning process. Whatever. In any event, feel free to use it whenever you want.) Qualitizing is the process of finding the right sound for the right part and making the most out of what you want that sound to be. In other words, with a synth you can decide not only that you want a string sound, but you can also decide what kind of string sound you want to match the vision you hear in your head. Qualitizing is the art of taking the sum total of the sound-manipulation capability you have and using it to create or modify a sound for a unique application.

Qualitizing involves first the creation, generation, and modification of the sound in the synth, and then the use of outboard gear to further refine it. The reason why I make a distinction between synth recording and recording with other instruments is that the synth sound is a complete fabrication, a fiction created by wave tables, algorithms, and other sci-fi stuff to conjure up sounds and let humans fool with them. I mean this in the best sense, of course.

Today's practically limitless sandbox full of synthesizer noises makes it impractical to deal with the treatment of specific sounds, so I think it most efficient to group the sounds into broad categories that share major characteristics. The categories are:

1. Bowed strings
2. Plucked strings, strummed strings
3. Pianos
4. Organs
5. Wind instruments (brasses and reeds)
6. Bass sounds
7. Percussive sounds
8. Buzzy sounds
9. Pads
10. Leads

Of course, the synth being as flexible as it is, you will often create sounds that are a combination of the above categories. If that's the case then you must determine which characteristic you want to dominate in the overall sound. When I speak about layered combinations I'm referring to a situation where one part is using more than one patch to create a sound; *e.g.*, guitar and bassoon to create a "guitoon." The level of each layer of course can be controlled to suit your needs. At the end of this chapter I'll give you a sort of EQ color chart for synth sound characteristics.

A note to keep in mind: the synthesizer, as the name implies, synthesizes its sound totally out of electronic stuff. The synth has no acoustic properties of its own (other than an expensive dull thump if you drop it). As a result you can radically alter the parameters of a sound electronically. This being the case, before you embark on outboard signal treatment such as EQ, get as close as you can to the sound you want by tweaking the synth itself. Then you can use the EQ for fine tuning.

Another note to keep in mind: Synths can take up a heck of a lot of room in a mix. Be sure you know how big the sound should be relative to the other instruments. Try not to get carried away with all the impressive stuff you can do with a sound and forget what role it's supposed to play in the composition.

1. Bowed Strings

This is certainly one of the key reasons for owning a synth. You got'chur whole dang orchestra in a box. No longer do you have to cram forty cranky, bow-waving fiddle players into your bedroom to record a string section. Nowadays all you need is a Roland or a Kurzweil or a Korg, two fingers, and a little AC current.

The key to cool string sounds is to mimic what happens in the real world of dueling violins. Generally speaking, in any section of violins, violas, and cellos there will be those in the group who are slightly out of tune on any given note. This isn't because they're uncaring or untalented; it's just that a violin doesn't have any frets, so slight differences in finger placement on the neck can result in one man's A440 being another's A442.

Another thing about real-world strings: no two players have exactly the same vibrato. In the case of a violin, *vibrato* is the rocking of the fretting finger on the string that causes the pitch of the note to bend slightly up and down. (Guitar players vibrato too. So do singers but they don't use their fingers.) When you get a group of strings playing together each player is beginning and ending the vibrato at a slightly different time and has greater or lesser enthusiasm about the amount of pitch variation. Our human ears for the most part have learned to average out these minor differences, and rather than hearing them as discrepancies (as you would if only two players were playing) we hear them as a pleasant blending.

To create that effect with synthesized strings is really the big challenge in getting realistic orchestra sounds. If you are able to use a sampled string section much of the problem is taken care of. The sample is an actual digital recording of a real string section, so the player variations are actually there. But if you are using a synth to generate the sound there are some little tricks you can play to fool the ear.

Building a String Sound

For the illusion of realism it is usually most effective to build a string section sound out of a composite of performances. For example, sequence a performance of violins, then a viola part, and then a cello part. Then use the sequencer to create copies of each of these parts to form stereo pairs. When you get done the idea is to have the like instruments balanced on each side of the stereo spectrum.

Tricks

- You can use the sequencer to "offset" the strings so they don't start and stop at exactly the same millisecond. You do this by having the part constructed of doubles, which are copies of the same part but "evented" at slightly different locations on the Midi Time Code.

- You can use a chorus device on one part of a string composite and leave the others without chorusing.

- You can have a varying rate of vibrato between and during string parts.

- You can detune one string double part very slightly flat.

- Of course you can also add other patches of strings into the mix. For instance, a large string orchestra sounds good layered behind a small string section. The small section gives you presence and the large section gives you body.

- Finally, if you have sampling capability and you want to really get crazy, here's something you can do have some fun. You can create your own acoustic lunacy by sending a string patch out to an amplifier (see Recipe 17 in "The Recipe Section") and miking the amp to add ambience. Then send the mic into your sampler to create your own sample. This is particularly effective in an obvious ambient setting like a tile bathroom or a big garage.

EQing Bowed Strings

(Note: The complete EQ guide is at the end of the chapter.) The areas of EQ in a string sound that you are most likely to affect are the sibilance range, pure tone, and the extreme top end.

2. Plucked Strings, Strummed Strings

These sounds would include things like harpsichords, guitars, banjos, pizzicato strings, and so on.

Tricks

- Slight detuning between doubles can give strumming sounds a choruslike effect.

- A very slight delay offset in the sequencer between doubled parts acts as a slap echo. Try tuning the delayed double up or down by a third, a fifth, or an octave for an unusual effect. This works best with plucked sounds of short duration like pizzicato strings.

- It has been my experience that the performance and dynamics of guitar-type sounds is typically unrealistic when played by us keyboard guys. This is particularly true of strummed or arpeggiated chords. If you want something that sounds like a guitar you have to think like a guitarist, and that means imitating the order of the notes struck in a guitar chord (usually from low strings to high). It is also a good idea to listen to guitar parts to discover which chord voicings are the most "guitarry."

EQing Plucked Strings

The EQ you will most likely go for would be that used to bring out attack, top end, and upper midrange.

3. Pianos (Synthesized or Sampled)

There are so many cyberpiano types that it almost seems overwhelming to deal with them all. I'm going to put them into two broad categories: acoustic pianos and electric pianos.

Tricks

- Acoustic pianos need to be chosen for their appropriateness to the type of music. A huge Bösendorfer sound will probably be too big for a sane rendition of "Great Balls of Fire." Your first mission is to, as someone with a lot of reverb on his voice once said, "Choose wisely, Luke, and may the Force be with you."

- One of my favorite sounds for slowish songs is a layered combination of piano and strings. The piano adds attack and the strings provide a lush quality.

- A chorus effect on an acoustic piano is a nice unexpected effect when the track is fairly open.

- For an electronic piano sound, the one most commonly used these days is the Fender Rhodes with a chorus effect. It is a staple of jazz and R&B ballads. It sounds great when layered or doubled with a picked guitar to give it a little more definition in the track.

- True stereo is possible with a synth piano sound. My preference is to split the keyboard only slightly left and right of center for accompanied vocal, say bass notes at ten o'clock and top notes at two o'clock. I know this is weird because I said earlier that I pan drums from the audience's perspective, and now I'm telling you to pan the piano from the performer's perspective. What can I say, I'm a keyboard player, that's how I hear a piano in the real world. You should do what's comfortable. For stereo rock piano tracks I will still split the keyboard, but I will put the parts on the same side of the stereo spectrum with the top register at two o'clock and the bottom register at four o'clock. In this manner I can treat the two halves differently.

EQing Piano Sounds

EQ the piano according to the amount of attack and brightness you want. Generally, to avoid muddiness, it is best to stay conservative when boosting the bottom end, particularly with the softer electric pianos.

4. Organ Sounds

You know, dear reader, I really enjoy an amusing and subtly piquant Hammond organ sound. It's so rich in rock-and-roll tradition, with such a delightfully full-bodied tone. In fact, now that I think of it, I love a full-on Hammond B-3, especially when I have 600 watts of twin blazing overdriven Leslies. I love the hammering Hammond percussion and the drawbars yanked to the maximum! I love jolting the organ back and forth! I love standing up to slam screaming chords, then ripping off a lead that howls at the rafters! I love the lights, the fans, the underwear thrown from the audience, I love the... oh, sorry. As I was saying, a nice organ sound is a good thing to have in your repertoire.

Tricks

- The reason why most synth organ sounds don't seem rock-and-roll enough is the constant rate of vibrato in the patch. To beef up a synth Hammond-type organ sound, play the part and record it to the sequencer, then in a separate playthrough go back and add vibrato in spots to mimic a Leslie. Speed up and slow down the rate and vary the amount to correspond to the way you want to shape the notes. (Listen to some old Emerson, Lake, and Palmer records for inspiration.)

- Try doubling the organ part with a marimba or log drum sound for added percussion.

- Try layering a percussive Hammond sound with a pipe organ sound for lead parts.

- If you have sampling capability, record the synth part with the vibrato and marimba to the sequencer and send the whole schmear out to an amplifier. Overdrive the amp slightly into distortion. Mic the amp and sample. *Voilà*, instant Deep Purplish sample sound.

EQing Organ Sounds
Look to boost attack range for a percussive sound, sibilance range for a distorted sound, and upper midrange for a lead sound.

5. Wind Instruments (Brasses and Reeds)

Generally speaking, synthesized wind instruments operate as a section much like the strings. Both brasses and reeds play a role, and the type of song will determinate which of these sounds dominates. Of course solo winds are often used for leads, but in the synth world I find it's difficult to get a patch that sounds right on its own. So rather than attempting to mimic a horn or sax solo I usually use some processing to create a deliberately different sound.

Tricks
- For a section sound I will often tune the double of a part slightly sharp. Horn players tend more often to "lip up" a note than to play flat, especially at an exciting part of the song.

- For an R&B-type horn section look to build the parts individually from one trumpet, one tenor sax, one alto sax, one trombone, and one baritone sax (or some combination thereof) and then double them. It is best to play the parts and record them to the sequencer individually without quantizing. Then go back and decide which notes must be quantized and which can sound a little ragged. Remember, real horn sections are tight but not perfectly together. We're used to hearing the imperfections.

- For fast-moving parts the attack of the notes becomes very important. Choose your horn section accordingly.

- For fast-moving, rhythmic, or exciting parts try moving the sequencing to the "front" of the beat (very slightly ahead of the track).

EQing Brass and Reed Sounds
For brass you will likely want the tone of the instrument to dominate, and some of the upper midrange for punch. Extreme top end will provide a breathy quality, but be sure you're not just adding noise. For reeds (rock saxes in particular) you will want the vibrating reed sound (around 5 K) and the tone of the instrument (500 Hz).

6. Bass Sounds

In this category I include not only bass guitar sounds but also all those strange and wonderful low noises you can only get from a demented synth. A little reminder: Just because the synth can generate a low sound doesn't mean that you can hear it. Make sure when creating your sound to cut off low frequencies below 50 Hz so they don't take up precious oxide molecules when you go to tape. Chances are that anything below that frequency will be largely lost to the ear but will still take up room on the tape.

Tricks

- For bass-guitar–type sounds treat the instrument exactly as you would a bass, except don't add compression. Control dynamics with the synth parameters to do the job. A compressor may just bring up the level of the noise floor.

- Try sending the bass sound out to an amplifier and recording a sample of the result.

- Use the flanging recipe to fatten up a bass sound (Recipe 15 in "The Recipe Section").

- Try doubles with pitched percussion such as marimba or log drum. An unusual sound is to mix a low marimba with a fretless bass.

- Try mixing a pizzicato bass viol with a soft bass guitar.

EQing Bass Sounds

As I said above, treat the synth bass as a bass guitar in terms of EQ. The exception would be if there is a "buzzy" quality, in which case you would EQ that component of the sound like a vibrating reed (à la sax).

7. Percussive Sounds

See "The Drum Chapter." But try experimenting by mixing percussion with more sustaining instruments to add color and attack.

8. Buzzy Sounds

It's difficult to be exact when describing sounds, but I would typify this category as anything that has a sonic component reminiscent of angry insects in a jar. I would include any distorted or reedy sound in this group, along with any preset labeled "laser" anything.

Tricks

- Try to reserve this type of sound for single-note melodies. The buzziness can interfere with upper-register instruments like cymbals and rhythm guitars.

- These sounds work best with very little reverb.

- Try affecting the sound with a phaser or flanger. The upper-register quality of the buzz is interesting when it is swirling around in phaserland.

- Try doubling a synth guitar with the laser/buzzy sound for leads.

EQing Buzzy Sounds

This one is a little tough because it really depends on how much of the buzz and how much of the tone you want in the sound. What I've found to work best is to combine two instruments in a double, one that is buzz-dominant and EQed with a boost at about 5 to 7 K, and one that is EQed for tone.

9. Pads

A *pad* could be defined as something you use to comfort your "sit-down" after too many hours in the studio. In this case, however, I'm referring to a *keyboard pad*, a soft amorphous sound that has little attack and a lot of held notes; sort of like a musical fog. Its function is usually to provide a warm color behind a lead vocal or lead instrument without calling attention to itself.

Tricks

- Pads lend themselves particularly well to signal processing with phasing, flanging, and chorusing effects.

- Pad chords are best structured when voiced either mostly above or below the body of the lead instrument so they are not competing for aural space.

- Pads lend themselves to swells and decrescendos. Try recording the pad part to the sequencer after you've done the lead vocal. In this way you can add dynamics to the pad by raising the pad volume slightly between vocal lines and lowering it under the singing. This trick also works well when you swell the pad just before a chorus to heighten anticipation.

- Try to choose pads that have an attack rate that is the slowest you can get away with, so that when you change chords the pad tends to follow the change rather than lead it. This contributes to a dreamy quality and smoothes out the track.

- Pads sound particularly good when they are given longer reverb treatments.

EQing Pads

In the case of the pad you want to de-emphasize presence so the part will move to the back. Therefore, generally speaking, you will want to emphasize the warm EQ range for these parts. A boost at the extreme top can also be useful, particularly if you are using phasing or flanging. The upper mids may interfere with the background role of the pad; if so, you may want to cut the 3–5 K range.

10. Leads

The lead is the synth part that plays the stellar role. Whether it is an instrumental solo or a recurring melodic theme, you want to treat the part with as much attention as a lead vocal. The first thing to do is to reserve as much control for this part as possible. By this I mean allocate as many voices or as much processing as you need and then distribute what's left over to the less important parts. When we get to the section on virtual mixing keep in mind that the most flexibility should be reserved for the parts that get the most notice.

Tricks

- Make sure that the sound you use is in keeping with the part you're playing. A comical burping noise for the lead may not go well in the context of a ballad.

- Balance the components of the sound so that they complement each other no matter what the volume of the playback. Buzzy lead sounds will sound buzzier at low volumes, while screaming leads may rip your head off at high decibels.

- Since the sound is exposed you can add a lot of signal processing if you choose. If you do, however, be aware of the components of any background sounds such as pads and string parts that may have conflicting frequency information. This usually occurs in the upper frequencies.

- This is one of the places where sending a sound to an amp and sampling it can pay the biggest dividends. Take the basic sound and add chorusing, slap echo, *etc.*, to the amp for a complex sample, then record it to your sampler.

- Have fun and experiment!

EQing Lead Sounds

It's impossible to lay down any rules here: check out the EQ component guide at the end of the chapter.

Synth EQ Color Chart

Boost or cut

100 Hz	Bass sound	Power
200 Hz	Muddiness	Cut
250 Hz	Warmth	Bottom for pads, strings
500 Hz	Tone	Horns, reeds, organ
1 K	Transient	Perussive or plucked sounds
2–3 K	Upper midrange	Leads
5–7 K	Sibilance	Distortion, buzz, string bow, esses
10 K	Top end	Phasing, flanging; cut for noise
22 K	Ridiculous	Dog whistle

SECTION FOUR

Doing It

The Mixdown Chapter: Where It All Comes Together

What is mixing? Just what the name implies. It is the blending of elements in a deliberate way. Not unlike making a James Bond vodka martini. A bit of this, a dash of that, and a whole lot of something else, shaken not stirred. Audio mixing is really no different (except it's not liquid). The object is to blend musical elements in pleasing proportions. The goal of a good mix is to combine musical elements in a way that establishes the mood of the music and calls attention to the elements that the artist wants the audience to hear. Most of all, the mix is where all of the hard work you've put into the recording is going to pay off. In this chapter and the next I hope to give you some concepts and practical tools to create great mixes.

A Balancing Act

Let me make one very important point here. Mixing is not an exercise in electronics. Other than the actual playing of the musical intruments, it is the most artistic part of the whole recording process. I truly think of a mix as a performance. I spend hours in preparation and setup trying to squeeze every ounce of emotional value out of the music. I learn every nuance of every part. I plan what I'm going to exploit and what warts I'm going to try to hide. Then and only then do I start the *takes,* the actual recording of mixes. It's not unusual for me to do eight to ten hours of taking and retaking in an effort to get just the right balance. Sometimes, however, I get it on the first take.

An Aside

When I was mixing Men at Work's "Down Under" I got the mix on the first take. Nailed it. At first I couldn't believe it, but everything seemed to be right. Unfortunately, being the perfectionist lunatic that I am, instead of going to the local joint to celebrate I hung out for a while so I could go back and listen to the mix with a reasonably fresh ear. I returned to the studio from half an hour of being abused by some video game and fired up the monitors. I closed my eyes and listened. It sounded pretty darn good, in fact it sounded grea... uh-oh. Midway through the song I noticed a subtle something. The reverb on the snare, which should have been stereo, was only on one side. I jumped up and looked in the patch bay, where all the connections are, and sure enough, the cable from one side of the reverb had come out of its little hole. There are several perfect Anglo-Saxon words for such occasions, and I made very loud repeated use of them. Then I sat down and went back to work retaking mixes. I tried for another four hours to come up with a mix that was as good as the first one but with all of its reverb bits intact. Guess what?

Next time you hear "Down Under" listen closely and you'll notice that one side of the snare drum reverb is missing. That first mix was the one. I couldn't top it. The record sold millions of copies and I never had one person complain that they would have bought it except for the snare reverb. Sometimes perfection ain't all it's cracked up to be.

The above little tale notwithstanding, mixing is about patience. It's a necessary requirement. Nonmusician friends who have come to the studio when I'm working to see the glamour of the music business go out of their minds with boredom. (From a spectator's point of view, watching the mixing process is about as exciting as watching paint dry; the only thing worse is being subjected to 297 takes of the same guitar overdub.) Sometimes it takes me twenty takes to figure out that it was the tambourine part that was bugging me. Without those twenty "wasted" takes I might never have found that out. And here I was fooling with the high-hat, thinking that was the problem. So as you can see, mixing is at least in part trial and error. For a recordist there is no shortcut. Mistakes are a necessary part of the process. You just have to ride them out and learn from them.

Doing the Mix

Perhaps the most instructive thing I can say about mixing is that it is first and foremost an exercise in artistic balance. All the gear in the world will not substitute for a keen sense of proportion and aesthetic judgment in the way you present the music.

The first step to any good mix is to have a picture in your mind of what you want it to sound like. This picture is the goal you work toward, the artistic target you want to hit. There is a single-mindedness to the act of mixing, but that isn't to say that you can't take advantage of fortunate accidents and discoveries. In fact, improvising is one of the truly exciting facets of the whole deal. The thing, however, is to keep an eye on the "big picture" and make sure that any new elements fit into the game plan. As we all know, it's easy to become sidetracked by technology. Getting into a new sound is part of the artistic action, but any sound (no matter how cool) that distracts from the overall musical vision has to be thought about very clearly because it will result in a change of perception on the part of the audience.

Making the Road Map, Avoiding the Potholes

A successful mix is part preparation, part inspiration, and part perspiration. I know that sounds like a halftime pep talk, but it's true.

The first thing to do when you're getting ready is to construct a clear game plan for the mix. You begin by asking yourself some questions to establish guidelines to work from:

- What kind of mood do I want to establish for the presentation of the music? Warm? romantic? aggressive? exciting? soothing? and so on.

- What resources do I have available to achieve my goal? How many reverb units and signal processors do I have? What about equalizers and compressors? Where can I borrow some and what will I use them on?

- Which performance elements do I want to emphasize and which do I need to move to the background?

- How will each musical element interact with all the others?

When you've answered these questions to the point that you can practically hear the mix in your head, you're ready to begin. But before we lay hands to faders, I want to take a fresh look at some concepts fundamental to the whole process of mixing. It is important that you understand these ideas because they act as the road map to your final musical destination.

Musical Space

There is an idea that I think is central to the discussion of recording and in my opinion is one of the most important concepts in record production. It's an intangible thing that I call musical space. A reasonable definition might be that musical space is the imaginary "room" that the recorded performance is emanating from. A sort of cyberplace where the musicians are. Musical space has a front-to-back dimension and a side-to-side dimension. It is within these dimensions that you place the recording. In my mind it's like the set of a film — the musical space sets the mood of the piece.

Using musical space is about placing psychological boundaries and informing the audience of the location of elements. Think of it as the architecture of recording. You're building a structure, shaping the environment, and then ultimately arranging the furniture for the musicians to sit on. How you manipulate the elements in the musical space you're working with will determine how the audience perceives the music. Carefully constructing your musical space can move an audience to the place where you wish them to be, toward understanding and sharing the emotional intent you had in mind when you started recording a piece of music.

Here's some of the kinds of stuff you can do by manipulating musical space. You can have the listeners believe the singer is practically sitting in their laps, or in a cavern miles deep. You can have a guitar solo go from one of their ears through their heads and out the other ear. You can have their imaginary room crowded with music and intensely claustrophobic, or spacious and peaceful. You can have the audience jumping or contemplating. And you can do all of this without changing one note of the music. You can do it by manipulating the space that contains the music. A portable studio and a few pieces of outboard gear can give you a considerable construction crew to work with.

The View from Here — Mono to Stereo

The architecture of musical space has changed over the years as new developments in recording technology have occurred, the biggest being the development of stereo in the 1950s. Stereo can be defined as the creation of three-dimensional audio space from two sources (the speakers). Stereo mimics the way your ears and brain work. When you get audio information through your ears, in your head you compare what your left ear is hearing versus what your right ear is hearing versus what both ears are hearing. From this comparison your brain can tell where the sound is coming from. For example, if both ears are hearing a noise equally your brain tells you it's right in front of you. If your left ear hears it louder the sound is on the left, while if your right ear hears it louder it is on the right, and so on. This fairly obvious idea has profound importance in the history of recording, because throughout most of recording history the public heard recorded music as if we were an auditory cyclops with only one ear in the center of our foreheads. That was the essence of mono recording.

To recap some ideas previously expressed, mono recording means that the music is coming from one source; and because your ear hears only one signal, the sound lacks dimension. An example from the real world will help illustrate what I mean. Imagine you're in the audience at a concert hall listening to Papa Yodell's Good Time Tuba Band. Papa Yodell is standing on the left of the stage, first son Lemuel is on the right, and all the other little Yodells are arrayed in a semicircle between them, fixin' to play their tiny tuba hearts out. Your experience in the real world tells you that you will hear Papa with your left ear and Lemuel with your right, with all the other Yodells somewhere in between. You don't think about this positioning — it's automatic and natural. But just before they strike up the band all the Yodells run over and line up one behind the other at center stage. Suddenly the walls of the concert hall narrow so that the sound only bounces around from front to back, not from side to side. And both your ears move around to the front of your head. Now you've got mono. The applicable dimension is only front to back, closer or farther away. And what determines how close or far away something is in the real world? Loudness. (Actually that's a lie; as you know, ambience enters into the perception picture. But for the moment let's say....) The only way you can tell the position of one tuba is by the difference in its relative volume from the others. That's the way music was recorded for most of the last hundred years. When it came time for the trumpet solo the trumpeter just played louder or walked up to the mic. Because everything was in the middle loudness was the determinant for what the audience payed attention to.

Then stereo came along and, wow, a recording sounded like the real world! There was a sense of "being there" that was very exciting to an audience that had only heard mono up until then. In fact the novelty of stereo itself was so attractive that there were a number of records of stuff like trains speeding from one speaker to the other and cars racing around a track. ("Experience the heart-stopping excitement of the Cinerama of sound! STEREO!")

From a recordist's standpoint the great news was that with the advent of stereo you could now place an instrument where you wanted it to appear in the stereo spectrum. You had the dimensions of left and right to work with. You could determine where you wanted to attract the audience's attention by manipulating both the loudness and the position of an instrument in musical space. In a stereo recording you could communicate to the audience where the musicians were placed on the "stage." For example, you could mimic the position of Papa Yodell and the kids on the stage and thereby give greater verisimilitude to the recording as a concert. Or if you wanted you could make Papa rocket around the stage or seem to be at odds with the other Yodells.

How Stereo Works

As I said, we humans determine the location of a sound by comparing what one ear hears to what the other hears. To describe and clarify, think of your hearing equipment as having a total of oe hundred percent capacity. Now, if only your left ear hears something you would say that you're hearing one hundred percent left, zero percent right. If only your right ear hears then it's one hundred percent right, zero percent left. If you hear something directly in front of you then each ear is hearing equally — fifty percent left, fifty percent right. This can be diagrammed as a continuum called the **stereo spectrum**.

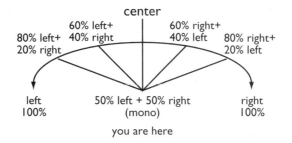

If you were standing on a corner and a car was to pass by you, your ears could continually tell you the car's position by giving you a report of which ear was hearing what percentage of the total sound.

Basic Principles of Mixing — The Stereo Spectrum

There are two components to stereo musical space, the left-to-right dimension and the front-to-back dimension.

The Left-to-Right Dimension

The process of creating stereo in the recording world uses a method that really is modeled pretty closely on how we hear. But instead of having two ears like us people, the stereo recording has two tracks as its source of information about the world. Let's pretend that your speakers replace your ears as a way of blasting audio information into your brain. Speaker L is your left ear and speaker R is your right. Where does a speaker get its information? From a signal coming from tape (forget amps and signal processors and stuff for now). Each speaker has its own tape track to respond to — that is the world it's hearing, a track of recorded material. For now let's say track 1 is going to the left speaker and track 2 is going to the right. If some sound is reported only to speaker L it would mean that none of that sound gets to the other speaker. The sound is therefore one hundred percent left. The reverse can also be true: Speaker R only = one hundred percent right.

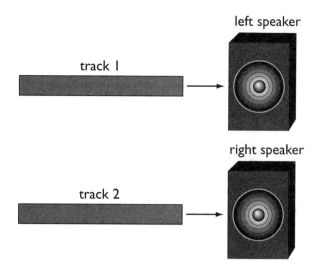

To beat the heck out of the speakers-as-ears analogy, if you hear something from your speaker ears that tells you the sound is directly in front of you, according to our model of hearing you would say that you are hearing fifty percent left and fifty percent right. Left is getting its info from track 1 and right is getting it from track 2. In order to hear something in the middle you would have to hear equal amounts of what's on track 1 and what's on track 2.

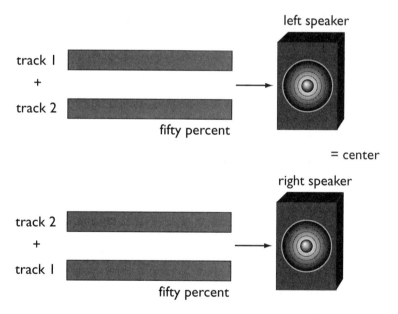

That's how stereo (two-track) recording works. Two tracks have separate information on them. The stuff that is unique to each will only appear on the appropriate side, left or right, but what they have in common will appear somewhere between these two extremes depending on percentages.

Here are some examples:

Guitar just left of center means that the guitar is sixty percent on the left track (1) and forty percent on the right (2).

High-hat just right of center means that the high-hat is sixty percent on the right track (2) and forty percent on the left (1).

Snare drum dead center means that it is fifty percent left and fifty percent right.

Keyboard far right means it is one hundred percent on the right track and only on track 2 (one hundred percent right, zero percent left).

(That, incidentally, is how a pan pot works. Even though it's only one knob it actually controls the percentage of information shared to two tracks.)

Don't confuse this with the notion of multitracking. When I'm talking about stereo here I'm referring to what is called the "mix" of the instruments; where in the stereo spectrum you place each instrument from the multitrack. The manipulation of stereo is a creative decision. It is the act of shaping the left-to-right dimension of your musical space. In other words, in your recording you can decide to put an instrument anywhere in the stereo spectrum that you feel is most suited to the music. The principal tool that you use to accomplish this is the **pan pot** on the console.

The next consideration in erecting your musical structure is deciding on the front-to-back dimension of musical space.

Establishing Depth in the Front-to-Back Dimension: Loudness, Equalization, and Ambience

In the left-to-right stereo world, the main tool for moving things around is the pan contol. There is a relatively direct and intuitive connection between the control and the result. Turn the knob to the left and the instrument images to the left and so on. But when you're dealing with the dimension of front-to-back space, or depth, there are a number of ways to move things around, and some of them are a little less obvious than others.

Loudness

As I discussed in the little section on mono recording, one way to make something appear closer is to make it louder; and to move something away from the audience you make it softer. Generally by making something louder you focus attention on it and make it more important to the listener. This method is a mainstay of mixing. To direct the listener to what you want to hear simply push the fader up. Guitar solo? Make the guitar louder at that spot to call attention to it. Vocal? Needs to be louder then the other instruments in order to be heard. So the first and most obvious tool for positioning something with regard to its depth in musical space is volume.

There is, however, one problem with using volume alone to create focus. If the instrument or voice is too loud it sounds as if it's not part of the rest of the music. The other instruments don't seem to support it. This is referred to as being too "out front" and can destroy the continuity of a mix.

As another example, what if you have a three-part harmony vocal, an ensemble that is the centerpiece of the action? How are you going to distinguish between the separate voices if they are all equally loud? The answer to both these situations is the manipulation of equalization.

Equalization

Equalization is a way to enhance the distinctions between musical elements, and it is a very effective tool for establishing depth placement. Just remember: EQ is the tool for estabishing clarity.

Earlier I spent some ink talking about the timbre and upper harmonics of a sound. I also mentioned that some frequencies are psychoacoustically active, meaning that we humans are hardwired to be more sensitive to certain sonic ranges than others. These two facts are the basis of EQ manipulation for placement.

To go back to our vocal group example, each singer has his or her own unique timbre. These timbre frequencies are in the upper range of the sound spectrum. Therefore if you want to distinguish between three equally loud voices you would boost the equalizer range where these differences lie to make the most of them — somewhere between 5 and 12 K depending on the situation. If you wanted the vocal group to blend together you might cut the same range, thereby eliminating individual distinctions and psychologically moving all the voices back in the musical space. This is effective in "block" background harmonies where you don't want the individual voices to compete with the lead vocal.

Another place where the equalizer is used in the front-to-back placement of an instrument is in the application of "apparent" volume. This is the situation when something seems to be louder than it's actually registering on the meter in dBs. What's really happening is that we humans are paying more attention to those frequencies. Have you ever heard a baby crying in a busy shopping mall? The sound cuts through the mall noise like an arrow. As you've no doubt guessed, that sound is full of those psychoacoustically active frequencies I referred to earlier.

Remember that if you rely on volume alone to attract attention to an instrument you run the risk of discontinuity in the track. Sort of a lump in the musical fabric. So you need another way to draw the audience's attention. Here's where the psychoacoustic characteristics of a sound come in handy.

Think of it this way: let's substitute the word "size" for volume, and "color" for EQ. Now think of a painting. You can make an element of a composition pop out by making it bigger, or by coloring it more brightly than anything else in the landscape. Using size alone to emphasize can make the object so big that it covers up the rest of the painting, overwhelming the landscape and leaving no room for anything else. It is "out there," unsupported by context. But if you use a dramatic color to call attention to an object you can still have it contained in the picture and keep landscape unbroken and balanced.

How do you do this? The most dramatic colors you have on your EQ palette are the psychoacoustic frequencies from around 2 to 4 K. By boosting the amount of 2 to 4 K you call attention to the instrument and allow it to cut through the track, like the baby in the shopping mall. A word to the wise, however: too much of this frequency range and the sound can become piercing. I would suggest that you reserve boosting these frequencies for things like solo instrument passages where the part is important thematically or is a lead instrument.

Ambience . . . ence . . . ence

The third way of manipulating the perception of depth is the use of ambience. Ambience, as you now know, is the sound of sound as it's bouncing off the walls, floor, and ceiling of a room. There are two aspects to this. First, when you're creating your imaginary environment you will determine its size by the time it takes for the reverberations to die away. A twelve-foot-long room will have a shorter reverb than a concert hall. Reverb decay time thus gives the listener a spatial frame of reference. The second aspect of ambience is the position of the sound source in the imaginary room. This we can control with the amount of reverb we apply to any sound source. In the real world we subconsciously use the amount of reverb to tell us how distant something is from us.

As a rule, the more ambience we hear relative to the source sound, the farther away we perceive the source sound to be. For example, if you are standing in the back of Notre Dame Cathedral and the Hunchback is right next to you grunting directly into your ear you would hear very little ambient effect. The reason is that you are closer to his voice than the walls are. You hear the sound before the environment has a chance to ineract with it. But if he is up in the bell tower yelling down at you the sound of his voice will reverberate off the walls before it gets to you. This will give you a subconscious, automatic clue as to the how fay away he is.

The moral of the story is when it comes to mixing ambience, first establish the size of your musical space with the *reverb decay time* and then determine how far back a sound should be in that space with the *amount of reverb*. If you want to move something to the back of the musical space add lots of reverb. If you want it to be at the front add less or use a delayed reverb.

There is another way that ambient sound gives the appearance of distance. The more reverb you add to a sound the less distinct it seems to be. In the real world, the farther something away is from us the less clear it sounds. Think of someone trying to talk to you from down at the end of a cave. The reflections off the walls garble the words. So the more reverb you add the less distinct the sound will be, and consequently the farther away it will appear.

Musical Continuity and the Mixdown

Now that you've seen some basics of how to manipulate sound in musical space the discussion naturally turns to what you want to accomplish when you move all that stuff around. There are two concepts that are at the heart of creating a successful mix. These are what I call the line **of focus** and the **energy center**, and maintaining them is the entire function of mixing in the first place.

The easiest way to explain these ideas is to borrow an analogy from the film world. Think about a movie script. Its purpose is to act as a blueprint for a film. It is the story that the entire production is trying to tell. Two key questions must be answered by the production in order for the story to be successful: Who is the central character in the story and what propels the action along? If either of these two questions is not answered clearly then you have people yawning in their seats, or confused, or throwing Milk Duds at the screen. You can have the best script in the world, but the film will be a failure if the production keeps obscuring the main points.

When you create a piece of music you have in effect written a script for the production. Everything should follow from the song. You still have to ask who the main character is and what gets the main character from point A to point B. But the answers are in musical instead of cinematic terms.

The Line of Focus

The line of focus is simply the path you want the audience to follow from the beginning of the song through to the end. The elements of focus are like the main characters of your song. They are what the audience is (or should be) paying attention to at any given moment. The line of focus is what keeps the audience interested and involved.

The element that you're directing the audience to focus on needn't be only one thing, but rather only one thing at a time. To do otherwise is to risk the murkiness of a really bad movie. Too many elements screaming for attention makes for confusion on the part of the listener, and — trust me — two seconds of confusion and you've lost them, total burnout, Milk Duds thrown at your speakers. So keeping your eye on the proverbial ball is critical.

What exactly is focus? It's anything that holds the listener's attention. It could be the lead vocal or a kazoo, whatever you feel is important. Think of it like a relay race where a baton is passed from one runner to another. There are many runners in the race but only one runner at a time has the baton. As an example let's diagram a bit of a song production. Below is a sequence of focal points. The audience's attention will be directed to these principal characters. The recordist will shine the spotlight on the artist's intent.

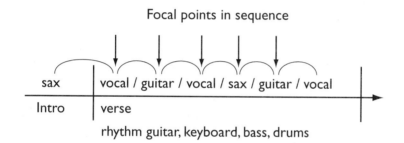

The intro and first verse of a song might follow a pattern like the one diagrammed above. The first element of focus is the saxophone lead line at the introduction of the song. The whole band is playing but the sax has center stage. When you get to the verse the sax hands off the focus to the singer, who sings a line and then in turn hands off to the guitar part between the first vocal line and the second. The singer gets the baton back for another line until it is handed off to the sax, which has a little line between vocals, and so on. The skill of mixing lies in making these transitions take place naturally so the audience is carried along. The goal of this continuity is also to always have one principal musical element for the audience to listen to. Ideally in a good mix there is no dead air for lack of a compelling musical idea or lyric; and conversely there should be no competition between elements for the audience's attention.

The Energy Center

The energy center is the musical undercurrent that propels the action along. It is the heartbeat of the song. To go back to our film analogy, it is like the pace of a movie. The energy center of a song is often referred to as the "feel" and it is what the audience feels that moves them, not necessarily what they are conscious of hearing. Put simply, it is the rhythm of the song. But it would be innacurate to describe the energy center as the "rhythm track" (drums, bass, and rhythm guitar) because the rhythm I'm talking about is the *feeling* of musical motion. This is created by the rhythmic bits and pieces that sweep an audience from one musical element to another. It is the grooves, daddy-o, and can come from anywhere in the track. The trick as a good mixologist is to identify what the energy center elements are and make sure they never get lost or obscured.

The concept is easiest to understand with an example. Let's say we're mixing an imaginary dance track called "Unghhh." The song is designed to pack a dance floor, so rhythm plays a very important part in its concept. You are on an energy hunt to get the most out of the groove. The first place you look is to the drums and bass. Seems obvious. So you listen to them for a while without any other instruments. So far so good. But when you put up the vocal, the track seems to lose energy. Maybe the singer is singing just a little behind the beat and the track is appearing to lag as a result. Obviously you have to have the singer, and you have to have drums and bass, but the combination doesn't work on its own. So you put up the sax part and the rhythm still isn't right. Now you add the backing vocals. That's nice in the chorus, but the verses still don't have the dynamism you want. Finally you put up a little guitar overdub that's going plinka on the two and the four of the measure. Suddenly the whole thing gels. Maybe the guitar is just that perfect amount out of time to blend synergistically between the vocal and the drums to supercharge the whole track.

If you were to guess where the energy center was before you went through this whole process you might quite reasonably have said that it was the drums. But as it turns out it was a little guitar part that was the key to unlocking the rhythm. So you make sure that the little guitar part is prominent in your mix and "Unghhh" goes on to move bodies all over the land.

The moral is that sometimes the thing that motivate a track can be what you least expect. I've had occasions where tambourine parts have been the energy center, or vocal punches, or trumpet blasts. A big one to look at is the high-hat. And much modern dance music is rhythmically successful because unusual elements like sampled vocals are featured to augment the drums and bass.

You know how you can tell when you've discovered the energy center? The flow of the track disappears when you pull it out of the mix. In other words, the best way to tell if the element is an energy center is that the track doesn't work if it's missing.

Bringing the Line of Focus and the Energy Center Together

In the final mix your job is to maintain the line of focus as it rides on the energy of the track. If you can keep these two elements in the front of your brain, then you will be clear as to where to place all the other elements so as not to muddy the waters.

Summary: A Review of Concepts

- **Mono** is the the production of sound from one source (one speaker).

- **Stereo** is the creation of three-dimensional musical space from two sources (two speakers).

- **Musical space** is the imaginary "room" the music is emanating from.

- The **left-to-right dimension** is the placement of instruments in a plane between and including the speakers. It is controlled primarily by the **pan pot**.

- The **back-to-front dimension** is the placement of instruments relative to their depth from the front of the speakers. This dimension is controlled by **volume, equalization,** and **ambience**.

- The **line of focus** is the sequence of elements to which you direct the audience's attention.

- The **energy center** is the "heartbeat" of a musical piece, the element that establishes the groove of the music.

The Step-by-Step Recording and Mixdown Chapter

Recording a Song from Beginning to End

This next section is designed to provide you with a walk-through of the entire process of recording a song. You will see how to record sixteen instruments on a portable studio, each with its own EQ, reverb, panning, and special effects. You will be able to have control over each instrument individually as it is being recorded and will be able to overdub to correct mistakes. We will begin by recording a basic rhythm track combining bass and drums. Next we will premix and bounce tracks to the two-track machine, returning the result to the portable studio. Along the way we will be adding effects and sound processors. The last step we will encounter is the final mix, which will result in our completed master recording. By the time we're done you will have the techniques to get what you hear in your head onto the tape. All it takes is some ingenuity and planning.

Submixing, Premixing, and Bouncing

Making the Most of Four Tracks

The object of the techniques of submixing, premixing, and bouncing is to make the most of a limited number of console channels and tracks. I've used these techniques when I've run out of room on a twenty four-track machine or a pro console, and the same techniques were used to record the Beatles' four-track masterpiece, *Sgt. Pepper's Lonely Hearts Club Band* (except that they didn't have synthesizers or drum machines, so they submixed actual instruments played by actual people). When you are working in a four-track universe with a limited number of inputs available to you it is essential to know how to use these techniques effectively.

Submixing

Submixing is the process of combining a number of instruments to a smaller number of input channels than there are instruments. It is accomplished by using an external mixer to combine the instruments before they reach the portable studio. For instance, to record a nine-piece band to a four-track and have the vocal remain separately controllable you would have to have at least ten channels on your recording console. By creating a submix you can bring all these instruments into the tape machine with a much smaller number of console channels. To do this you would use the separate external mixer to act as the input depot for all the instruments except the vocals. You would use the capabilities of this mixer to blend the instruments into a stereo mix. Then you would bring the stereo outputs of the submixer into two channels of the portable studio. The vocal would be brought into the portable studio through a separate channel and recorded on its own track. In this manner the EQ and reverb settings on the vocal would be independent of the rest of the instruments. Thus you would be able to record the whole band, have some control over the elements, and use only three portable studio channels — two for the instruments and one for the vocal.

Premixing

Premixing is the process of balancing musical elements before they get to tape. For instance, in most synths you can premix several sounds internally, then send them out on a collective output to the portable studio. Drum machines are frequently used in this fashion (as you will shortly see). The advantage is that you are able to bring a lot of sounds into the portable studio without having separate console channels for each one. By using the internal mixing capabilities of the synth or drum machine you can pan, position, and in some cases EQ several instruments before they get to the console. (Note: remember that in order for the instruments that are panned internally to come out panned in stereo on tape they will require two tracks of tape, each fed by a left or right output of the synth.) You'll see an example of this in recording the drum machine in Step 1 of the process.

Bouncing

Bouncing is the process of balancing and combining elements that have been previously recorded on tape. This is accomplished by playing back the already recorded tracks together and rerecording the combination of playbacks onto another track. It treats the recorded tracks as if they were live instruments bussed to the same track(s).

Bouncing is usually done one of two ways: internal bouncing, or external bouncing. An **internal bounce** combines already-recorded tracks to another track of the same machine. For instance, let's say you have guitar 1 on track 1 and guitar 2 on track 2 and you want to combine them to the same track. You can accomplish this by playing them back and assigning them to record on track 4. The two guitars can be balanced and mixed and will end up together on the same track. You can then erase tracks 1 and 2 and use them to record more instruments.

An **external bounce** is done exactly the same way except that the combination of playbacks is sent out of the stereo buss of the portable studio to be recorded onto a track (or tracks) of a separate machine (*i.e.*, a two-track tape deck). The result from the external machine is then recorded back into the portable studio using the channel inputs. For example, say you have four different guitars on tracks 1 through 4. You could mix, pan, reverb, and EQ them together and send them to the stereo buss and out to the two-track exactly as you would do in any other mixdown procedure. After you record the mix to the two-track you could feed it back into the portable studio via two console channels, where it is recorded on tracks 1 and 2 of the portable studio. Tracks 3 and 4 could then be cleared of their former occupants and used to record more stuff.

Before You Bounce

There is an important thing to keep in mind as you go about bouncing things together. Each bounce is in effect a miniature mixdown, and the same care and caution that you would apply to a final mix must be applied to a bounce.

The mechanics of premixing and bouncing are relatively straightforward, but the implementation requires considerable attention to detail to get good results. The single most intrusive problem you face, the one that will require the most attention, is noise. This is where you need to be hyper-alert. If you record it noisy it stays noisy. If in the process of bouncing you combine noise from several tracks then you are in effect amplifying the noise with each bounce. Noise is cumulative. The more times you bounce, the more noise you get. So you have to minimize the noise in the first place by using good recording technique for each track. You have to be aware of any buzzes and squeaks the instruments may be making. You have to be aware of the environment and old lady Hanlon's vacuuming. Most of all you have to be aware of getting the best signal-to-noise ratio you can on tape. If you aren't particular and aware during each step of the process then you'll end up with something that sounds like a recording of a song in a windstorm.

Getting Started: Our Imaginary Studio

The whole purpose of this section is to show you some ways to get the most performance from the equipment you have. By making the equipment perform multiple duty you can go a long way toward overcoming budgetary limitations. However, there are certain equipment basics that you should have in order to accomplish the techniques I outline. If these aren't available to you, you will have to accommodate your recording to your circumstances (or borrow some gear from a buddy, always a decent option).

The type of imaginary portable studio I have chosen for this exercise cruises somewhere down the middle of the road when it comes to features. It is more than the most basic machine but less than the ultimate. You will have to modify your own recording to accommodate to the features on your machine. If your machine has fewer channels than our model you will be required to perform more recording operations. If you have more channels than our model you will have more flexibility to take advantage of.

Imaginary Portable Studio Specs

Manufactured by Pete's Imaginary Audio Corp.

- six input channels

- one auxiliary send

- four-track cassette (two tracks discrete record simultaneously)

- EQ top — cut and boost +/-12 dB @ 5 K

- EQ bottom — cut and boost +/-12 dB @ 100 Hz

- noise reduction

- two-track master output

Additional Equipment

There are some pieces of equipment beyond the portable studio itself that are required to perform the operations outlined here:

Two-Track Machine

The first and probably most costly purchase you will have to make is a two-track tape recorder for mixing down your portable studio four-track recordings. I highly recommend that if at all possible you bite the financial bullet and get a DAT (digital audiotape) machine for the processes covered. As I've said elsewhere, using a digital machine for bouncing and mixing will go a very long way to eliminating the noise problems usually associated with multiple bouncing/combining operations. I will give you some tips on how to deal with unwanted noise, but for now let me say that the best way is to invest in a DAT machine.

If you don't have the budget for a DAT, I would recommend a good reel-to-reel two-track tape deck, preferably with the capability of running at fifteen inches per second — although by the time you read this the cost of a used DAT may be comparable to that of a decent reel-to-reel machine.

A definite last in the two-track mixdown machine derby is a cassette deck. Its low speed of operation and relatively inexpensive circuitry will prove noisy. But you gotta start somewhere, and budget is a consideration. I started out on a beat-up mono tape recorder, so don't give up hope of getting decent recordings.

Reverb Unit

Another key ingredient to enhance recording is a decent reverb unit. Part of the object of the exercise in this chapter is to show you how to get the most out of one reverb unit. In the examples that follow I approach things as if I had only one unit, which I will use as a straight reverb, a delayed reverb, a slap echo, and a delay line. This is done by changing the settings of the reverb for each stage of the process and recording it as you go along. Obviously, the more flexible the reverb unit the better off you are. In the first step I show two options for the use of the reverb unit, one as a direct feed from the drum machine, and the other providing a special mono reverb for the snare. If you have more than one unit available, you can of course perform both options.

Signal Processors

When you see all the instruments you're going to squeeze onto your four-track you will be grateful for anything that can help make some elbow room. Two items that are very helpful are **compressors** and **equalizers**. This section is, I think, where you'll see why I recommend that you get your hands on at least two channels of each unit.

In General

Of course there are all sorts of other bells and whistles out there that can make your recording more interesting. Tricks like **chorusing, phasing,** and **flanging** can add to an instrument's color in much the same way as reverb or echo. But I have to insert a note of caution here. Incorporating too many effects can be distracting, so unless your express intent is to feature the special effects be careful not to overdo them.

Keeping Out the Noise

As I've said, the bouncing process is inherently noisy, but there are a couple of things you can do to help defeat the beast of a thousand frequencies. The first thing to remember is that there is no substitute for good basic recording technique. The more track combining you do the more critical the noise issue becomes. So record each track with the best signal-to-noise ratio you can get. The more molecules of oxide excited by the music (up to the point of distortion, of course) the fewer molecules are available for noise.

Another noise medicine is a healthy dose of planning. By knowing which tracks are going to be bounced you can EQ the original recording of the instrument to accommodate it to the process. Here's what I mean. As you know by now, the frequencies that distinguish one instrument from another lie in the upper frequency registers, so a natural tendency when you are mixing to bounce would be to boost these frequencies to get the most clarity from each element. The problem is that noise also becomes more pronounced when the upper frequencies are boosted. If you're combining tracks you are also combining their noise. So you get gang o'noise. How to get both clarity and noise reduction? By doing the opposite of what makes sense. Huh? What you do is overboost the top end when you first record the track. This way you are sure that you have the upper harmonics covered. But won't this bring up the noise too (you say quite reasonably)? The answer is yes, for that part of the process it will. However, bouncing is a two-stage process. You get to affect the sound twice, once when you record and once when you mix. What you are going to do when you combine the top-end over-EQed original tracks in the mix is to cut the high end slightly on them before you perform the bounce. In this manner you retain the upper end of the instrument and reduce the amount of noise at the same time.

Another possibility in the war on noise is the use of gates to clamp down on noise between notes. As was noted earlier, however, you need to be careful not to interfere with the musicality of the part by having the gate clip off decaying notes.

A big noise culprit is the reverb unit. Most of these units can be optimized by keeping the input level as high as possible and the output level as low as practical. In other words, you want to what goes in to be loud. If the signal going in is low you will hear a higher proportion of circuit noise from the reverb unit itself. The more you bring up the output the more you bring up the noise. If you boost the reverb output because you need to hear more of the reverb sound, you are also boosting the noise that the circuits make.

The final thing I'm going to suggest on the subject of sonic disease is that you should use whatever noise reduction you have available to you at every step of the process. In most portable studio machines there is either Dolby or DBX or some other noise-reduction protocol. Read your manual to find out which you have and use it.

Getting Down to It

Okay, now that you've been given the surgeon general's warning on noise pollution, let's move on to the matter at hand — recording some music. You have all the bits and pieces of information rolling around in your cranium. Your synapses are all atingle with musical vibrations, and you want to get down to it. What's the first thing you do? Fire up the Les Paul and rumble, right? Nope.

You plan — carefully. You need to know where to point the ol' Harley, 'cause if you don't you may end up going ninty down some dead-end road. You need a road map. What I mean is that the complications of committing to premixes which will themselves be mixed together warrants that you sit down and figure out how and when to allocate your resources, which are talent, equipment, and tracks.

One question that needs to be answered in this planning stage is the order in which you are going to record the instruments. There are a number of concerns involved in this. For example, if you are going to add background vocals behind the lead then the final lead vocal must be done first so that the background singers have something to phrase with. However, if you want more than one background vocal track you need the tracks to do this. Therefore you may want to do a lead vocal and bounce it with the stereo mix, leaving yourself two open tracks for harmonies. As another example, if you have only one compressor and you'd like to use it on both the bass and the guitar then you will want to record the two separately so you can use separate compressor settings on each. This idea of sequential use of outboard gear and allocation of tracks will become much clearer when we get into the step-by-step diagrams.

A Note on Notes

As if the above planning doesn't sound paper-intensive enough, I highly recommend that you keep a journal listing any pertinent information of what you did when recording a track. I can tell you from personal experience that it is real ugly when you go to duplicate a great sound and you can't remember exactly what you did. I've included a journal template that you can copy for your notebooks. Remember, after fourteen hours of recording, your mind is likely to be a trash heap of stuff you tried and discarded. It is a drag to have to sort through all that again just to get back a sound because you forgot to write it down.

About the Mix Diagrams

The following diagrams are set up to show the process of recording a complete imaginary song. They are included to be an easy reference for how to perform various recording functions. It's a good idea to refer to them periodically, because in addition to their basic value they can also be a trigger for a burst of invention and some new ways to do things.

And Away We Go

Our imaginary song is performed by an invisible band consisting of drums, bass, two guitars, four backing vocals, and a lead singer. I have tried to diagram what I find to be a relatively common set of musical circumstance and have included some variations that I hope will be illustrative. The approach I adopted here was to show what can be done with a very basic system. There is no attempt in the diagrams to address how to use any specific special gear.

The steps you will take at home will of course depend on the equipment you have available to you. For instance, if you have additional outboard EQ beyond what's available on the portable studio you already know that I recommend using it. If you have favorite sound-processing gear by all means incorporate it. With regard to reverb and ambient effects I have been deliberately vague; you have to let circumstances dictate how these colors will be used.

Finally, these diagrams are guidelines that you can use as a jumping-off place for exploring new and better ways of expressing your artistic vision. The last thing I want is for anyone to stick slavishly to mine or anyone else's formula. What I most want you to get from the information in this book is the skill that will allow you to create.

Basics Revisited

Here are a few tips and reminders to keep mentally handy to help you through the sonic jungle.

- Check each instrument for any noise-generating stuff and be sure the signal-to-noise ratio is optimized for each piece of outboard gear.

- Remember when you premix: once a track is combined with another track the two cannot be separated. Make sure that you are happy with each musical element before you commit to it.

- Take frequent reality checks. Make sure that each step of the way is leading you toward your musical vision.

- Plan what you are going to do and in what order.

- Take notes! Don't even trust your pizza order to memory, much less your favorite guitar sound.

- Remember, it ain't brain surgery; nobody's gonna die if you screw up. Experiment and have some fun.

Good luck. Now go ye forth and multitrack.

Step 1: Mixing and Recording Drum Machine, Stereo Reverb, Snare Reverb, and Bass to Tracks 1 and 2 of the Portable Studio

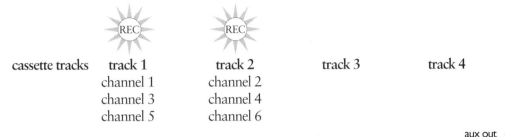

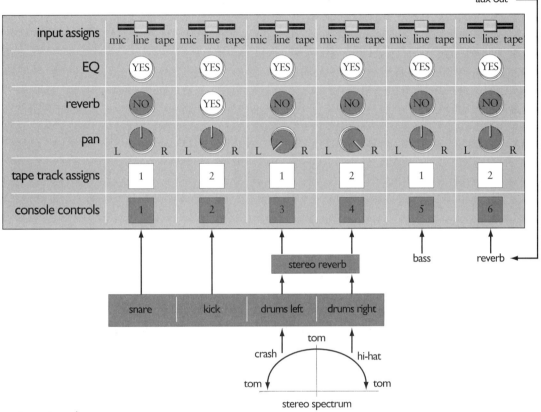

1. Plugging in the setup

- Set up drum machine as below:
  a. Kick (bass) drum sent to output 1
  b. Snare drum sent to output 2
  c. Other drums left and right as shown, or variation as desired
  d. Combination of cymbals and drums left and right sent to the stereo outputs
- Plug left stereo out of drum machine to left stereo in of reverb (reverb 1).
- Plug right stereo out of drum machine into right stereo in of reverb.
- Plug kick drum out of drum machine into channel 1 of portable studio.
- Plug snare drum out of drum machine into channel 2 of portable studio.
- Plug left output of stereo reverb into channel 3 of portable studio.
- Plug right output of stereo reverb into channel 4 of portable studio.
- Plug bass guitar into channel 5 of portable studio. To use a compressor insert it between the bass and the console channel, then set the parameters.
- Plug effect output of portable studio into reverb 2.
- Plug one side of reverb 2 into channel 6 of portable studio.

2. Inputting to the portable studio console

- In this case all channels are set to "line in."
- Set fader to manufacturer's zero or middle-mark level.
- Use line trim (if available) to control level of instrument.
- Input level to channel should not exceed +6 on peaks.

3. Inputting to tape

- Set the portable studio to record on tracks 1 and 2.
- Monitor on cue 1 and 2.

4. Balancing reverbs

- Play drum machine and balance reverb 1, with a mix of straight signal to effect as desired.
- Set reverb to desired program and parameters.

5. Panning

- Pan all portable studio channels as shown. (Note: The panning at this stage is buss assignment, so tracks panned up the middle will go equally to tracks 1 and 2, just as in a stereo mix.)

6. Send to auxiliary

- The snare drum auxiliary (effect) send will be engaged to send signal to reverb 2.
- Set reverb 2 to desired program (*i.e.*, gated reverb, *etc.*).

7. Equalizing the channels

- Play drum machine and EQ kick drum on portable studio as discussed.
- Play drum machine and EQ snare drum on portable studio as discussed.
- Play drum machine and EQ other drums and cymbals on portable studio as discussed.
- EQ bass guitar on portable studio as discussed.
- EQ snare reverb 2 on portable studio to enhance snare sound.

8. Balance the total mix

- Final tweaking of EQ and reverb.
- Using faders, blend volume of elements in pleasing proportions.

9. Record to tracks 1 and 2

10. Play back tracks 1 and 2 for critical listening

- If it isn't right adjust the levels and record again. Remember, these are your fundamental tracks — make sure you're happy with them before you go on.

The stereo spectrum after the first-stage mix:

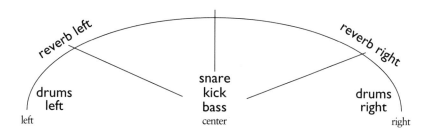

The mix is set up in the following manner: The **kick drum** and **bass guitar** are panned to the center of the mix. They will work in concert to provide the heart-beat of the track. Since they are both low-frequency instruments they also are best put in the center (mono). There is no reverb applied to either because I want them to be very upfront in the mix. Being low-frequency they can be quite loud and not interfere with the other elements I plan for the middle.

The **snare drum** is panned center as the principal rhythm instrument. I have used a snare drum preset with a nonlinear reverb to fatten the snare sound.

The **drums left and right** are the culmination of an internal bounce in the drum machine. I chose to use the American drum perspective and put the high-hat at about one o'clock and the crash at about ten o'clock. I also set the toms to go from high to low, right to left. To these drums I want to add some reverb to move them back a little in the stereo spectrum. As I have no more console channel inputs I will have to use the reverb as a **chained** instrument, meaning that the instrument signal will have to go through the unit, be mixed with the effect internally, and then that combination inputted to the console. As you know from "The Effects Chapter," this is not the most desirable way do it, but in this case it's the only option. The output of the **reverb**, which is a combination of drums, cymbals, and reverb, is then sent out the stereo outputs of the reverb to channels 3 and 4 of the portable studio. These channels are assigned to tracks 1 and 2 respectively, creating the stereo spread.

Step 2: Recording Rhythm Guitar and Lead Vocal to Tracks 3 and 4; Monitoring Stereo Mix on Tracks 1 and 2 with Reverb to Cue

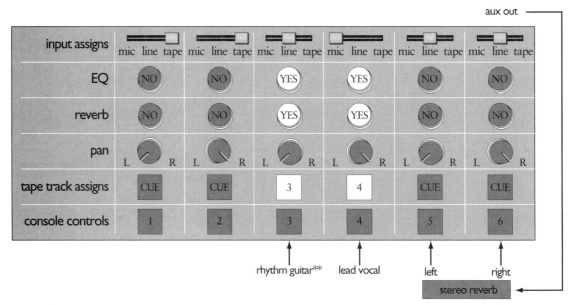

* EQ if necessary
**Record before the lead vocal

1. Setting up to monitor for overdubbing

- Assign tracks 1 and 2 to tape return. Pan them hard left and right for stereo mix.
- Plug auxiliary (effect) out of portable studio into stereo reverb input.
- Plug output of reverb into portable studio channel and send to cue, not to tape. (In this fashion reverb can be used for listening and not be recorded to tape.)
  (Note: See your owner's manual for routing configuration.)

2. Recording the guitar

- Plug guitar into portable studio channel and bring into console using "line in" (if recording direct) or "mic in" (if miked amplifier).
- Assign guitar to record on track 3.
- Enable track 3 record input.
- EQ guitar as discussed.
- Set record level to track 3.

- Record on track 3.
- When done, set track 3 to tape return for monitoring.

3. Recording the vocal

- Plug vocal mic into portable studio channel and bring into console using "mic in."
- Assign vocal to record on track 4.
- Enable track 4 record input.
- Insert compressor if desired (see "The Recipe Section").
- EQ vocal as discussed.
- Set monitor level in headphones (remember to use headphones if there is an open mic).
- Set record level to track 4.
- Record on track 4.
- Without monitoring tracks 1 and 2, review tracks 3 and 4 to make sure that the overdubs are right and as free of noise as possible.

Step 3: Mixing to the Two-Track (First Bounce)

In this step you'll combine the original stereo mix from tracks 1 and 2 with the new elements on tracks 3 and 4 into a new stereo mix.

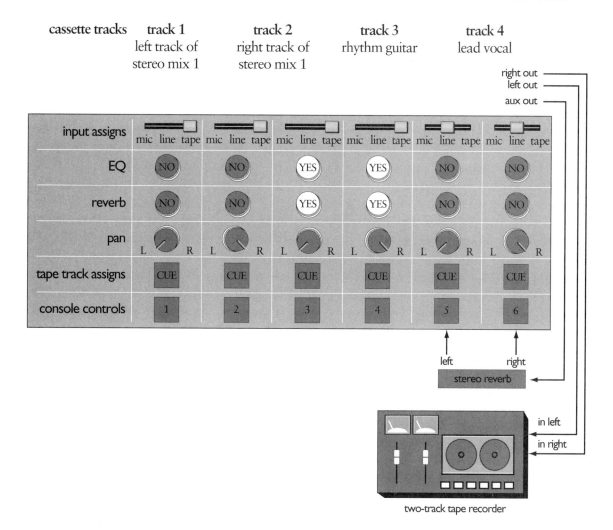

1. Setting up for the mix

- Put all four tracks in tape return.
- Pan tracks as shown (or as desired).
- Apply reverb as shown. (Note: I am bringing the reverb back into two portable studio channels so that I can EQ it. Some consoles may not have EQ on these "extra" channels.)
- Apply EQ as discussed. (Remember to check out top-end boost.)
- Send all tracks to stereo mix (or "stereo buss," "master," "two-track out," *etc.*, whatever your manufacturer calls it).

2. Setting record levels of two-track machine

- Plug stereo left of portable studio into stereo left of two-track.
- Plug stereo right of portable studio into stereo right of two-track.
- Place the two-track into "input," ready to record.
- Play some of the mix from the portable studio and watch the meters on the two-track.
- Adjust the master output fader on the portable studio and the input control on the two-track to establish a good signal-to-noise ratio.
- To check if your mix is balanced left and right, listen for the snare drum and watch the meters on the two-track. The left and right meters should read equal level on a given snare hit. This means that the snare is in the middle, which means that there is a correct amount of level from both sides. If one meter is reading higher than the other, the sides are out of balance and the fader of one of the portable studio channels needs to be adjusted.

3. Engage noise reduction on two-track

4. Record to two-track

The stereo spectrum after the first external bounce:

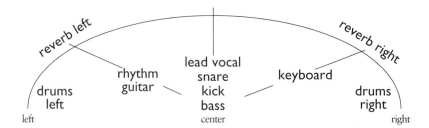

The first thing I did was to record the **rhythm guitar** to act as a support and reference point for the vocalist. That way I have some control over how loud the guitar is for the singer. If it was already premixed then the singer would have no choice of headphone balance between the guitar and the rest of the track.

Next I want to record the final **lead vocal** so that all other overdubs will have the vocal as a reference point. As in most songs the vocal will be the center of attention and all the other instruments will act as supporting players. By recording the vocal early in the process I'll immediately know if any overdubs I record are distracting. Remembering the line of focus, I want to have the lead vocal in the center of the stereo spectrum. I will EQ it to make the most of the top end, and I will be sure that it is loud enough in the mix that it will not get lost when other instruments are added (even if it sounds a little over-loud at this early stage). Finally I add a reverb to it and the rhythm guitar, delayed to keep the front end of the sound clear before the reverb is heard. I will add relatively more reverb to the guitar to make it appear farther back in the track.

The process of mixing a vocal is a little different from other instruments in that it often requires "riding" the fader. This means raising the level smoothly to catch quiet or indistinct words and lowering the level to keep the dynamics under control. It is the mixdown version of hand compression.

Step 4: Returning the Mix to the Portable Studio from the Two-Track

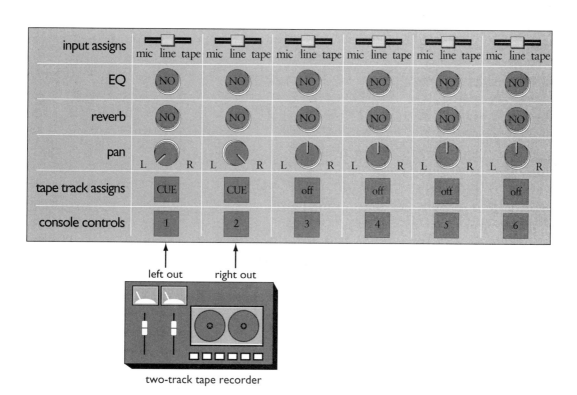

two-track tape recorder

- Plug the left output of the two-track into channel 1 of the portable studio.
- Plug the right output of the two-track into channel 2 of the portable studio.
- Set channels 1 and 2 to line in.
- Pan channels 1 and 2 of the portable studio to left and right, respectively.
- Play the two-track mix and monitor it to make sure that the mix is the way you want it.
- If desired, EQ channels 1 and 2 to EQ entire mix from the two-track.
- Enable input to record to tracks 1 and 2 of the portable studio.
- Set record levels of tracks 1 and 2 with faders on portable studio channels.
- Engage noise reduction on portable studio.
- Record on portable studio tracks 1 and 2.
- Erase tracks 3 and 4.

You will repeat this step each time you return a bounced mix to the portable studio.

Step 5: Recording Lead Guitar and Keyboard to Tracks 3 and 4 while Monitoring Stereo Mix Tracks 1 and 2 with Reverb to Cue

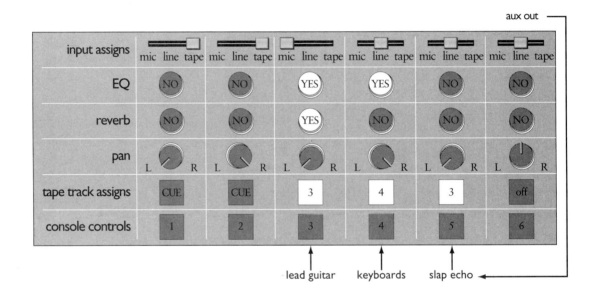

1. Setting up to monitor for overdubbing

- Assign tracks 1 and 2 to tape return.
- Pan them hard left and right for stereo mix.
- Plug auxiliary (effect) out of portable studio into stereo reverb input.

2. Recording the guitar and slap echo

- Plug guitar into portable studio and bring into console using line in (if guitar direct) or mic in (if miked amplifier).
- Assign guitar (pan left) to record on track 3.
- Enable track 3 record input.
- EQ guitar as discussed.
- Plug mono output of reverb into portable studio channel 5.
- Set to line in channel 5.
- Set slap echo as desired.
- Balance and EQ slap echo level with guitar level.
- Pan channel 5 left to record on track 3.
- Set record level of channels 3 and 5 to track 3.
- Record on track 3.
- When done assign track 3 to tape in for monitoring.

3. Recording the keyboard

- Plug keyboard into channel 4 line in.
- Assign keyboard to record on track 4.
- Enable track 4 record input.
- EQ keyboard as discussed.
- Set record level to track 4.
- Record on track 4.

Without monitoring tracks 1 and 2, review tracks 3 and 4 to make sure that the overdubs are right and free of noise as possible.

Step 6: Mixing to the Two-Track (Second Bounce)

In this step you'll combine the original stereo mix from tracks 1 and 2 with the lead guitar, slap echo, and keyboard on tracks 3 and 4 into a new stereo mix.

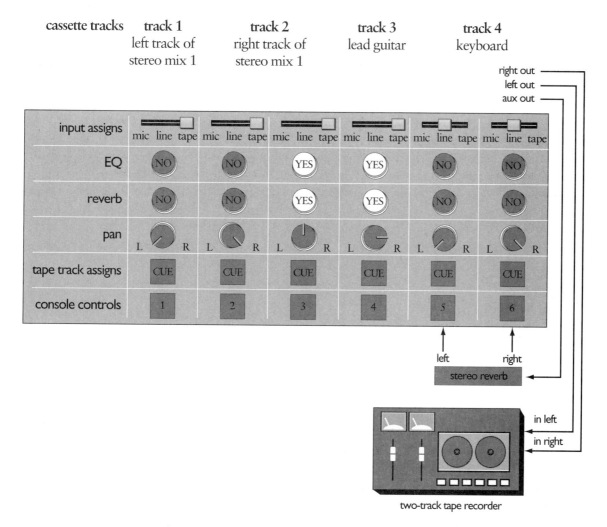

cassette tracks	track 1	track 2	track 3	track 4
	left track of stereo mix 1	right track of stereo mix 1	lead guitar	keyboard

two-track tape recorder

1. Setting up for the mix

- Put all four tracks in tape return.
- Pan tracks as shown (or as desired).
- Apply reverb as shown.
- Apply EQ as discussed (remember to check out top-end boost).
- Send all tracks to stereo mix.

2. Reminders to set record levels of two-track machine

- Plug stereo left of portable studio into stereo left of two-track.
- Plug stereo right of portable studio into stereo right of two-track.
- Place the two-track into input ready to record.
- Play some of the mix from the portable studio and watch the meters on the two-track.
- Adjust the master output fader on the portable studio and the input control on the two-track to establish a good signal-to-noise ratio.
- Check to make sure your mix is balanced left and right by using the snare drum (see Step 3).

3. Engage noise reduction on two-track

4. Record to two-track machine

The stereo spectrum after the Step-6 mix:

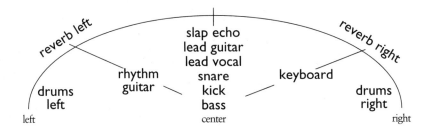

At one point in this song the lead guitar plays a solo. I have determined that at that point I want the lead guitar to take center stage literally and figuratively. So I will pan the lead to the center of the mix and EQ it to boost the psychoacoustically active upper midrange (2 to 3 K) to attract focus.

I also want to do a special ambient treatment to get the lead to stand out from the rest of the instruments. Since they're getting a straight reverb I chose a slap echo for this guitar. Since this reverb is in mono I will pan it to the middle and consider it a component of the guitar sound. For this reason I may EQ it a little differently from the guitar itself. Adding a little bottom will add warmth and also move the slap farther back behind the guitar.

The keyboard is panned to offset the rhythm guitar previously mixed on the opposite side. There is no rule about this but I like there to be support elements on both sides of the stereo spectrum. I EQ the keys keeping in mind that I want them to blend in the background and not intrude on the vocal. I might emphasize the low mids or bottom end and less of the top frequencies. I also added a fair amount of straight reverb because I want the keys to sustain and fade smoothly.

Repeat Step 4 to return this two-track mix to portable studio.

Step 7: Recording Two Background Vocals and Reverb "Doubles" to Tracks 3 and 4 while Monitoring Stereo Mix Tracks 1 and 2

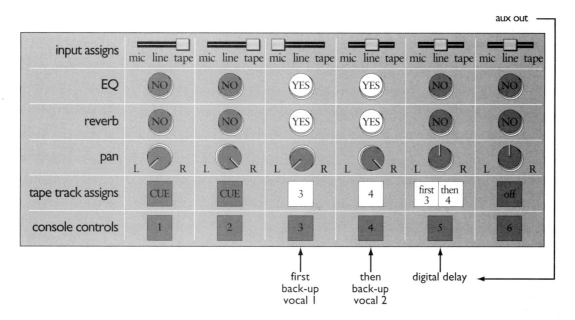

1. Setting up to monitor for overdubbing

- Assign tracks 1 and 2 to tape return.
- Pan them hard left and right for stereo mix.
- Plug auxiliary (effect) out of portable studio into stereo reverb input.
- Plug mono output of reverb into channel 5 line in.
- Set reverb as delay (see " The Effects Chapter").

2. Recording vocal and electronic double

- Plug vocal mic into portable studio channel and bring into console using mic in.
- Assign vocal to record on track 3.
- Enable track 3 record input.
- Insert compressor if desired (see "The Recipe Section").
- EQ vocal as discussed.
- Enable effect send to send to reverb from channel 3.
- Set monitor level to headphones (remember to use headphones when there is an open mic).
- Assign reverb channel (5) to record on track 3.
- Balance amount of reverb "double" with background vocal.
- Set record level of combination of channels 3 and 5 to track 3.
- Record on track 3.

Repeat the process, recording to track 4. Then, without monitoring tracks 1 and 2, review tracks 3 and 4 to make sure they are right and as free of noise as possible.

Step 8: Mixing to the Two-Track (Third Bounce)

In this step combine the stereo mix from tracks 1 and 2 with the first set of background vocals and electronic "doubles" on tracks 3 and 4 into a new stereo mix.

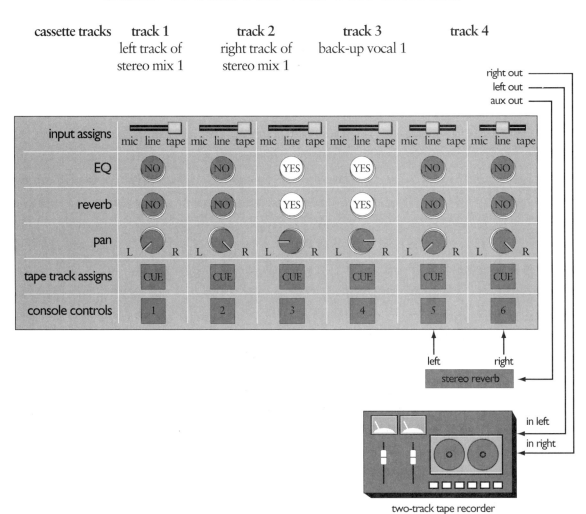

cassette tracks	track 1	track 2	track 3	track 4
	left track of stereo mix 1	right track of stereo mix 1	back-up vocal 1	

two-track tape recorder

1. Setting up for the mix

- Set all four tracks in tape return.
- Pan tracks as shown (tracks 3 and 4 are both panned mid-left).
- Apply reverb as shown.
- Apply EQ as discussed (remember to check out top-end boost).
- Send all tracks to stereo mix.

2. Reminders to set record levels of two-track machine

- Place the two-track into input ready to record.
- Play some of the mix from the portable studio and watch the meters on the two-track.
- Adjust the master output fader on the portable studio and the input control on the two-track to establish a good signal-to-noise ratio.
- Check to make sure your mix is balanced left and right by using the snare drum (see Step 3).

3. Engage noise reduction on two-track

4. Record to two-track machine

The stereo spectrum after the Step-8 mix:

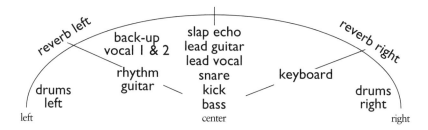

The object here is to get the effect of an eight-voice background harmony group with only one actual voice. The way you do it is to add an electronic delay, or *mult,* to the vocal being sung. Actually the mult is a single-repeat echo set very close in time to the original signal. The idea is to get it to sound as if there are twice as many voices rather than a slap echo. This takes a little fooling around with delay times (usually in milliseconds). Another very pleasing option is to use chorusing as an alternative to the delay.

We record one voice and its delay to track 3, in much the same way that we recorded the snare and its reverb to track 2. The next step is to repeat the process and go to track 4. This will in effect create a four-voice harmony section. The final harmony step will be to repeat the whole process again in Step 9, thereby giving you eight voices.

By the way, if this is a two-part harmony I would record part 1 first, then part 2, then combine them to the left side on the first bounce. Then I would record part 1 and part 2 again and combine them to the right side in the final mix.

Repeat Step 4 to return this two-track mix to the portable studio.

Step 9: Mixing to the Two-Track (Final Mix)

In this step combine the stereo mix from tracks 1 and 2 with the second set of background vocals and electronic "doubles" on tracks 3 and 4 into a new stereo mix. The, you can EQ the overall mix and add level rides.

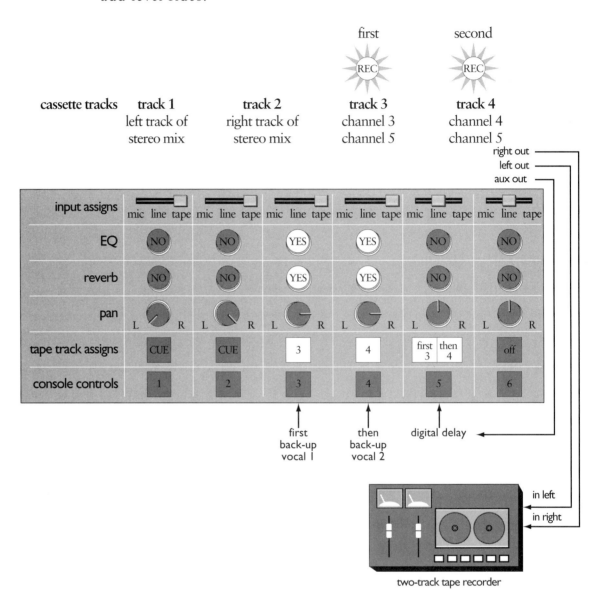

1. Setting up for the mix

- Set all four tracks in tape return.
- Pan tracks as shown (tracks 3 and 4 are both panned mid-right).
- Apply reverb as shown.
- Apply EQ as shown (remember to check out top-end boost).
- Send all tracks to stereo mix.

2. Reminders to set record levels of two-track machine

- Place the two-track into input ready to record.
- Play some of the mix from the portable studio and watch the meters on the two-track.
- Adjust the master output fader on the portable studio and the input control on the two-track to establish a good signal-to-noise ratio on the two-track.
- Check to make sure your mix is balanced left and right by using the snare drum (see Step 3).

3. Engage noise reduction on the two-track

4. Record to two-track machine

The stereo spectrum after the Step-9 mix:

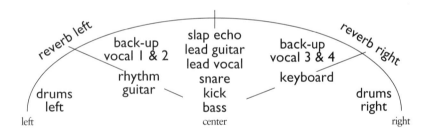

The Final Mix

This is more or less the last stage of the mix. At this point I will complete the background vocals and move them in opposite balance to the backgrounds on the last pass. This time, however, when I go to the two-track I am going to do some overall coloration. I'm going to insert a stereo equalizer between the portable studio and the two-track to equalize each side of the mix (left and right) from the portable studio simultaneously. This will allow me to bring out some mix characteristics (punch and clarity, for instance) and hide others (harshness, muddiness). At the same time I can also compress the entire mix to help eliminate wild dynamic swings. I will use this opportunity to EQ the stereo mix on tracks 1 and 2 if I think it will benefit by it.

Another trick I employ in the mix is to actually create some desirable dynamic changes as the song goes along. For instance, I might want to raise the volume of the whole song at the chorus and bring it down for the verses, thereby introducing a little added excitement. I do this by "riding" the master output fader. Alternatively, if I only want to create a "move" on one side of the mix I can open up the input of the two-track on that side.

The last thing I do is the fade. This is the final mix, so you want to fade the song evenly. An effective fade usually dips as follows: first third fairly rapidly so people know you're fading; middle third more gradually; last third fairly rapidly, ending on some musical part that makes sense as the period on the sentence, so to speak.

By the way, you always bring the faders down after a mix to eliminate bias noise even if the song is an ending rather than a fade. You don't want someone's last impression of your music to be noise.

Well, my friends, the fat lady has sung — this song is done. Time to move on to the rest of your career. Best of luck.

The Recipe Section:
How to Do Things
You Thought You Couldn't Do
with a Portable Studio

This section of the book is designed to provide step-by-step instructions on how to make your portable studio do things it doesn't usually do. To get the most out of this section read the following guidelines before you dive in.

- Read the text first. Follow good basic recording practices. Remember: garbage in, garbage out.

- When stuff doesn't work, it's usually pilot error. (But if someone you're trying to impress is in the room, go ahead and blame it on the machine.)

- The specific channel and track numbers used in these instructions are for example only. In most cases any combination can be used.

- Often a technique described for one application can be used with good results for instruments other than those in the example.

- Connector types may vary from one piece of gear to another. Be sure to check for proper connectors.

- When combining instruments or mics, check for phase relationships (see "The Microphone Chapter") to be sure one signal isn't out of phase with another.

- Experiment!

RECIPE 1 (EQUALIZER)
USING AN OUTBOARD EQUALIZER TO RECORD AN INSTRUMENT "DIRECT IN"

Application: Additional EQ for sound enhancement and problem solving when recording a direct in track.

Requirement: Outboard equalizer

1. Plug instrument into input of outboard EQ.
2. Plug output of EQ into input (line) channel of portable studio.
3. Set EQ.
4. Check level to record.
5. Record track.

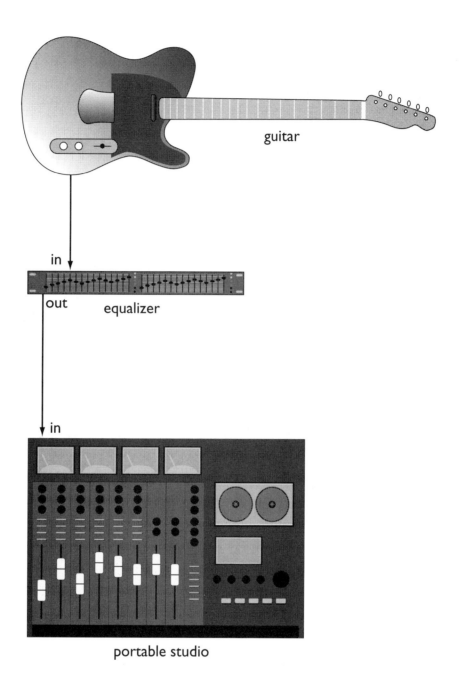

guitar

in

out   equalizer

in

portable studio

assign channel I
record track ❶

Recipe 2 (Equalizer)
Using an Outboard Equalizer to Record a Miked Instrument

Application: Additional EQ for sound enhancement and problem solving when recording an acoustic or amplified instrument track.

Requirement: Outboard equalizer

1. Mic instrument or amp.
2. Plug microphone into portable studio channel 1 (mic in).
3. Plug effect send output of portable studio into outboard EQ in.
4. Plug output of EQ into channel 3 of portable studio.
5. Use channel 1 effect send to route signal to EQ.
6. Set EQ.
7. Assign *only* channel 3 to record on track 1.
8. Check level to record.
9. Record on track 1.

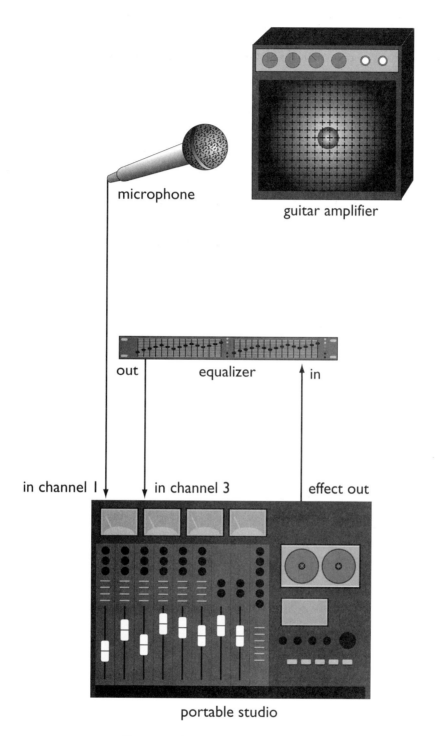

guitar amplifier

microphone

out   equalizer   in

in channel 1   in channel 3   effect out

portable studio

use effect send channel 1
assign channel 3
record track ❶

RECIPE 3 (EQUALIZER)
RECORDING USING A COMPRESSOR AND OUTBOARD EQ

Application: Particularly useful for vocals, bass, or any situation where large dynamic changes need to be controlled. The EQ is used after the compressor to recapture frequencies and add life that may have been lost in the compression process.

Requirements: Compressor, outboard equalizer

1. Mic instrument or amp.
2. Plug microphone into portable studio channel 1 (mic in).
3. Plug effect send output of portable studio into compressor in.
4. Plug output of compressor into input of outboard EQ.
5. Plug output of EQ into channel 3 input (line) of portable studio.
6. Use channel 1 effect send to route signal to compressor and EQ.
7. Set compressor.
8. Set EQ.
9. Assign *only* channel 3 to record on track 1.
10. Check level to record.
11. Record on track 1.

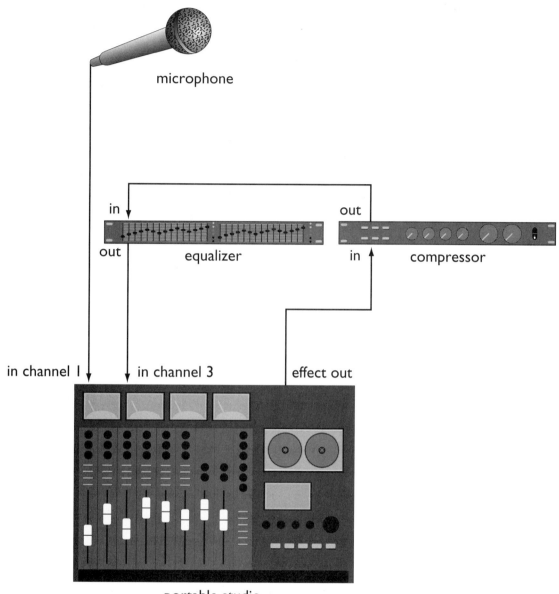

microphone

in

out

out

in

equalizer

compressor

in channel 1

in channel 3

effect out

portable studio

use effect send channel 1
assign channel 3
record track ❶

Recipe 4 (Compressor)
Using an Equalizer and a Compressor

Application: To control dynamic range that is frequency-dependent. Particularly useful for "de-essing" vocals or for removing instrumental harshness. Used in the following manner the compressor will only compress when the undesirable frequency appears (*e.g.*, de-ess @ 7 K).

Requirements: Compressor, outboard equalizer

1. Mic instrument or amp.
2. Plug microphone into portable studio channel 1 (mic in).
3. Plug effect send output of portable studio into outboard EQ in.
4. Plug output of EQ into input of compressor.
5. Plug output of compressor into channel 3 input (line) of portable studio.
6. Use channel 1 effect send to route signal to EQ and compressor.
7. Set EQ to boost offending frequency slightly.
8. Set compressor (quick attack and release) to dip slightly only on the peaks of offending frequency.
9. Assign *only* channel 3 to record on track 1.
10. Check level to record.
11. Record on track 1.

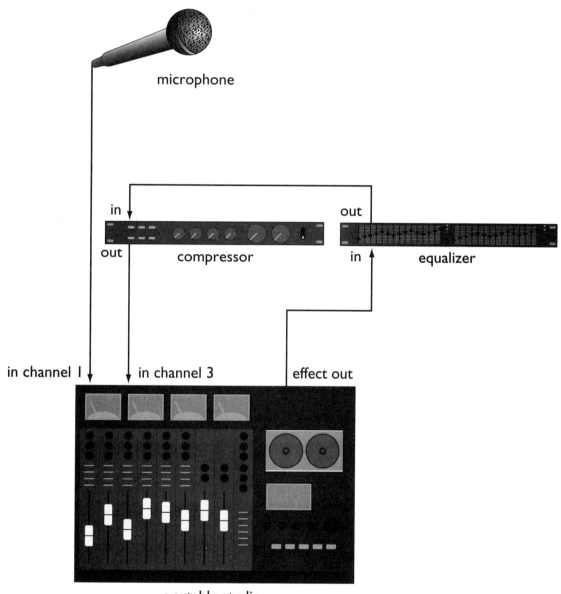

microphone

in

out   compressor

out

in   equalizer

in channel 1   in channel 3   effect out

portable studio

use effect send channel 1
assign channel 3
record track ❶

RECIPE 5 (EQUALIZER)
EQUALIZING A STEREO MIX

Application: To enhance the overall sound of a final mix as it is being recorded to two-track. (Can be used in the external bouncing procedure as well.)

Requirements: Stereo equalizer or two mono equalizers

1. Set up mix at desired levels as described in "The Mixdown Chapter."
2. Plug left master output of portable studio into left input of equalizer.
3. Plug left output of equalizer into left input of two-track mixdown machine.
4. Plug right master output of portable studio into right input of equalizer.
5. Plug right output of equalizer into right input of two-track mixdown machine.
6. Set desired equalization.
7. Set record levels on two-track mixdown machine.
8. Record to two-track mixdown machine.

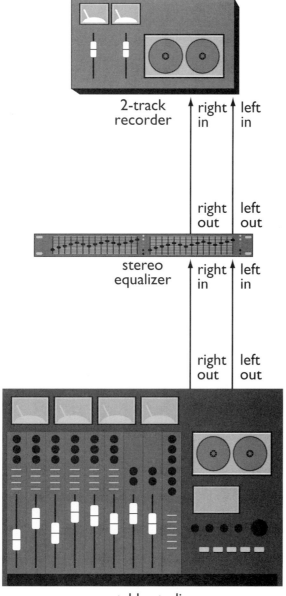

2-track
recorder

right | left
in | in

right | left
out | out

stereo
equalizer

right | left
in | in

right | left
out | out

portable studio

Recipe 6 (Equalizer)
Equalizing Several Instruments at the Same Time Using Only One Equalizer

Application: To enhance the sound of a blend of instruments or to eliminate harshness. Particularly good for vocals. This process can be done either while recording the original tracks or while combining after the tracks have been recorded.

Requirement: Equalizer

1. Plug portable studio effect send output into input of equalizer.
2. Plug output of equalizer into channel 3 line in.
3. Assign *only* channel 3 to record on track 3.
4. Bring mic/instrument 1 into channel 1; *do not* assign to record.
5. Bring mic/instrument 2 into channel 2; *do not* assign to record.
6. Send signal from channels 1 and 2 out to effect send.
7. Monitor track 3.
8. EQ channels 1 and 2 for differences.
9. Set outboard EQ to blend instruments.
10. Record combination on track 3.

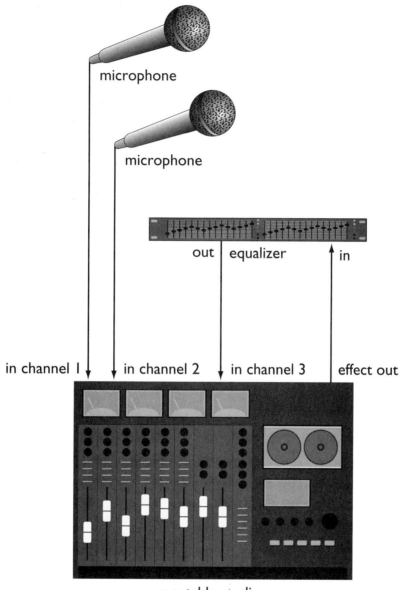

microphone

microphone

out | equalizer | in

in channel 1   in channel 2   in channel 3   effect out

portable studio

use effect sends channel 1 and channel 2
assign channel 3
record track ❸

Recipe 7 (Compressor)
Compressing an Instrument while Recording Direct In

Application: Basic compression used to control dynamic range. Particularly useful for bass and to add sustain to acoustic guitar.

Requirement: Mono compressor

1. Plug instrument into input of compressor.
2. Plug output of compressor into channel 1 line in.
3. Set compressor (start at 4:1 ratio).
4. Play instrument; set compressor to 3 dB gain reduction to begin; adjust accordingly.
5. EQ channel 1.
6. Assign channel 1 to record on track 1.
7. Check record level of track 1.
8. Record on track 1.

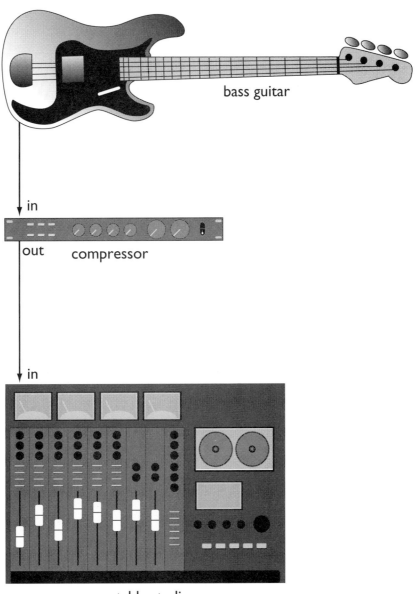

bass guitar

in

compressor

out

in

portable studio

assign channel 1
record track ❶

Recipe 8 (Compressor)
Compressing a Microphone Signal

Application: Basic compression used to control dynamic range. Particularly useful for vocals and to add sustain to acoustic guitar.

Requirement: Mono compressor

1. Plug microphone into channel 1 mic input.
2. Plug portable studio effect send output into input of compressor.
3. Plug output of compressor into channel 2 line in.
4. Set compressor (start at 4:1 ratio, quick attack, slow release).
5. Use channel 1 effect send to route signal to compressor.
6. Assign *only* channel 2 to record on track 2.
7. Monitor track 2.
8. Vocalize or play instrument and set compressor to 3 dB gain reduction to begin; adjust settings according to taste.
9. EQ channel 1. (Do *not* assign to track 2.)
10. EQ channel 2.
11. Check record level of track 2.
12. Record on track 2.

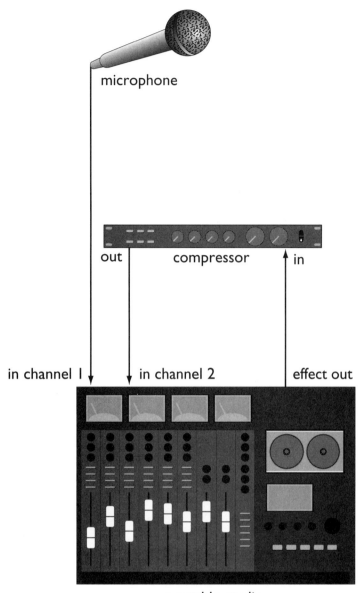

microphone

out   compressor   in

in channel 1   in channel 2   effect out

portable studio

use effect send channel 1
assign channel 2
record track ❷

RECIPE 9 (COMPRESSOR)
COMPRESSING A STEREO MIX

Application: To enhance the overall sound of a final mix as it is being recorded to two-track. (Can be used in the external bouncing procedure as well.)

Requirements: Stereo compressor or two mono compressors

1. Set up mix at desired levels as described in "The Mixdown Chapter."
2. Plug left master output of portable studio into left input of compressor.
3. Plug left output of compressor into left input of two-track mixdown machine.
4. Plug right master output of portable studio into right input of compressor.
5. Plug right output of compressor into right input of two-track mixdown machine.
6. Set desired compression. (For natural-sounding compression; ratio usually 4:1, gain reduction less than 3 dB at peaks, quick gentle release.)
7. Set record levels on two-track mixdown machine.
8. Record to two-track.

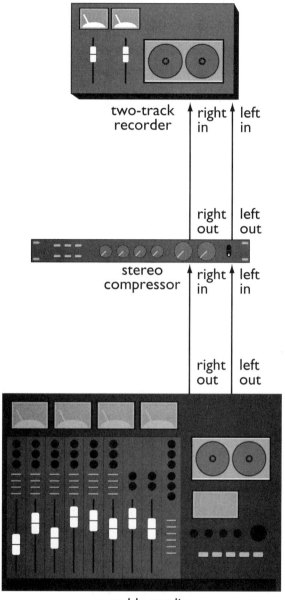

two-track
recorder

right
in

left
in

right
out

left
out

stereo
compressor

right
in

left
in

right
out

left
out

portable studio

RECIPE 10 (COMPRESSOR)
COMPRESSING SEVERAL INSTRUMENTS AT THE SAME TIME USING ONLY ONE COMPRESSOR

Application: To enhance the sound of a blend of instruments or to eliminate harshness. Particularly good for vocals or multiple guitars. This process can be done either while recording the original tracks or while combining after the tracks have been recorded.

Requirement: Compressor

1. Plug portable studio effect send output into input of compressor.
2. Plug output of compressor into channel 3 line in.
3. Assign *only* channel 3 to record on track 3.
4. Plug mic/instrument 1 into channel 1; do *not* assign to record.
5. Plug mic/instrument 2 into channel 2; do *not* assign to record.
6. Send signal from channels 1 and 2 out to effect send.
7. Monitor track 3.
8. EQ channels 1 and 2 for differences.
9. Set compressor.
10. Record combination on track 3.

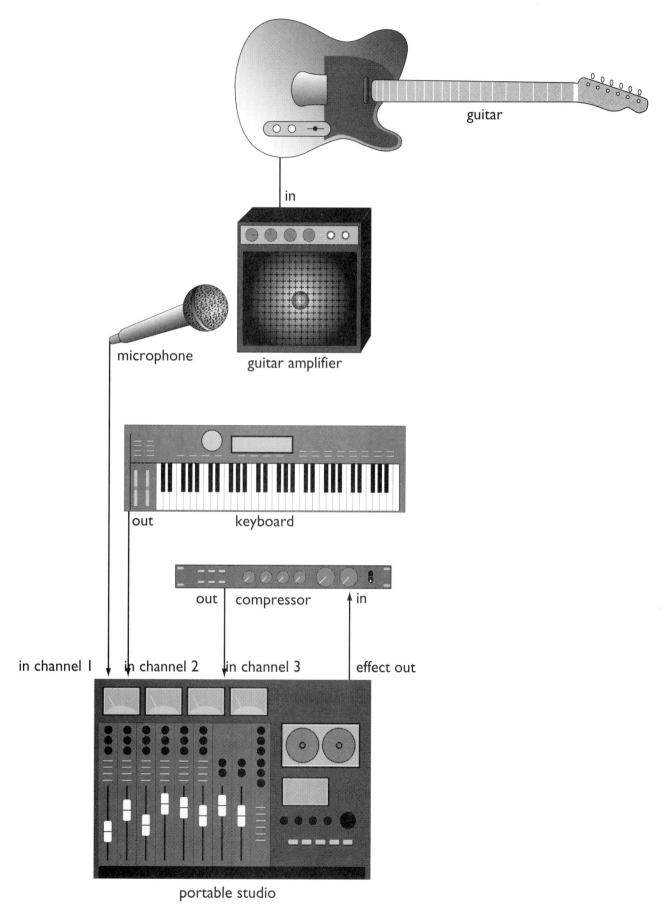

guitar

in

microphone

guitar amplifier

out   keyboard

out │ compressor   ↑ in

in channel 1   in channel 2   in channel 3   effect out

portable studio

use effect sends channel 1 and channel 2
assign channel 3
record track ❸

Recipe 11 (Effect)
Recording an Effect with a Track

Application: Use when you wish to apply a specific reverb to enhance a sound. Useful also when you want a variety of reverbs in the final mix but are limited in the amount of effects you have available. For example, recording a keyboard sound *with* a chorused reverb means you can reset the reverb for another effect in the mix.

Requirement: Signal processor (*e.g.*, reverb)

1. Plug instrument into channel 1 line in.
2. Plug portable studio effect send output into signal processor input.
3. Plug mono out of signal processor into channel 2 line in.
4. Assign channel 1 to record on track 3.
5. Assign channel 2 to record on track 3.
6. Use channel 1 effect send to route signal to reverb.
7. Monitor track 3.
8. EQ and balance channels 1 and 2.
9. Record on track 3.

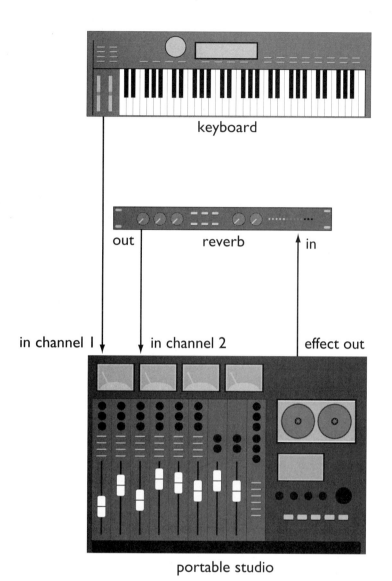

keyboard

out   reverb   in

in channel 1   in channel 2   effect out

portable studio

use effect send channel 1
assign channels 1 and 2
record track ❸

Recipe 12 (Effect)
Stereo Guitar 1

Application: Use this method while recording a track to create a stereo effect from the same signal without altering the characteristics of the sound (*i.e.*, no chorusing, etc.). Particularly good on guitars, but can be used for any instrument.

Requirements: Delay, Y-splitter or direct box

1. Split guitar signal.
2. Plug signal 1 into channel 1 line in.
3. Plug signal 2 into delay input.
4. Plug delay output into channel 2 line in.
5. Set delay time as desired; check for phase problems (see "The Microphone Chapter").
6. EQ channels 1 and 2.
7. Record channel 1 on track 1.
8. Record channel 2 on track 2.
9. After recording tracks, pan track 1 to the left and track 2 to the right.

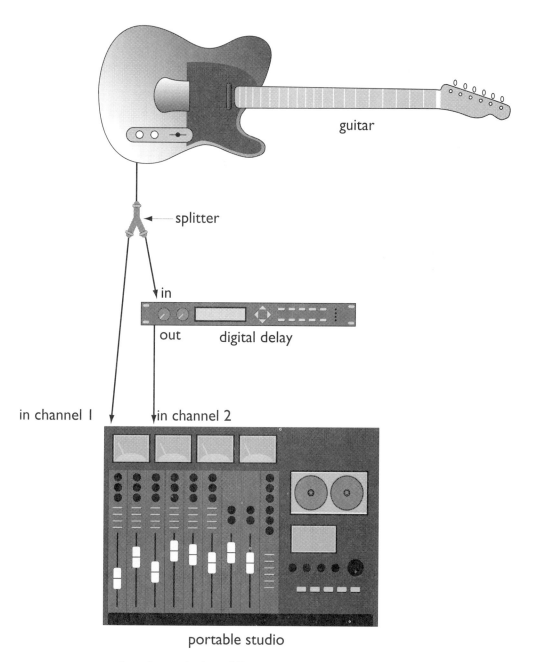

guitar

splitter

in

out   digital delay

in channel 1   in channel 2

portable studio

assign channels 1 and 2
record tracks ❶ and ❷

RECIPE 13 (EFFECT)
STEREO GUITAR 2

Application: Use this method while premixing or bouncing tracks to create a stereo effect from the same signal without altering the characteristics of the sound (*i.e.*, no chorusing, etc.). This method allows use of the portable studio on the delay. Particularly good on guitars but can be used for any instrument. Can be used with either direct in or miked signal or combination. Example is with a miked amp.

Requirement: Delay

1. Plug mic into channel 1 mic in.
2. Plug portable studio effect send output into delay input.
3. Plug delay output into channel 2 line in.
4. Set delay time as desired; check for phase problems (see "The Microphone Chapter").
5. EQ channels 1 and 2.
6. Assign channel 1 to record on track 1.
7. Assign channel 2 to record on track 2.
8. Record on tracks 1 and 2.
9. After recording tracks, pan track 1 to the left and track 2 to the right.

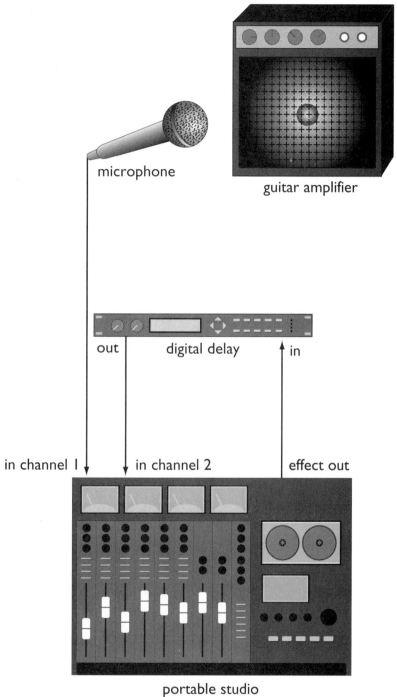

microphone

guitar amplifier

out   digital delay   in

in channel 1   in channel 2   effect out

portable studio

use effect send channel 1
assign channels 1 and 2
record tracks ❶ and ❷

RECIPE 14 (EFFECT)
BIG GUITAR

Application: To increase the apparent size of a "room" in which the instrument is recorded by using a second microphone and a delay. Effective for expanding power sounds (guitars, organ, synth leads, *etc.*) in situations where a reverb may be too "sweet."

Requirements: Hallway or suitably large room, two microphones, delay

1. Follow procedure for close-mic recording of amplified guitar (see "The Guitar Chapter").
2. Set up another microphone four to six feet back from first amp mic. Check for phase problems (see "The Microphone Chapter").
3. Bring distant mic (1) into channel 1 line in.
4. Bring close mic (2) into channel 2 line in.
5. Plug portable studio effect send output into input of delay.
6. Plug delay output into channel 3 line in.
7. Activate effect send of channel 1 to route signal to delay; do not assign channel 1 to record on a track.
8. Set delay time as desired; check for phase problems.
9. Assign channels 2 and 3 to record on track 3.
10. Monitor track 3 and EQ channels 2 and 3 separately (mute the channel not being worked on):
    Close mic: Accentuate 3 K and below.
    Distant mic: Accentuate 5 K and above.
11. Balance channels 2 and 3 for desired effect.
12. Record on track 3.

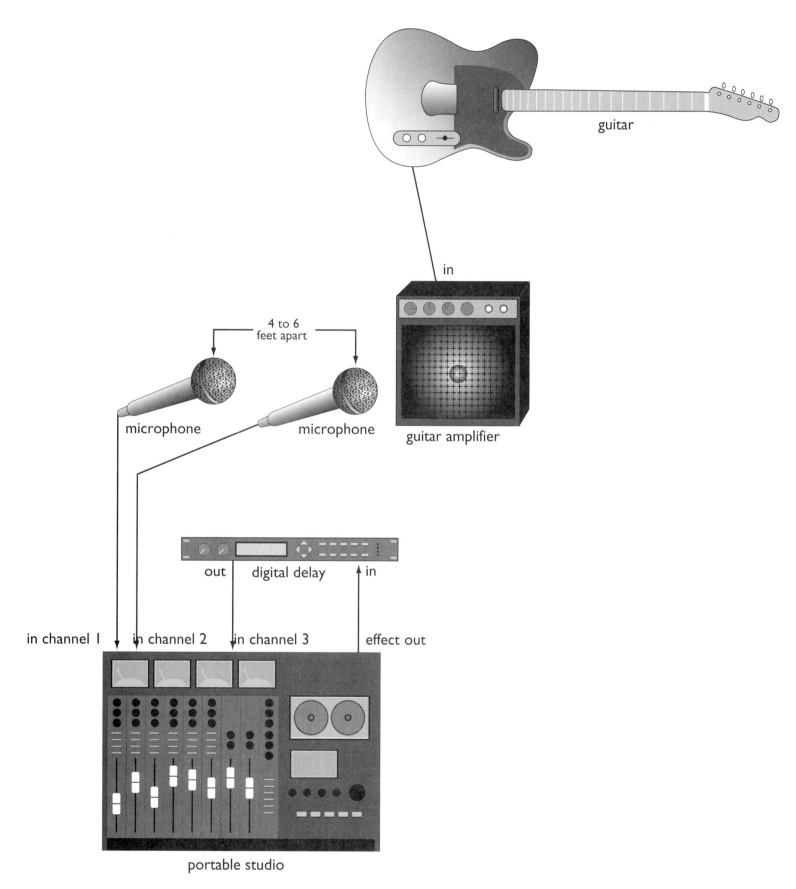

guitar

in

4 to 6
feet apart

microphone   microphone   guitar amplifier

out   digital delay   in

in channel 1   in channel 2   in channel 3   effect out

portable studio

use effect send channel 1
assign channels 2 and 3
record track ❸

268 ⊕ THE RECIPE SECTION: HOW TO DO THINGS YOU THOUGHT YOU COULDN'T DO WITH A PORTABLE STUDIO

RECIPE 15 (EFFECT)
BIG BASS 1

Application: To add additional color and expand bass or keyboard bass without having to use an amplifier. Ideal for apartments or limited acoustic environments.

Requirements: Splitter box, flanger

1. Plug bass into splitter box.
2. Plug one output of splitter into channel 2 line in.
3. Plug other output of splitter into input of flanger.
4. Plug mono output of flanger into channel 1 line in; set flanger as desired.
5. Assign channels 1 and 2 to record on track 4.
6. Monitor track 4.
7. EQ each bass separately (mute the input not being worked on) to complement overall sound:
   Flanger sound: Boost upper mids for clarity.
   Direct sound: Boost lows for punch.
8. Balance levels of channels 1 and 2 for desired combination sound; check for phase problems (see "The Microphone Chapter').
9. Set record level to track 4.
10. Record on track 4.

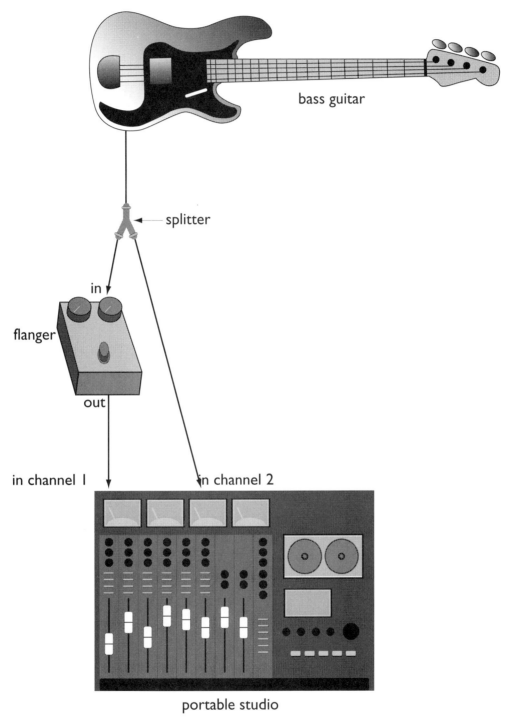

bass guitar

splitter

in

flanger

out

in channel 1

in channel 2

portable studio

assign channels 1 and 2
record track ❹

RECIPE 16 (EFFECT)
BIG BASS 2

Application: To expand a bass sound by adding a miked amplifier to the direct in signal. (Note: In acoustically limited situations, a line out of the preamplifier may be substituted for the microphone/speaker setup.) Especially good for enhancing a keyboard bass.

Requirements: Amplifier, splitter box, microphone, compressor

1. Plug bass into splitter box.
2. Plug one output of splitter into channel 1 line in.
3. Plug other output of splitter into input of amplifier.
4. Mic bass amplifier (as described in "The Bass Chapter").
5. Plug microphone into channel 2 mic in.
6. Plug output of portable studio effect send into input of compressor.
7. Plug output of compressor into channel 3 line in.
8. Use effect sends on channels 1 and 2 to send signal to compressor. Do not assign channels 1 and 2 to record on a track.
9. Assign only channel 3 to record on track 3.
10. Monitor track 3.
11. EQ each bass separately (mute the input not being worked on) to complement overall sound:
    Amp sound: Boost upper mids for clarity.
    Direct sound: Boost lows for punch.
12. Balance levels of channels 1 and 2 for desired compressor level and combination sound; check for phase problems (see "The Microphone Chapter").
13. Set record level to track 3.
14. Record on track 3.

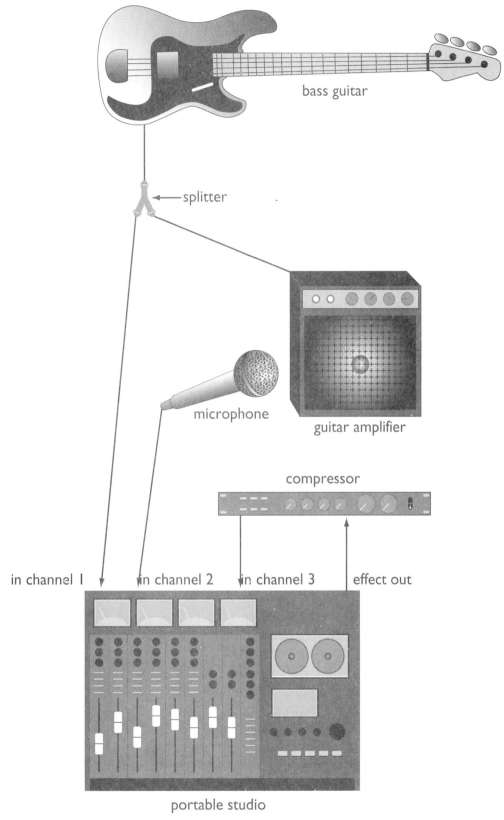

bass guitar

splitter

microphone

guitar amplifier

compressor

in channel 1   in channel 2   in channel 3   effect out

portable studio

use effect sends channels 1 and 2
assign channel 3
record track ❸

Recipe 17 (Effect)
Big Bang Snare

Application: To add a "live" room sound to a drum machine snare.

Requirements: Tile bathroom or similar "bright" acoustic space, amplifier, microphone

1. Plug output of drum machine into channel 1 line in.
2. Plug portable studio effect send output into amplifier input.
3. Place amp in a live room with the speaker facing the most distant wall.
4. Place mic three feet from amp.
5. Plug mic into channel 3 mic in.
6. Use channel 1 effect send to send drum machine to amplifier. Do not assign channel 1 to record on a track.
7. Assign channel 3 to record on track 3
8. EQ channel 3.
9. Set record level to track 3.
10. Record on track 3.

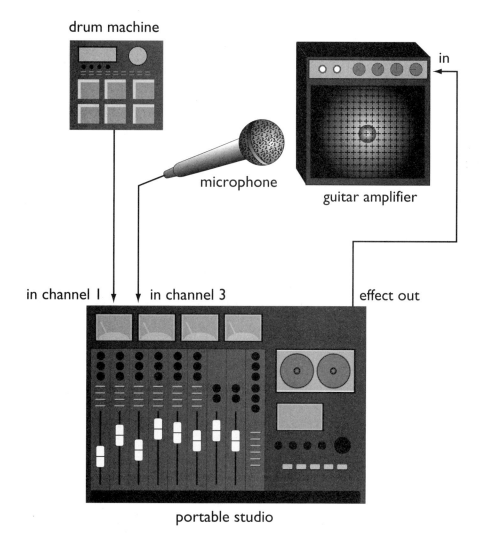

drum machine

microphone

guitar amplifier

in

in channel 1

in channel 3

effect out

portable studio

use effect send channels 1
assign channel 3
record track ❸

RECIPE 18 (EFFECT)
BIG VOCALS

Application: To make a few backup singers sound like a much larger group.

Requirements: Splitter, delay, harmonizer (a chorus can be substituted for the harmonizer but is less effective)

1. Record vocals to tracks 1 and 2 (see "The Vocal Chapter").
2. Assign tracks 1 and 2 to record to track 3.
3. Plug portable studio effect send output into splitter box.
4. Plug one side of splitter box into input of delay.
5. Plug delay output into channel 3 line in.
6. Plug other side of splitter box into input of harmonizer.
7. Plug harmonizer output into channel 4 line in.
8. Set delay time (see "The Effects Chapter").
9. Set harmonizer pitch change to ±6 to 9 cents.
10. Balance inputs of delay and harmonizer for proper signal-to-noise ratio and check for distortion (see "The Effects Chapter").
11. Assign channels 3 and 4 to record on track 3.
12. Monitor channel 3 and EQ channels 1, 2, 3, and 4 separately (mute channels not being worked on).
13. Check balance between channels 1, 2, 3, and 4 for musicality and desired effect.
14. Record on track 3.

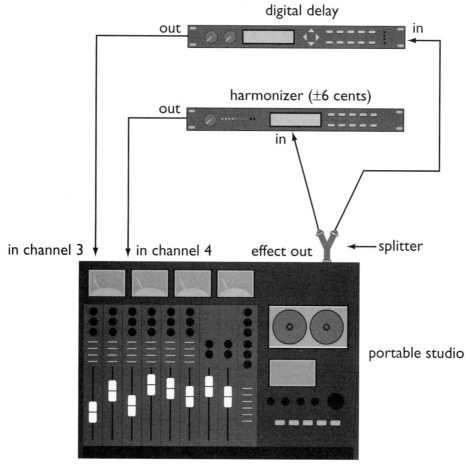

digital delay

out — in

harmonizer (±6 cents)

out — in

in channel 3   in channel 4   effect out   ← splitter

portable studio

Vocal   Vocal
track I   track 2

use effect sends channels I and 2
assign channels I, 2, and 3
record tracks ❸

RECIPE 19 (EFFECT)
DOUBLE LEAD VOCAL

Application: To use a delay to strengthen a lead vocal sound (also called a *mult*).

Requirement: Delay

1. Plug mic into channel 1 mic in.
2. Plug portable studio effect send output into delay input.
3. Plug delay output into channel 2 line in.
4. Use channel 1 effect send to route vocal to delay.
5. Set delay at desired time interval (usually very short, so delay is nearly indistinguishable from original signal). Set feedback very low so there is no more than one repeat (see "The Effects Chapter").
6. Check delay for proper signal-to-noise ratio.
7. Assign channels 1 and 2 to record on track 3.
8. Monitor track 3 and add desired amount of delay to original signal.
9. EQ channels 1 and 2 to blend them together as one sound.
10. Set record level to track 3.
11. Record on track 3.

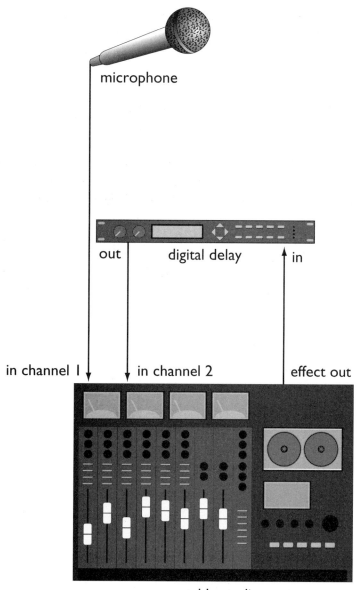

microphone

out digital delay in

in channel 1 in channel 2 effect out

portable studio

use effect send channel 1
assign channels 1 and 2
record track ❸

RECIPE 20 (EFFECT)
BOUNCE AND "STEREOIZE" (INTERNAL COMBINING)

Application: To create a stereo "image" of a group of instruments previously combined to a mono track.

Requirement: Harmonizer (delay or chorus may be substituted, but are less effective)

1. Record instruments on tracks 1 and 2.
2. Assign tracks 1 and 2 to record to track 3.
3. EQ and balance channels 1 and 2; record to track 3.
4. Plug portable studio effect send output into input of harmonizer.
5. Plug harmonizer output into channel 1 line in.
6. Use channel 3 effect send to route signal to harmonizer.
7. Set harmonizer pitch change to ±6 to 9 cents.
8. Assign channel 1 to record on track 1.
9. After recording, pan channel 1 to left and channel 3 to right.

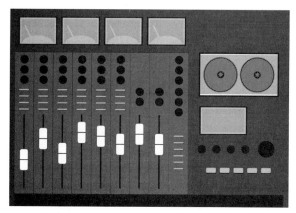

guitar   guitar
track 1   track 2

assign channels 1 and 2
record tracks ❸

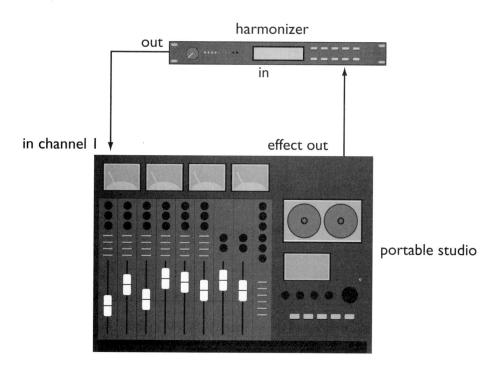

portable studio

use effect send channel 3
assign channels 1
record tracks ❶

Recipe 21 (Effect)
Bounce, Double, and "Stereoize" (External Combining)

Application: To create a stereo "image" and double a group of instruments during an external submix. This configuration uses the effect send to process any reverb, echo, etc.; the harmonizer uses the stereo buss and is placed last in the portable studio audio chain.

Requirements: Harmonizer (delay or chorus may be substituted, but are less effective), two-track machine

1. Record instruments on tracks.
2. Assign channels to be bounced to left and right (stereo buss) (see "The Step-by-Step Recording and Mixdown Chapter").
3. EQ and balance for premix.
4. Plug left master output of portable studio into left input of two-track.
5. Plug right master output of portable studio into input of harmonizer.
6. Plug harmonizer output into right input of two-track.
7. Pan all instruments to be combined to the *center* (this will route signal to both the left and right of the stereo buss).
8. Set harmonizer pitch change to ±6 to 9 cents.
9. Balance record levels on left and right of two-track.
10. Record on left and right of two-track.
11. Complete bounce back to portable studio (see "The Step-by-Step Recording and Mixdown Chapter").
12. Pan returned bounce tracks to opposite sides.

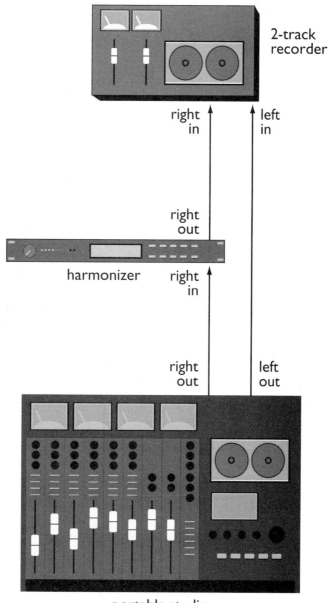

2-track
recorder

right
in

left
in

right
out

harmonizer

right
in

right
out

left
out

portable studio

Recipe 22 (Effect)
Delayed Reverb

Application: Use to provide a brief instant of "dry" sound before the reverb is activated by the source signal. This will help provide clarity when using reverb. Particularly effective on vocals and snare drum.

Requirements: Delay, reverb

1. Plug the effect send output of the portable studio into the input of the delay.
2. Plug the delay output into the input of the reverb.
3. Plug the left out of the reverb into the left effect return; activate return.
4. Plug the right out of the reverb into the right effect return; activate return.
5. Plug a metronome or drum machine into channel 1 line in, then play quarter notes.
6. Use channel 1 effect send to route signal to delay.
7. Set delay timing.
8. Proceed with processing.

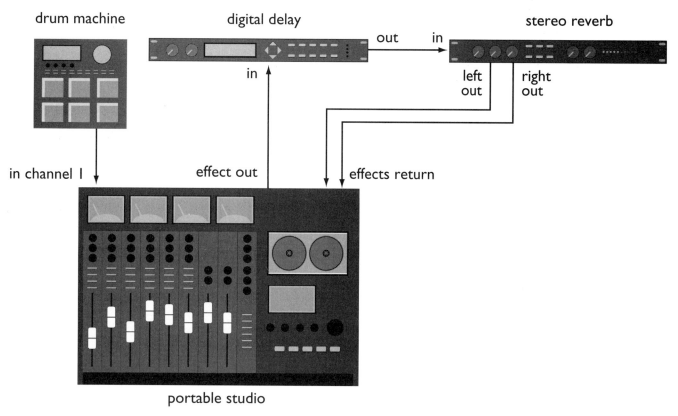

drum machine   digital delay   stereo reverb

out   in

in

left out   right out

in channel 1

effect out   effects return

portable studio

use effect send channel 1

Recipe 23 (Effect)
Gated Reverb

Application: This reverb sound was used on the snare of the Men at Work records. It provides additional "bang" to drums. (Some signal processors have a built-in gated reverb, but this method allows for greater flexibility.)

Requirements: Two gates, reverb

1. Plug effect send output of portable studio into input of reverb.
2. Plug left output of reverb into gate 1 input.
3. Plug right output of reverb into gate 2 input.
4. Plug output of gate 1 into left effect return; activate return.
5. Plug output of gate 2 into right effect return; activate return.
6. Plug drum machine into channel 1 line in; play quarter notes on snare.
7. Use channel 1 effect send to route signal to reverb.
8. Set reverb to desired decay time (see "The Effects Chapter"). I usually use 1.5 to 2.5 seconds.
9. Use gate 1 and gate 2 to chop the reverb return decay to add to the desired sound.

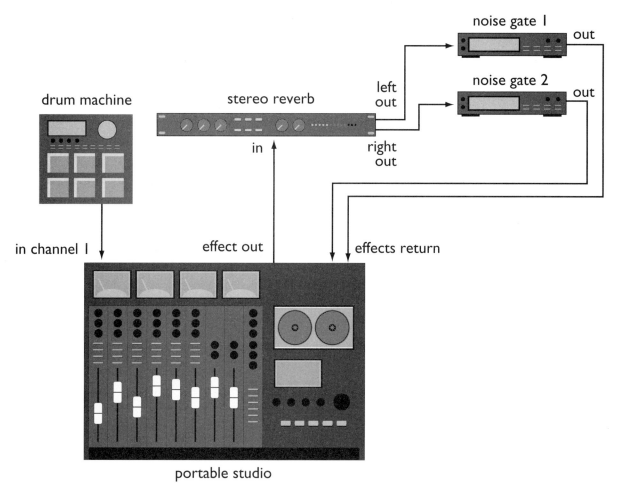

drum machine

stereo reverb

left out

noise gate 1   out

noise gate 2   out

in

right out

in channel 1

effect out

effects return

portable studio

use effect send channel 1

RECIPE 24 (EFFECT)
DIRECT IN AND AMPED GUITAR

Application: To add a distorted amp to a direct in "clean" guitar. Also good for adding a clean amp sound for fullness and warmth to a clear direct sound. This method allows you to mix in and control the amount of amp sound versus direct in sound.

Requirements: Amplifier, microphone

1. Plug guitar into channel 1 line in.
2. Plug portable studio effect send output into input of amplifier.
3. Mic amplifier.
4. Plug microphone into channel 3 mic in.
5. Use channel 1 effect send to route signal to the amplifier.
6. Assign channels 1 and 3 to record on track 3.
7. Monitor track 3.
8. EQ channels 1 and 3 separately; balance for desired combination. Check for phase problems (see "The Microphone Chapter").
9. Record on track 3.

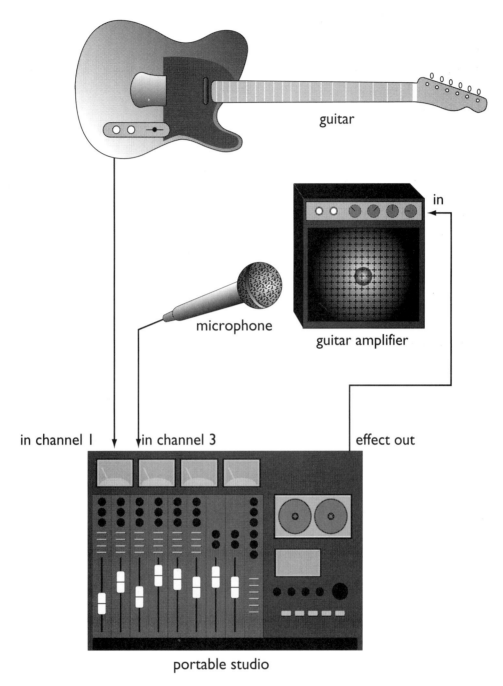

guitar

in

microphone

guitar amplifier

in channel 1   in channel 3   effect out

portable studio

use effect send channel 1
assign channels 1 and 3
record track ❸

Recipe 25 (Effect)
Eliminating Noise on a Bounce

Application: When combining tracks, noise can be a problem. This method is useful for limiting noise during gaps in a performance; *e.g.*, headphone leakage between background vocal lines, hum between guitar solo lines, *etc.*

Requirement: Noise gate

1. Plug portable studio effect send output into input of gate.
2. Plug output of gate into channel 3 line in.
3. Use effect sends to route tracks to be combined through gate.
4. Assign only channel 3 to record on track 3.
5. Monitor track 3.
6. Play tracks to EQ, blend, and set gate.
7. EQ channel 3 for overall mix.
8. Record on track 3.

noise gate

out

in

in channel 3

effect out

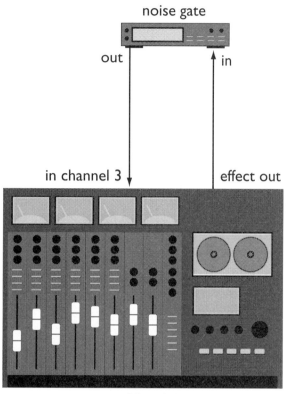

portable studio

use effect send channels 1 and 2
assign channel 3
record track ❸

Recipe 26 (Effect)
Echoing One Instrument with Another

Application: Use to add a nice ethereal effect; for instance, a string sound becomes the repeat "echo" of a piano part.

Requirements: Two synths or multiple-output synth, echo (delay line, analog echo, *etc.*)

1. Plug synth 1 into channel 1 line in.
2. Plug synth 2 into channel 2 line in.
3. Plug portable studio effect send output into input of echo.
4. Plug echo output into channel 3 line in.
5. Assign channel 1 to record on track 3.
6. Use channel 2 effect send to route signal to echo. Do not assign channel 2 to record on a track.
7. Assign channel 3 to record on track 3.
8. Monitor track 3.
9. Set echo for desired number of repeats (you should hear repeats of synth 2 only).
10. Balance channels 1 and 3.
11. Record on track 3.

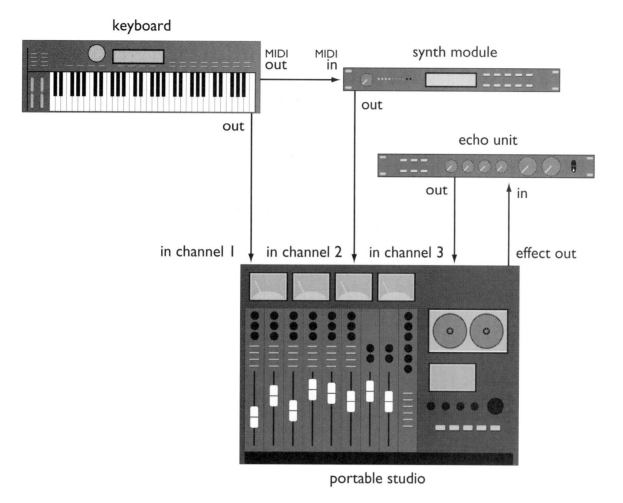

keyboard

MIDI out → MIDI in   synth module

out

echo unit

out

out   in

in channel 1   in channel 2   in channel 3   effect out

portable studio

use effect send on channel 2
assign channel 1 and 3 only
record track ❸

Recipe 27 (Effect)
Monster Keyboard Sounds

Application: To use a distorted amp to create lead sounds for solos, *etc.* Particularly good for using keyboards to imitate power guitar. Works great with a Hammond B-3, and like any amp application can also be used with real guitars.

Requirements: Splitter box, amplifer, harmonizer, compressor, two microphones

1. Plug keyboard into splitter box.
2. Plug one side of splitter box into amplifier.
3. Plug other side of splitter box into channel 1 line in.
4. Plug mic 1 into channel 3 mic in.
5. Plug mic 2 into channel 2 mic in.
6. Plug portable studio effect send output into input of compressor.
7. Plug compressor output into input of harmonizer.
8. Plug harmonizer output into channel 4 line in.
9. Use channel 2 effect send to route mic 2 to compressor. Do not assign channel 2 to record on a track.
10. Assign channels 1, 3, and 4 to record on track 3.
11. Set compressor to -3 dB gain reduction (see "The Effects Chapter").
12. Set harmonizer pitch change to ±6 to 9 cents or as desired. The more pitch change the more radical the effect.
13. Monitor track 3.
14. EQ channels 1, 3, and 4 separately, then blend for desired combination sound.
15. Record on track 3.

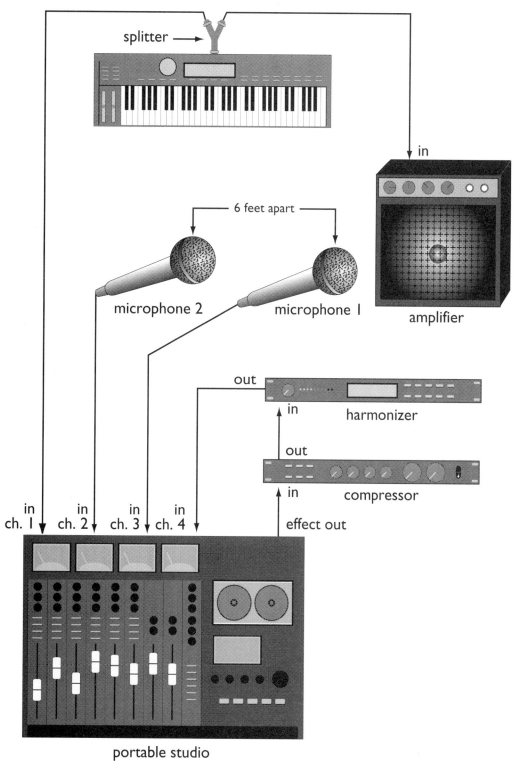

splitter ⟶

6 feet apart

microphone 2   microphone 1   amplifier

in

out   harmonizer
in

out   compressor
in

in   in   in   in
ch. 1   ch. 2   ch. 3   ch. 4   effect out

portable studio
use effect send channel 2
assign channels 1, 3, and 4
record track ❸

Index